The Emil and Kathleen Sick Lecture-Book Series
in Western History and Biography

Carlos A. Schwantes is associate professor of
history at Walla Walla College.

The Emil and Kathleen Sick Lecture-Book Series
in Western History and Biography

The Great Columbia Plain: A Historical Geography, 1805–1910,
by Donald W. Meinig
*Mills and Markets: A History of the Pacific Coast Lumber Industry
to 1900*, by Thomas R. Cox
*Radical Heritage: Labor, Socialism, and Reform in Washington
and British Columbia, 1885–1917*, by Carlos A. Schwantes

Radical Heritage

Labor, Socialism, and Reform in Washington and British Columbia, 1885-1917

Carlos A. Schwantes

UNIVERSITY OF WASHINGTON PRESS

Seattle and London

Copyright © 1979 by the University of Washington Press
Printed in the United States of America

Library of Congress Cataloging in Publication Data

Schwantes, Carlos A   1945–
   Radical heritage.

   (The Emil and Kathleen Sick lecture-book series in
western history and biography; 3)
   Bibliography: p.
   Includes index.
   1.   Trade-unions—Washington (State)—Political
activity—History.   2.   Trade-unions—British Columbia—
Political activity—History.   3.   Socialism in Washington
(State)—History.   4.   Socialism in British Columbia—
History.   I.   Title.   II.   Series.
   HD8079.W3S38   309.1'711'03   78-21757
   ISBN 0-295-95653-4

To Mary,
my beloved partner

The Emil and Kathleen Sick
Lecture-Book Series
in Western History and Biography

Under the provisions of a Fund established by the children of Mr. and Mrs. Emil Sick, whose deep interest in the history and culture of the American West was inspired by their own experience in the region, distinguished scholars are brought to the University of Washington to deliver public lectures based on original research in the fields of Western history and biography. The terms of the gift also provide for the publication by the University of Washington Press of the books resulting from the research upon which the lectures are based. This book is the third volume in the series.

Preface

At no time is the visitor to the Pacific Northwest more likely to deceive himself than upon crossing the Canadian-American border at Blaine, Washington. In summer he might pause there to enjoy the international gardens that form the highway median. Standing amid the flowers he would probably notice the relative ease with which the stream of traffic crossed from one country to the other. He might also admire the massive white Peace Arch that marks the boundary with the simple inscription: "Children of a Common Mother." If, however, those words produce in the mind's eye a picture of Britannia's offspring as fraternal twins, the process of self-deception has begun. The observer merely compounds the error if he applies that image to Washington and British Columbia. That is easy enough to do since, together with Oregon, they have long evoked the notion of a misty Northwest commonwealth of mountain, forest, and sea, and in the historical sense they were nurtured in the womb of the Old Oregon Country. The process of self-deception becomes complete when the visitor concludes that for the most part the border is a meaningless formality.

How ironic that while the uninitiated frequently believe in an almost insignificant line of separation, many historians are tempted to picture the 49th parallel as a kind of partition across which the researcher need not glance after the 1850s and 1860s. As this study hopes to demonstrate, however, Washington and British Columbia constitute a unique historical laboratory in which to reexamine the response to industrialism in the late nineteenth and early twentieth centuries.

Between 1885 and 1917 both areas underwent a rapid, often turbulent transformation from frontier to urban, industrialized societies. The process was by no means completed when World War I began, but during those thirty-odd years we can see how geographical neighbors looked over one another's shoulders as they sought to discover and apply effective remedies for the common ills plaguing the world's jerry-built industrial civilization.

As might be expected, disparate political, economic, and social systems sometimes caused Washingtonians and British Columbians to apply the same nostrums in markedly different ways. This will become clearer as we examine anew the familiar remedies offered by the trade unionism of Samuel Gompers and the socialism of Eugene Debs. In the process, new understanding may be gained as to why the general-welfare state developed as it did in the United States, or, more specifically, why organized labor in America failed to develop a viable socialist-labor-reform party comparable to the Labour party in Great Britain or the New Democratic party in Canada.

Organized labor played a more prominent role in the evolution of society in Washington and British Columbia than perhaps in any other frontier region in North America. To be sure, the percentage of nonagricultural workers unionized in those two areas has frequently been higher than in any other part of the United States or Canada. Largely because of the interrelated nature of labor, socialism, and reform in Washington and British Columbia, both areas have long been pictured by observers as being advanced, even radical, in terms of social legislation. [1]

Both Washington and British Columbia have also been described as "puzzling" and somehow different from the other states and provinces of the nations of which they are a part. Actually, the puzzling aspect is not the misleading similarity but rather the separateness that marks the political environments of the two; the governor of Washington and the premier of British Columbia did not exchange official visits to discuss matters of common concern until 1973. Governor Daniel Evans of Washington, the first man to serve three consecutive terms in that office, a "straight arrow" engineer and liberal Republican technocrat, contrasted sharply with Premier Dave Barrett, the earthy social worker best described as a "lumpy free-enterprise socialist."[2] Both men, however, were recognized as innovators within the framework of two very different political traditions.

When the New Democratic party captured thirty-eight of the fifty-five seats in British Columbia's legislative assembly in the election of August 1972, Dave Barrett, at the age of forty-five, became the premier of the first of Canada's wealthier provinces to choose socialism. Educated in universities in Seattle and St. Louis and having spent at least one summer working in the pea harvest of eastern Washington, Barrett was no doubt mindful of the way his minority party had been able to use the parliamentary system to gain power. "The Americans," he observed, "have a tremendous history of radical movements. But the problem is they don't have direct access to power. Canadians do."[3]

In any comparative study of labor in politics, access to power is a key element, but not the only element. In searching for that elusive quality known as the American character, the historian David Potter at one time believed that he had discovered the essential ingredient in the unparalleled American abundance. Later, after contemplating the comparative aspects of the American and Canadian experiences, he was forced to temper his environmental view by adding a plea for consideration of the historical and cultural dimensions of the problem.[4] Indeed, the contrast between the demise of the socialist movement in Washington and its continuing viability in British Columbia cannot be fully explained without reference to historical and cultural influences.

I have placed relatively greater emphasis in this study on Canadian history, government, and politics than on the often more familiar American institutional and political framework. Similarly, I have tended to emphasize the general newspapers and periodicals of Canada and British Columbia more than those of Washington because the Canadian publications are less well known and can sometimes answer questions that have seldom been asked of them. Although I have attempted to test familiar generalizations about American history in a new setting and have even suggested that some of those generalizations may be inapplicable in the sometimes exotic setting of Washington and British Columbia, I have tried to refrain from reasoning that they were not applicable in other parts of the United States.

Finally, I must provide a few important definitions. The American Pacific Northwest qualifies as a distinct region, and the same is true of British Columbia. Nonetheless, the terms "Pacific Northwest" and "North Pacific industrial frontier" will be used throughout this study to designate Washington and British Columbia combined. My working definition of the adjective "radical" is contained in *Webster's Seventh New Collegiate Dictionary*: "marked by a considerable departure from the usual or traditional." I have sought, however, to confine my attention to people and ideas supporting the evolution of the modern welfare state. Hence, several radicalisms, notably anarchism, are discussed only briefly or not at all. This study also confirms the insight offered in Ambrose Bierce's cynical definition of radicalism: "the conservatism of tomorrow injected into the affairs of today."

The research for this book has been aided by the kind and efficient staffs at a number of libraries and historical societies. I want particularly to thank Willard Ireland and his staff at the Public Archives of British Columbia, Anne Yandle and her staff in the Special Collections Division, University of British Columbia Library, Richard C. Berner of the Archives and Manuscripts Division, University of Washington Library, Merle Wells of the Idaho State Historical Society, and Lawrence Dodd and Marilyn Sparks of the Whitman College Library. Helen Sickler and Lee Johnston of the Walla Walla College Library rendered invaluable service by helping me obtain an incredible mass of interlibrary loan materials. During the past seven years no person did more to provide me with the time needed to pursue the research and writing than Robert Reynolds, former President of Walla Walla College. I also owe a debt of gratitude to the Walla Walla College Faculty Grants Committee.

Guiding me through the intricacies of labor history and reform thought in the pre–World War I era was my mentor at the University of Michigan, Professor Sidney Fine. Also sharing their insights with me were Professors Gerald S. Brown, Shaw Livermore, Jr., and Charles Rehmus, all of the University of Michigan. Professor David Bercuson of the University of Calgary shared with me his trenchant observations on western working-class radicalism. I alone, however, am responsible for errors of fact or judgment that may appear in the following pages.

A special acknowledgment is also due Professor Robert E. Burke of the University of Washington. Though I made his acquaintance only late in the history of this project, he played a crucial role in facilitating its publication. I count myself fortunate to have received his generous encouragement and support.

Contents

Abbreviations

AFL	American Federation of Labor
ALU	American Labor Union
ARU	American Railway Union
CCC	Canadian Cooperative Commonwealth
CCF	Cooperative Commonwealth Federation
CIO	Congress of Industrial Organizations
CLC	Central Labor Council of Seattle and Vicinity
CSL	Canadian Socialist League
ILP	Independent Labor Party
IWA	International Workingmen's Association
IWW	Industrial Workers of the World
NEC	National Executive Committee of the Socialist Party
NDP	New Democratic Party
SDA	Social Democracy of America
SDP	Social Democratic Party (in America, 1898–1901; in Canada, 1911–19)
SLP	Socialist Labor Party
SPA	Socialist Party of America
SPC	Socialist Party of Canada
STLA	Socialist Trades and Labor Alliance
TLC	Trades and Labor Congress of Canada
UBRE	United Brotherhood of Railway Employees
UMW	United Mine Workers of America
USLP	United Socialist Labor Party

WCLU	Western Central Labor Union
WFM	Western Federation of Miners
WLU	Western Labor Union

Radical Heritage

CHAPTER 1

The North Pacific
Industrial Frontier:

Washington and British Columbia
in the late Nineteenth Century

The radical heritage of the Pacific Northwest resulted from the interaction of people and ideas with an environment that nurtured the most bizarre proposals for social, economic, and political change. In fact, during the years from 1885 to 1917, the Pacific Northwest was a land of unusual opportunity for world savers and fortune seekers alike. Many settlers believed it was the promised land where opportunity combined with personal determination would allow them to realize the dreams created by the promotional literature they had read back in Kansas, Kentucky, or Great Britain. Especially for working-class immigrants from older, more established societies, the North Pacific industrial frontier seemed a land of new possibilities.

REALITY AND MYTH

Statistically and descriptively, the North Pacific region lent itself to the most outlandish claims and characterizations—and no wonder. In size alone, the reality of the Pacific Northwest almost defied comprehension. British Columbia encompassed an enormous expanse of land larger than the combined area of the United Kingdom, Ireland, France, Netherlands, and Denmark. Washington, by contrast, although equal to the combined area of the six New England states, was but one-fifth the size of her northern neighbor. Despite its great physical size, however, British Columbia by the turn of the century had a distinctly urban character; almost two-thirds of the province's population by 1901 lived within one hundred miles of Victoria and Vancouver.

Geographically and politically, the province and state were divided into two main units. British Columbia was split by the Georgia Strait into mainland and island, Vancouver Island itself being a landform the size of Belgium. The Cascade Range divided Washington into an extensive semi-arid, but fertile plateau known locally as the Inland Empire and a wet, evergreen lowland surrounding Puget Sound. Western Washington's major urban centers, Seattle and Tacoma, benefited from an excellent water highway that enabled them to establish trade links with San Francisco and the Orient. The Inland Empire until the coming of the railroads remained relatively isolated. Spokane Falls, attracting railroads as "metal to a magnet," had established itself by the twentieth century as the trade nexus for the Inland Empire.[1]

Mainland British Columbia was riven by a series of mountain ranges, the most formidable being the fifty-mile wide Rocky Mountain barrier that formed the eastern boundary of the province. If British Columbia had an equivalent to the Inland Empire, it was the Kootenay region, an area of long, canoe-shaped valleys running perpendicular to the international boundary. The peculiar configuration of the Kootenay area made it a natural tributary to Spokane. Before World War I Spokane had better rail access to the Kootenays than any Canadian city, and people in Kootenay towns were able to acquire any item from Spokane by merely telegraphing for it. Newspapers in the Kootenays closely followed American political contests and affairs on Wall Street.

The beautiful Kootenay region was once described as "the only place God made—and completed." The region's most alluring quality, however, lay not in its deep, azure lakes and snowcapped mountains, but in its mineral wealth. The idyllic character of life in the Kootenays changed dramatically in the early 1890s following the discovery of gold and silver in the West Kootenay. Between 1890 and 1897 almost two hundred Spokane-based mining companies were formed to exploit the riches of the West Kootenay. Although the Kootenays remained for years extremely remote from the commercial and governmental centers of British Columbia, radical unions such as the Western Federation of Miners that swept in

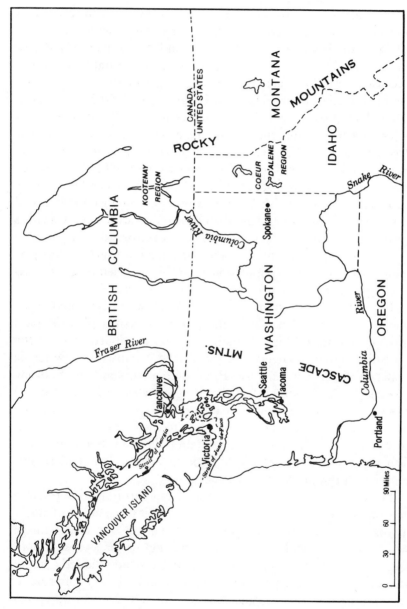

Map 1. The North Pacific Industrial Frontier

from the Coeur d'Alenes of Idaho had a marked impact on the labor movement in the Pacific province.[2]

Political debate in British Columbia came to reflect the province's markedly urban character, the inordinately large influence of radical ideas on Kootenay metal miners and Vancouver Island coal miners, and the absence of a significant agricultural community. Because of a lack of factual knowledge regarding the true agricultural potential of the Old Oregon Country, the British and American diplomats who divided that remote region in 1846 had little idea of just how inequitably the tillable land had been distributed by their decision to extend the international boundary along the 49th parallel from the crest of the Rocky Mountains to the Pacific. Washington received a vast expanse of agricultural land both east and west of the Cascades; in time British Columbia became convinced that it had less potential agricultural land than Prince Edward Island, Canada's smallest province. At the turn of the century, British Columbia reported the smallest number of agrarians in all of Canada: 13.4 percent of the province's population engaged in agricultural pursuits as compared with a national average of 46 percent.[3]

The farmers in Washington's Walla Walla area discovered in the mid-1860s that, given water, the rolling semi-arid plateau could produce an agricultural bonanza far more important than the sporadic mining discoveries in the Pacific Northwest. The fertile Walla Walla Valley and the Palouse country south of Spokane proved to be well suited to the raising of wheat and other cereal crops. Wheat became such an important crop that by the 1890s numerous counties in eastern Washington were marked by a one-crop economy, which fostered agrarian radicalism. Soon organized farmers joined with organized labor to form a powerful reform coalition in the pre-World War I era.

The reality of the Pacific Northwest can hardly be described in geographic and statistical terms alone, for in the minds of many immigrants the "Great Northwest" was part of that dream image which does not lend itself to quantification or facile description. Puget Sound, for example, was in reality an island-studded body of salt water and Mt. Hood a volcanic peak, but in the eyes of promoters and settlers the volcano was as "graceful" as an Egyptian pyramid, and the Sound became an "agricultural Venice," the "Mediterranean of America."

The image of the Pacific Northwest as a promised land had an especially powerful influence on the many working-class immigrants first attracted to the region in the 1880s and 1890s. At a time when the mills of Lawrence, Pittsburgh, and Hamilton were already becoming blackened with age, communities in Washington and British Columbia remained largely untouched by the industrial revolution. In fact, not until the mid-1880s was the misty solitude of the North Pacific region broken by railway links to the rest of the United States and Canada. As a result, social, economic, and political structures, especially in Washington, still seemed malleable to the newcomers.

Many a worker immigrating to the North Pacific industrial frontier was thus encouraged to develop a somewhat altered concept of his role in society. A worker moving to Washington in the 1880s might have perceived himself as a carpenter or miner when he left St. Louis or Scranton, but once in the expansive environment of Puget Sound he might see himself as a miner or molder or carpenter—*and* a participant in the creation of a new and more equitable society than the one he left behind.

To measure the attitudes of workingmen in that age before opinion polls is without question a most difficult task. It may, however, be possible to apprehend in a rough fashion the general outlook of the larger community in which workers lived by using the images· created by promoters and found in the travel literature. The travelers who roamed the Canadian and American wests after 1865 typically noted minor traits and magnified them into characteristics of a region or a nation. Despite their tendency to make grand generalization from limited evidence, they did make explicit and vivid what local residents took for granted. These observations complemented the images that were being projected by promoters.[4]

As a young man living in Boston, Stewart Holbrook found that the booster pamphlets "somehow left the impression that one could have a decent living in Oregon and Washington simply by eating the gorgeous scenery. . . ."[5] The promotion of real estate that had been practiced with such a vengeance in Kansas and Southern California spread to the Pacific Northwest in the late nineteenth and early twentieth centuries. Townsite gambling became an epidemic, a regional vice. The amount of money and energy that promoters spent in describing the resources, capabilities, and wonders of the Pacific Northwest was prodigious. The Northern Pacific and Canadian Pacific railroads deluged the public with promotional circulars, as did chambers of commerce, private associations, and local immigration boards. The states of Oregon and Washington did little official publicizing of their resources, but both the Canadian and British Columbia governments actively promoted settlement.

The promotional literature was predicated upon that trait of mobility peculiar to the United States and, to a lesser extent, western Canada. "The American," one observer declared, "is so constituted that if he were assured that superior conditions of climate and soil were to be encountered on the planet Mars, he would yearn to leave his own land and get there." It was widely believed that this restlessness was a selective process: only the enterprising and adventurous would seek homes in a new country.[6] If so, society in the western United States and western Canada could have been expected to be less structured and more accepting of change than society in eastern portions of the two countries—and indeed this frequently appears to be the case.

The migration process was selective in another way as well. Dorothy Johansen has found that immigrants who chose one far western location over another, specifically Oregon or California, had in common a range of expectations that were a factor in establishing local and regional variations in outlook. The first settlers actually determined the character of a community by communicating their sense of satisfaction or dissatisfaction to potential immigrants, and thus further refined the process of westward migration and settlement.

The contrast between the Pacific Northwest and California as conveyed by the travel and promotional literature was vivid and clear, and as Dorothy Johansen and others have noted, Oregon attracted a different kind of population than California. The same is true of Washington and British Columbia.[7]

New Eden and New Eldorado

The physical image typically projected for Washington and Oregon was one of boundless resources and get-rich-quick opportunities. Washington was portrayed as having a "vast and inexhaustible" supply of natural resources. The coal deposits on Puget Sound were the "largest in the United States"; Washington was the "Pennsylvania of the Pacific." Other authors, impressed by the seemingly endless expanse of pines and firs, wrote that it would "scarcely be possible to exaggerate the extent and value of the forests of the Pacific North West." The Northwest was also described as a health-seekers paradise, filled with hot springs and mineral baths. Wasthington had an ideal climate, sunstroke was practically unknown there, and evenings were "cool and conducive to sound slumber." There were fewer fevers. Compared to the southwestern part of the United States, Washington was a "quiet and pleasant home."[8]

British Columbia was frequently portrayed as a distinctly different type of promised land, a sterile region where life was hard and the climate harsh. Some of the early literature described British Columbia as a land of perpetual snow. Although that image was soon abandoned and Vancouver Island became the "England of the Pacific," the prospective immigrant was still warned that the area was not suited for development as an agricultural or pastoral colony. The timber on that island was so dense, it was reported, that a farmer would spend a lifetime clearing his land. The interior was supposed to be extremely rugged. One or two generations grew up believing that British Columbia was a land of "rugged mountains, unfit for tillage." In time the fertility of the scattered valleys of the mainland became known, but many a prospective immigrant was warned that such land had already been monopolized by a few individuals. In 1884 the future of British Columbia lay in her mineral resources, and even the official publications minimized agricultural possibilities. Though the province became "Canada's El Dorado" as a result of an abundance of mineral wealth, and the image of harsh weather gave way to a new vision of a "singularly British climate," not until the beginning of the twentieth century would land seekers come to the province en masse, and even then the literature concluded that land in British Columbia could be won only with great effort and by resolute men.[9]

The greatest point of contrast between the images of the two regions resulted from the differences in agricultural opportunity. If in time British Columbia became the New Eldorado, Washington became the New Eden, a veritable farmers' paradise. Crop failures were allegedly unknown and because the harvest in both eastern and western Washington came in the dry season, the farmer was supposedly relieved "from all anxiety in securing his crops." The region around Walla Walla by 1886 was being promoted as the "finest stretch of wheat country in the world." [10]

The differential image projected regarding agricultural opportunities was reflected in the consideration of who should be encouraged to migrate. Washington, from the beginning, projected the image of a bountiful country offering special inducements to the poor man who came armed with little more than determination and "plenty of every day sense." If a person could not bring money, he should bring "plenty of pluck." Promoters of Washington in the 1880s promised success to any farmer who was willing to work. In fact, it was noted, everyone seemed ahead except the proverbial Missourians—popularly regarded as perennial losers. [11]

A much more cautious invitation was extended from British Columbia and Canada. Persons immigrating, it was reported, frequently formed inflated expectations of becoming "suddenly wealthy, and therefore become too soon disappointed. . . ." Emphasis in the literature was placed on the immigrant's having some kind of capital to sustain himself until his own lands became remunerative or to buy an already improved piece of land. "Indiscriminate immigration," it was advised, "is not desirable." People who were tempted to move to British Columbia in the hopes of bettering themselves were advised to pause, since Canada was allegedly already too full of such people. The man with a trade, the clerk, the accountant, or the semiprofessional were warned that "chances for employment are by no means good." British Columbia seemed to want "two classes only—capitalists and laborers. Both classes will do well." Not only was there an emphasis on hard work and hard living, but the immigrant to British Columbia was told that he must have one extra quality: "He must be loyal." [12]

Loyalty had to be emphasized since in the competition for the European immigrant, the Canadians found themselves at a disadvantage during most of the nineteenth century. Great Britain was not only flooded by American promotional publications, but once the immigrant came to Canada there was every inducement for him to keep on moving into the United States. That was especially true for farmers emigrating to Canada's Pacific slope. The temptation was to pursue social advancement and economic success south of the 49th parallel.[13]

While for workers Washington and British Columbia represented a common industrial frontier, the contrasting images projected for these two neighbors reveal marked differences in the general opportunity structure. And a society that offers special inducements to immigrants who are agriculturalists and small entrepreneurs is bound to be different from one that puts a premium on factory hands or miners. To be sure, metal mining, for example, was the same occupation on either side of the 49th parallel. Similarly, working-class life in isolated mining camps could produce identical feelings of class consciousness regardless of whether the camps were in the United States or Canada. Metal miners, however, were also part of a larger community, a state or province which reflected whatever political, economic, and social differences resulted from communicating dissimilar appeals to potential immigrants. Such differences became especially meaningful when workers and their allies entered the political arena to secure economic justice. The debate between capital and labor in the legislative chambers of Olympia and Victoria was unquestionably influenced by the contrasting attitudes and opportunities communicated in the travel and promotional literature.

WASHINGTON AND *British* COLUMBIA

The radical notions that flourished in the still tentative and experimental societies that characterized Washington and, to a lesser degree, British Columbia at the turn of the century sprang from many identical sources. The same tracts, books, ideas, and agitators circulated freely across the international boundary. In the actual implementation of such schemes, however, history and culture were as important determinants as geography and the opportunity structure.

Although Washington and British Columbia had both been a part of the Old Oregon Country, the histories and cultures of the two areas diverged widely. In Washington, the movement of people preceded the establishment of effective government, and the elements of American nationalism brought by settlers were typically regarded as "vestal fires." In British Columbia, on the other hand, government usually preceded settlement, and Canadian nationalism was a painstakingly difficult creation. The transition of Washington from territory to state largely followed the familiar pattern introduced by Congress a century earlier. Throughout the territorial period the ultimate goal had been to achieve statehood, which many believed had a quality akin to magic as far as the prosperity of the region was concerned. The achievement of statehood in 1889 was simply the final step of a journey begun some thirty years earlier. The realization of that goal was marked by those qualities so typical of the territorial period, formality combined with a casual pragmatism. The constitutional convention was painstakingly laborious, yet the state seal simply consisted of a portrait of George Washington copied by an Olympia jewelry store from an advertisement for patent medicine.[14]

Far more complex is the story of British Columbia's transition from colony to province. In contrast to Washington, British Columbia had a crown colony tradition going back to 1849 and a history of strong central government that stemmed from the monopoly fur-trading days of the Hudson's Bay Company. The local governing officials sent from London promoted respect for imperial authority as a means of coping with the problem of being an isolated colony containing a large and boisterous American population.

After the Dominion of Canada was formed in 1867 a three-way debate ensued in Victoria as to whether British Columbia should continue to eke out a pitiful existence as a crown colony on the fringe of her republican neighbor, join the American union, or become the Pacific entrepôt for the new Dominion. The idea of annexation to the United States was not popular among leaders of the debate, but neither was the thought of joining Canada, a country some three thousand miles distant. Canada, which had established no direct means of communication or transportation with the North Pacific region, was regarded by British Columbians as a land of poor, mean, and slow people. Canadians were scornfully characterized in British Columbia as "North American Chinamen." British Columbians only reluctantly joined the Canadian confederation in 1871.[15]

The union of British Columbia to Canada was not the natural consequence of sentiment or geography. In fact, the imperial tie and a sense of geographic separateness combined to create a provincial pride that was marked by indifference and even hostility to the remainder of Canada. In 1884 a traveler noted that British Columbians "do not call themselves Canadians," and still later British Columbia's attempt to discriminate against extraprovincial companies was denounced by the Canadian Association of Manufacturers as a failure to grasp the meaning of confederation.[16]

Even the problems of British Columbia, particularly the labor problem, seemed to have an individuality that set them off from those of the rest of the Dominion. Indeed, after visiting the province in the first decade of the twentieth century, Rudyard Kipling wrote that he had heard more about problems and crises in British Columbia than anywhere else on his world travels.[17]

A good deal of the province's individuality was rooted in a determination to remain British. A majority of the officials who governed the colony prior to 1871 looked to Britain as home, and this official element was very important in setting the whole tone of society in Victoria. They were acutely conscious of the need to maintain proper British manners, religion, law, and political traditions on the fringe of civilization. That attitude changed little even after British Columbia became a Canadian province. The maintenance of British political institutions in British Columbia was one of the primary reasons why radicals in the province had far greater access to genuine political power than their counterparts south of the 49th parallel.[18]

Compared to Washington and the Dominion as a whole, a high proportion of the population in British Columbia was British born; in 1910 settlers born in the British Isles accounted for almost 30 percent of British Columbia's nonaboriginal population as compared to approximately 11.4 percent in Canada as a whole and 3.4 percent in Washington. These percentages did not change significantly over the next several decades. Until 1941, in fact, the number of British-born persons living in British Columbia usually exceeded the number of Canadians born east of the Rocky Mountains. As a result of this British connection, several English newspapers were available in Victoria, and even the local papers provided space for "London Letters." British medals and titles rewarded achievement in this far corner of the British Empire. Not surprisingly, motorists in British Columbia drove on the left, as in

Great Britain, until in 1919 the province sought conformity with the rest of Canada.[19]

The British formed an influential part of organized labor in the province. Working-class immigrants from Great Britain generally went into those occupations with which they had been previously familiar: mining, fishing, shipping, and dock work. Many of these immigrants had been members of British trade unions and were familiar with the tenets of socialism. The British became leaders in unionizing such areas as the coal fields of the Pacific Northwest. In the United States, the Briton was encouraged to become a good American; in British Columbia he was encouraged to remain a good Briton and, as such, was tacitly encouraged to emulate the trade-union activities of fellow workers in Great Britain, Australia, and New Zealand, about which so much information was available in the province.[20]

The high percentage of British-born workers in British Columbia not only helped to prevent the intellectual isolation of the provincial labor movement from the mainstream of reform thought in Britain and other parts of the Empire, but it also created a cohesiveness among local workers that militated against employers' attempts to play off one European nationality against another in an effort to break strikes or disrupt labor organization—as often happened in the industrialized communities of eastern America. The same thing was more or less true in Washington, for, unlike the United States as a whole, Washington continued to attract most of its immigrants in the late nineteenth and early twentieth centuries from northern and western Europe. Large numbers of Scandinavians began arriving in the Puget Sound country in the 1880s, but Norwegians and Swedes, unlike the British in British Columbia, never accounted for more than 7 or 8 percent of the state's population. The bulk of those immigrating to Washington prior to World War I came from other parts of the United States.[21]

"A Boom of the Boomiest"

No matter whether they labored in a Tacoma iron foundry or searched for the glittering "paystreak" deep in a Kootenay metal mine, Pacific Northwest workers were all a part of a fast-growing, urban-oriented society. At the turn of the century Washington's population of 518,103 was 41 percent urban, by census definition, and British Columbia's 178,657 was over 50 percent urban. Within the next ten years, more than 50 percent of all Pacific Northwesterners lived in urban areas, which meant that the population of the region was far more urbanized than that of either the United States or Canada as a whole. The transformation from frontier rawness to urban respectability, however, was characterized by several periods of unusually rapid population growth and concomitant economic and social dislocation. In the formative but turbulent 1880s, Washington had one of the fastest rates of growth in the United States. During that decade the population of Washington quadrupled, and that of British Columbia nearly doubled. In the first decade of the twentieth century, both areas increased by at least 120 percent. Thus, despite a close physical and chronological proximity to primitive frontier conditions, the Pacific Northwest labor movement was nurtured in a highly developed urban environment dominated by a few important centers of trade and commerce.

The three settlements of Seattle, Tacoma, and Spokane generally contained at least one-third of the population of Washington; the same is true of Vancouver and Victoria in British Columbia. Of these five major urban areas, all but Victoria experienced the unsettling conditions that typified periods of rapid urban growth. These communities were not large by eastern standards, but the rate at which they grew was startling. During the 1880s Seattle's population had increased by over 1,000 percent to 42,837. Tacoma during the same decade grew by more than 3,000 percent, attaining a population of 36,006; and Spokane increased by almost 6,000 percent to 19,922 people. Vancouver's growth spurt came between 1901 and 1911, when the population increased by 271 percent, to 100,401. The population of Seattle at that time was over 237,000, while that of Victoria stood at a modest 31,660. Even the farmer who moved to Washington and British Columbia saw himself less as a member of an isolated, self-sufficient farm community than as a part of the rapidly evolving urban world of the Pacific Northwest.

Each urban area of the Pacific Northwest projected its own image. Victoria was noted for its Englishness, its slow pace of life, its quaint appearance, and its way of observing a decorous Sunday. Victoria was blessed with a number of shrubs and plants native to England and with lovely lanes where honeysuckle and sweetbriar abounded. British immigrants were naturally attracted to the capital of British Columbia, which some Americans called a habitation of "Mossbacks." [22]

Vancouver, unlike Victoria, was an instant city created in 1886 as the terminus for the Canadian Pacific Railway. It grew to some five thousand people in its first year, but it was a sleepy town compared to its American neighbors. Unlike Seattle it had less rowdyism, "revolvering," and lynch law spirit, but unlike Victoria it had a distinctly materialistic culture. As J. A. Hobson noted in 1906, its inhabitants "must be a race of financiers, concerned purely with money and stocks and shares." [23] Vancouver's powerful rival to the south was Seattle. Both cities carried on vigorous advertising campaigns, but Seattle's efforts in this area like Seattle's crime statistics tended to dwarf Vancouver's.

Seattle was noted for the "hustling" spirit so admired by Americans and so detested by the British. The "Seattle Spirit" was believed by many, especially those living in Seattle, to be an irresistible force destined to make her the Queen City of Puget Sound. Both Seattle and her rival to the south, Tacoma, were considered "marvelous examples of sudden growth." Tacoma, while less showy than Seattle, rapidly earned fame as a city full of stumps and enterprise. Kipling found Tacoma "literally staggering under a boom of the boomiest." The dizzying pace of Tacoma caused him to withdraw to British territory to "draw breath." Seattle eventually won preeminence on Puget Sound by convincing the Northern Pacific Railway to build a line to the city and the rival Great Northern to select Seattle as its Pacific terminus. Until World War I, however, Seattle, like the other major cities of the Pacific Northwest, suffered from its dependence upon extractive industries and outside capital. [24]

A community's projected image is not always an accurate indicator of the general character of the local labor movement, but nowhere in the Pacific Northwest were labor leaders such models of restraint and caution as in Portland, Oregon. Portland, in contrast to the communities further north, never earned fame as a boom town. She was much older and much more settled than her chief rivals. Growth for Portland, as for Victoria, had been a slow and natural process; in the eyes of her brash and energetic rivals she was almost a declining city. Visitors to Portland, especially on a Sunday, were often reminded of a rural New England town.[25]

Portland, Tacoma, Seattle, Vancouver, and Victoria all had a common maritime outlook, a cosmopolitan atmosphere, and close ties to San Francisco. Spokane, on the other hand, enjoyed unparalleled sway over the agricultural and mining areas of the Inland Empire and the Kootenays. Its ties were with Butte and Denver. Consequently, the Spokane labor movement acquired a regional, radical orientation markedly different from that which developed west of the Cascades.

URBAN AMENITIES

To be sure, many a migratory lumberjack or hardrock miner saw only the seamy side of these communities—the skid row jungle of employment agencies, soup kitchens, and brothels; nonetheless, in many important ways, the urban world inhabited by Pacific Northwest workers in the late nineteenth century provided a number of positive cultural and intellectual advantages.

The region's urban promoters and builders were often interested in far more than the mere pursuit of material gain. Cultural institutions, churches, physical amenities, and a sense of tidiness and cleanliness could give an upstart community a settled air and dispel any notion that might lurk in Eastern minds regarding the West's "fancied lack of social advantage."[26]

As small as these settlements were in the 1880s and 1890s, community leaders were creating philharmonic societies and art associations, and the professionals were organizing into medical societies, pharmaceutical societies, and bar associations. The whole community took pride in the installation of the latest type of street car or telephone equipment. These organizational and technological changes were seen as signs of stability, as evidence of the permanence of the settlement.

The public schools were a special source of pride. The territory and the province from very early times provided for public, nonsectarian education, with British Columbia having perhaps the most highly centralized system of public education in North America. These schools of the region contributed to the low rate of illiteracy long a significant feature of working-class life in the Pacific Northwest. Literate and educated workers were well prepared to read and discuss the many reform tracts that filtered into the region. The schools were also powerful disseminators of national identity in a far corner of North America. While educators in Washington taught children about the glories of the American Constitution and the egalitarian republic, teachers in British Columbia helped to reinforce the province's sense of Britishness. School children in British Columbia were taught that the flag of England floated over all public buildings "in token of safety and protection," and they were drilled in a knowledge of British history. A portrait of Queen Victoria and the British flag could be found in most British Columbia classrooms.[27]

Libraries, like the public schools, were established at an early date in the Pacific Northwest. The Hudson's Bay Company had attempted to stock its posts with the lastest reading material from England, and many clubs and union halls contained reading rooms until free libraries became available. Newspapers, theaters, clubs, and churches were also sources of cultural influence. Although there was no state church in the Pacific Northwest, the preeminence of the Anglican church, or the Church of England in Canada as it was officially known, strengthened the British tie in British Columbia. Athletic, polo, and yacht clubs were popular in certain coastal areas; in the Kootenays the union halls and the socialist clubs formed an important part of the social scene. In the 1890s reform clubs proliferated to discuss temperance, socialist, Populist, and other reform ideas. Women's clubs discussed female suffrage, contributed to the social and literary awareness of these settlements, and conveyed a sense of dignity and order.

WORK AND WORKERS

The cities of the Pacific Northwest were primarily commercial entrepôts rather than manufacturing centers. The economy of Washington and British Columbia placed primary emphasis on logging and timber products, agriculture, fishing, and mining, and Seattle and Vancouver were centers for these four seasonal industries. The nature of this work produced a large pool of migratory labor and led to periodic unemployment. The peculiarity of the

Pacific Northwest job market eventually contributed to the coexistence of conservative trade unions and labor radicalism.

If one held a steady job, wages were comparable to the national average, and in British Columbia in 1901 they were the highest in Canada. In 1903–04 wage earners in Washington received an average income of $789 a year; about 40 percent owned their own homes and about 80 percent were married. It seemed, though, that these wage earners had little in common with the migrants in mining, logging, and railway construction camps that dotted the Pacific Northwest in the years before World War I.

The migratory workers, numbering among them such men as the future head of the American Communist party, William Z. Foster, and future Supreme Court Justice, William O. Douglas, traveled from place to place, riding the rods and trucks of railway cars. Suspended some ten inches above sudden death, the migrant on a fast-moving train might be blasted with the cinders or the sand and dust of the deserts of eastern Washington. To fall asleep meant certain death beneath the wheels. In the winter, he sometimes nearly froze to death riding in the open gondolas, and he might be tossed from a moving train by an unsympathetic brakeman or crushed by a shifting load of timber. Migrants felt that "yard bulls" or railway police in dusty junction hamlets like Pasco, Washington, often used them for target practice. The migrants sometimes moved from the timber or mining operations to work the fall harvest in the Palouse country, which in the eyes of many a migrant worker was a land of dust storms; too often it meant bedding down under an open sky with the rattlesnakes. William O. Douglas remembered one migrant whose worldly possessions consisted of a battered suitcase, a pair of high heels he had purchased for a girl friend in Seattle, and a single shirt.[28]

At the beginning of the twentieth century, the trend toward the consolidation of industry and the splitting of management from ownership was particularly pronounced in the Pacific Northwest, where the major extractive industries required large accumulations of capital. The lack of local capital made the area dependent on outside investors, who were especially welcome in British Columbia to develop the province's vast resources.

By enlarging the size of manufacturing enterprises, the combination movement increased the number of workers in a given location and thus contributed to a rise in class consciousness. By 1901 British Columbia had the greatest number of employees per establishment in the Dominion and almost three times the comparative figure for Washington. In the Pacific Northwest, however, the number of employees in a given establishment in urban areas was usually low compared to the great concentration of workers that occurred in the forest and wood-products establishments scattered throughout the timbered areas: in 1910, for example, the forest industries in Washington employed an average of 63.3 percent of all wage workers in the state. The size of the logging operations ranged from small "gyppo" outfits to concerns employing hundreds of men. The typical sawmill required some fifty to one hundred hands, but in 1907 the Sutton Lumber Company erected a mill on the west coast of Vancouver Island that employed between four and five hundred men. Thirty-eight of the thirty-nine companies employing one hundred or more workers in British Columbia in 1910 were lumber mills, the exception being the Vancouver Engineering Works. Unfortunately this official accounting did not include the employees in the all-important fisheries, canneries, and mines.[29]

Class consciousness, the awareness on the part of an individual worker of a bond of interest with his fellow workers that united them into a class distinct from all other classes, may well be one of the most overworked concepts in labor history. It was, nonetheless, a fact of life in the mining and logging areas of the Pacific Northwest, where workers congregated in semi-isolated camps often ruled by petty autocrats and endured the economic insecurity and special hazards characteristic of labor in an extractive industry.

Although the forests and the fisheries were scenes of monumental labor conflicts, class-conscious Vancouver Island coal miners and hardrock miners in the Kootenay region comprised the radical element that dominated the British Columbia labor movement. Furthermore, no other occupational group in the Pacific Northwest, including the numerous Cascade-area coal miners, acquired the political influence of the British Columbia miners. In the Slocan riding of the West Kootenay, for example, miners comprised almost one-third of the eligible voters and in the Nanaimo city riding, about one-half. In the legislative assembly, miners became proficient operators of the machinery of government. Hardrock miners in the Northern Rockies also formed the backbone of a colorful regional labor movement that centered in Spokane and Butte and provided the basis for dual unionism in Washington long before the Industrial Workers of the World began attracting attention with their free-speech fights.

British economist J. A. Hobson observed of British Columbia in 1906 that nowhere else in Canada was the labor question so prominent and class sentiment so bitter, a view reitereated by a royal commission in 1914 which noted "an ever widening gulf" between employer and employee in the Pacific province. Hobson attributed class consciousness in British Columbia to the socialistic labor movement on the Pacific Coast and to labor agitators who came into the province from Washington, but the major reason was that class consciousness was a natural response of workers reacting to the labor policies of ruthless entrepreneurs—of which there were many on both sides of the 49th parallel.

The notion that the labor movement was a product of the workers' job consciousness rather than class consciousness does not fully apply to the Pacific Northwest. As a consequence of the sudden development of large extractive enterprises, conservative craft unionism had little appeal for the class-conscious workers of the region, who saw industrial unionism and reform politics as better suited to the unique environment in which they found themselves.[30]

CHAPTER 2

A Pacific Northwest Labor Movement

The trade-union movement in Washington and Oregon began in 1853 with the formation of an organization among printers, and this was followed in the late 1860s by union activity among locomotive engineers and longshoremen. In 1859 the bakers of Victoria organized what was apparently the first union in British Columbia. Unions among the carpenters and shipwrights of Victoria appeared in 1862. Not until the 1880s, though, did union organization become widespread in the Pacific Northwest. Until then, most Pacific Northwesterners had not concerned themselves with matters of trade unionism, labor violence, or radicalism.[1]

SINOPHOBIA

In 1877 British Columbia and Washington Territory were still relatively isolated Pacific outposts. Perhaps a merchant living in the placid atmosphere of Olympia or Victoria even felt a sense of smugness as he read newspaper accounts of the widespread labor violence in eastern and midwestern centers such as Pittsburgh and Chicago, disturbances that led a later historian to label 1877 as a "Year of Violence."[2] But if the Pacific Northwesterner drew the unwarranted conclusion that the superior quality of life along the shores of Puget Sound or the Strait of Juan de Fuca militated against such outbursts, events eight years later proved sobering.

Completion of the Northern Pacific and Canadian Pacific railway lines in the mid-1880s represented an important step toward the integration of Washington and British Columbia into the urbanizing, industrializing world. An economic and social evolution that in eastern Canada and the United States had required decades was telescoped into a few years in the Pacific Northwest, creating the illusion that "in the Northwest everything seems to have happened within the last ten years. . . ."[3]

The corporation and the labor union were heralds of a new and often disconcerting pattern of economic relationships. Logging operations employing fifty to one hundred men were moving in where the small outfit had once dominated. The prospector, with his mule and pan, was giving way to the mining company employing dozens of hardrock miners as wage workers. As disturbing as these changes were, none seemed quite as foreboding to Northwest workers as competition from Oriental labor. In the minds of countless laborers, the Chinese were intimately connected with the threatening aspects of economic change.

During the decade following 1870, Washington Territory had experienced a thirteenfold increase in Chinese residents, from a little more than two hundred to approximately three thousand. Although the Chinese accounted for only 4 percent of the territory's population in 1880, significant Oriental communities were developing by that time in Seattle and Tacoma. Until passage of the Chinese Exclusion Act of 1882 large numbers of Chinese workers were imported as contract laborers to help build the railroads of the Pacific Northwest. When the two transcontinental lines were completed, the Chinese were thrown on the labor market, creating an unemployment problem in urban areas. White laborers perceived a threat to their jobs from the unemployed Chinese at the same time as destitute whites looked hungrily at the menial jobs held by the employed Chinese. Workingmen were frightened by the steady, hard-working Chinese, who supposedly did not drink liquor, ate little, and were often used as pawns by the new entrepreneurs to drive wages down and disrupt union organization.[4]

The economic competition from reduced wages was not the only threat felt by whites. When the ways of the Chinese were pictured as "so dark and furtive that their tricks cannot be detected and unearthed," anxious whites easily accepted notions of conspiracy. Rumors spread that the Chinese were planning to massacre whites in Washington. The remedy was strongly hinted at by the anti-Chinese newspapers of Puget Sound which claimed that the Chinese were "here in defiance of our laws" and thus had "forfeited the protection of our laws."[5]

Sinophobia, a common characteristic of white workers in the western United States and Canada, Australia, and New Zealand, blatantly combined job consciousness and class consciousness under the banner of white solidarity. Thus when legislative remedies seemed inadequate to cope with the perceived threat, white workers in the Pacific Northwest were inclined to take collective action. Using techniques developed earlier by agitators in California, local labor organizers in Washington and British Columbia fanned the flames of anti-Chinese sentiment.

Outrages against the Chinese in Wyoming triggered violence in Washington. On 7 September 1885, three Chinese hop pickers were murdered in the Squak Valley. Three days later, at the Newcastle mines of the Oregon Improvement Company, one of the largest and most powerful coal operations in the territory, a dozen masked men set fire to the quarters where thirty-seven Chinese workers slept. The Chinese lost their belongings in the blaze, and the next day they all fled the area. On 3 November a mob of some three thousand whites in Tacoma drove scores of Chinese from the city. Success led to a transference of activity to Seattle, where three months later racial antagonism and worsening economic conditions led to mob violence and compelled the territorial governor to declare martial law. The following year in Vancouver, British Columbia, workers threatened to drive out the Chinese by the same methods used in Washington.[6]

By 1886 or 1887 most participants in the anti-Chinese outrages seemed convinced that they had attained their immediate goal, and the furor died down. Probably few of these people stopped to wonder what would happen if society ever came to perceive organized labor as a dire threat and took frenzied and sometimes extralegal steps to deal with it—as indeed happened a few years later. Some of the anti-Chinese agitators remained outspoken labor radicals, others quietly sought release through communitarianism, and still others went off in search of legislative remedies for society's ills. In short, while some participants adopted progressively more radical ideas, others, upon reflection, became far more conservative.

Though the anti-Chinese outbursts obviously touched the lives of a diverse group of people, the episode is probably most important in the impact it had on the evolution of organized labor in the Pacific Northwest, especially in Washington. During the formative years from 1885 to 1902, the local labor movement often revealed a heritage rooted in the sometimes contradictory lessons of the mid-1880s.

One popular lesson was that in a young and impatient society, radical action might offer a quick solution to the complex social and economic problems vexing the industrial world. In fact, the first national labor organization to attract a mass following in the North Pacific region, the Knights of Labor, was largely predicated on that assertion.

THE RISE OF LEFT-WING UNIONISM

Originating in Philadelphia in 1869, the Noble and Holy Order of the Knights of Labor sought to unite all branches of honorable toil in an ungainly structure that contained elements of both craft and industrial unionism. Although some assemblies were composed of the members of a single craft, most were mixed assemblies that placed less emphasis on collective bargaining than on labor solidarity and reform politics. Some of the mixed assemblies were little more than reform groups or social organizations that supported reading rooms, study groups, and guest lecturers. Although a number of the Knights' reformist schemes derived from the ideology of Jacksonian America and were designed less to cope with modern industrialism than to escape it, the Knights also pioneered such reforms as equal pay for both sexes and elimination of child labor.[7]

Almost ten years after its founding, the Order determined to become a truly national labor organization. The West Coast was not represented at the Knights' first general assembly in 1878 in Reading, Pennsylvania, but later that year a special session of the general assembly issued a one-year commission for an organizer in Portland, Oregon. The commission apparently went unused. In contrast to the growing strength of the Knights in the San Francisco Bay area, the North Pacific region was not actively organized by the Knights until the early 1880s. Because there was no rail connection between California and the Pacific Northwest until 1887, the Knights expanded their influence along the shipping lanes that linked San Francisco to the coal mining towns of Vancouver Island and the Puget Sound region.[8]

The Order grew rapidly in Tacoma and Seattle in late 1885 by capitalizing on the ugly mood created by the depression and unemployment that followed completion of the Pacific railway lines. Sinophobia and the phenomenal growth of the Knights in the region were irrefutably linked. In early September 1885, the Knights built a local assembly from the unsound timber of anti-Chinese sentiment in Tacoma. Later in the month the Knights and their allies held a territorial anti-Chinese congress. In September, likewise, the Knights in Victoria, British Columbia, staged a torchlight parade with banners reading "Chinese Serfs in Competition with White Labor" and "Land and Mineral Monopolies." The Knights of Victoria also began to publish a reform journal. "Being a labor paper," publisher J. M. Duval noted, "it must of necessity be a strong anti-Chinese journal."[9]

Many of those involved in the anti-Chinese activity in Tacoma and Seattle had no aim except to get rid of the Chinese, but Daniel Cronin, an agitator from the timber country around Eureka, California, dismissed the Chinese question as being subordinate to the real issue, the conflict between capital and labor. Cronin exemplified the close connection between the left wing of the Knights of Labor and the International Workingmen's Association (IWA), a radical organization that appeared in San Francisco in 1881 as a byproduct of anti-Chinese agitation.[10]

The Pacific Coast division of the IWA claimed to be a part of the Marxist Red International, but it was really an indigenous organization that reflected the perverse eclecticism of Burnette Haskell, an enigmatic young San Francisco lawyer noted for his indiscriminate advocacy of the reforms that swept America in the late nineteenth century. In addition to having established the IWA on the Pacific Coast, Haskell edited the IWA organ, the *Truth*, which he used to focus attention on the problems of Chinese immigration and monopoly and to support the left wing of the Knights of Labor. The IWA, which held agitation meetings and established labor libraries and lyceums, was linked to socialism but also espoused a brand of anarchism that generally rejected overt violence in favor of education. Haskell, however, the perennial adolescent, was fascinated by the political possibilities of explosives, and he once offered readers detailed instructions on how to make dynamite.[11]

IWA organizers such as Daniel Cronin actively sought converts from among the working class on the Pacific slope. Haskell himself visited the Pacific Northwest in February 1886, and on several occasions issued a lisping appeal to workers to rid the area of Chinese by Washington's birthday; the following year he claimed that adherents in Oregon and Washington accounted for almost one-third of the IWA's six thousand members. That figure was certainly greatly inflated, for the IWA had clearly declined after the Seattle disturbances. A number of IWA members joined the Socialist Labor party (see chapter 6) to continue their search for a solution to the problems created by the new industrialism; others, including Haskell and Cronin, embraced the gospel of communitarianism.

In retrospect, the IWA, which once described itself as a "secret, mysterious, world-wide" organization that was "quietly honeycombing society," appears more ludicrous than sinister. Nonetheless, many frightened citizens in Seattle probably agreed with a grand jury claim that the IWA was using the anti-Chinese turmoil to produce a social revolution. A bloody explosion during a labor demonstration in Chicago's Haymarket Square resulted in similar if unfounded fears about the aims of the Knights of Labor.[12]

The total membership of the Knights of Labor rose to 729,677 in July 1886. Seattle's District Assembly 115, having jurisdiction over all Washington local assemblies west of the Cascades, reported more than two thousand members in its nineteen affiliates. The number of local assemblies in the district climbed to thirty-two in 1887; ominously, however, membership had fallen by more than one-third. The newly formed Spokane District Assembly reported 127 members, but aside from Canada and the Inland Empire region, the Knights of Labor were clearly on the wane. The loss of several major strikes and mounting anti-labor hysteria limited the effectiveness and appeal of the Knights as a national labor organization.

Frustrated by the rapid decline in the Pacific Northwest, Burnette Haskell, the self-appointed spokesman for the left wing of the Knights, accused Knights' leader Terence Powderly of having sold

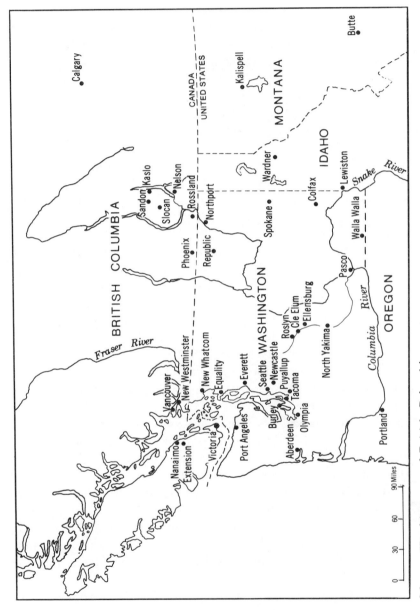

Map 2. Washington and British Columbia

out the Order on the North Pacific coast. In truth, Powderly deserved less blame for the decline than did the local Knights who had sought to capitalize on anti-Chinese sentiment in an effort to recruit members. Both the Knights and the IWA lost most of their popular support when anti-Chinese passions cooled. A number of trade unionists in western Washington came to believe that the Knights' reliance on anti-Chinese hysteria to improve the lot of workingmen had discredited it as a bona fide labor organization. In any case, however, members of the IWA and the left wing of the Knights were the first labor radicals in the Pacific Northwest.[13]

TROUBLE IN THE COAL FIELDS

In the coal fields of Washington and British Columbia, where the local assemblies were built on a more substantial basis than in Tacoma, Seattle, or Victoria, the Knights continued to test their strength against the mine operators. Because of its inclusive structure, the Knights of Labor appealed to the semi-skilled, often mobile workers drawn to the coal mines and kept in a state of submission by powerful companies that threatened to employ Chinese labor. Unprotected against Chinese incursions by sharply defined lines of skill, white miners sought to invoke the lines of status and prestige that membership in the Knights provided.

Coal had been discovered in the area east of Seattle and Tacoma in the early 1870s; by 1883 Wilkeson, Carbonado, and Newcastle were the largest and most boisterous mining towns in the territory. Like most coal towns in eastern America, those in Washington were characterized by their isolation, company housing, and the proverbial company store. The Oregon Improvement Company, an influential mine, railroad, and shipping enterprise, owned the largest mines on the west slope of the Cascades in the mid-1880s, but its operations were soon surpassed by those of a Northern Pacific Railroad subsidiary that operated mines at Roslyn and Cle Elum on the drier east side of the Cascades near Ellensburg. By 1905 the more than two thousand miners employed by the Northern Pacific enterprise produced 51 percent of the coal in the state and helped make Washington the second largest source of coal in the western United States.[14]

Many of the early Cascade area miners had become familiar with unionism in the mines of the East or abroad. Their concern for mine safety prompted one of the earliest strikes in the Washington mines, a dispute between the Knights and the Oregon Improvement Company at Newcastle in the spring of 1886 that evolved into a bitter seven-month struggle marked by violence on both sides. Before the conflict ended in victory for the Knights, the territorial militia had been sent to the camp and martial law declared. The isolation of the various camps and the presence of several different nationalities, however, prevented a general strike of Cascade region miners to obtain uniform working conditions and wages.[15]

Serious labor conflict in the Cascade coal fields erupted several more times in the late 1880s. One such confrontation occurred at Roslyn, an isolated company town of two thousand people, mostly miners and their families who lived in the shanties that clustered about the mines. The miners received an average wage of $34 a month even when they worked ten hours a day and six days a week, and even this soon vanished at the "pluck me" or company store. Miners had grumbled about the low wages and poor working conditions ever since the Northern Pacific subsidiary opened the field in 1885, but they were unable to agree among themselves on a plan of action until 1888, when they called a strike because the company brought in almost fifty black miners, who worked for longer hours and lower wages than white miners. The company protected the black miners in their tent quarters with armed guards.[16]

Labor troubles in the coal fields were particularly disturbing to Territorial Governor Eugene Semple, a man described by his biographer as an outspoken if ineffectual champion of white workingmen. Semple had come west in 1863 and earned a comfortable living offering legal counsel to miners during the Bannack City, Montana, gold rush. He became a member of the "Copperhead" wing of the Democratic party in Oregon but almost ruined his chance of being appointed territorial governor by supporting the anti-Chinese agitation that periodically swept the West Coast. Semple's personal sympathies lay with the miners in the Roslyn struggle of 1888, although he tried to remain officially neutral. In his report to the secretary of the interior, however, he deplored what he described as outrages committed by an absentee-owned coal company. He was particularly upset by the company's use of a private army of detectives that he considered a "direct menace" to the peace. The Master Workman of the Spokane District Assembly urged the governor to intervene in the struggle, which the Knights' leader described as a fight between all workers and a tyrannical management, but Semple first wanted to clarify some of the facts in this very murky dispute.[17]

The Knights claimed that the work force at Roslyn was being supplanted by company lackeys, mainly Portland rowdies and blacks. They also blamed the trouble on the rival United Miners' and Mine Laborers' Society, sometimes known simply as the Miners' Union. The Knights accused the Miners' Union of being a company organization composed of scabs. The Miners' Union denied this, claiming that they were simply an organization of former Knights who had broken with the Order. In any event, the coal company used the rivalry to destroy both organizations at Roslyn.[18]

Semple was territorial governor when labor conflict broke out once again at Newcastle. After the 1886 strike, work stoppages and sporadic clashes between the Knights and the Miners' Union had become increasingly frequent. When the Oregon Improvement Company in May 1888 replaced a foreman who was a member of the Knights with one who belonged to the Miners' Union, the Knights refused to work, claiming that the new man was a company hireling. After Knights from nearby mines at Franklin and Gilman arrived in Newcastle to join the protest, the Oregon Improvement Company appealed to Governor Semple to send troops to help protect its property.

Semple, who tried to remain officially neutral and allow local law enforcement officers to maintain the peace, was outraged when the company brought in a private army of detectives on the pretext that local authorities were not adequately protecting company property. The struggle, which dragged on into early 1889, ended in an illusory victory for the Knights.

For the next two years, while the Knights proudly flexed their organizational muscle, the Oregon Improvement Company waited for a change in the political climate and quietly planned for a victorious showdown with the union. Carefully copying the successful union-smashing tactics of the Roslyn operators, the company launched a brutal assault on the Knights in May 1891. Intimidated by a small army of private detectives and imported strikebreakers and lacking the kind of political support they had enjoyed in the late 1880s, the Knights nonetheless fought back for several months before being finally driven from the Cascade coal fields. In 1890, coal miners who had lost confidence in the Knights met in Columbus, Ohio, to form the United Mine Workers of America, destined to become one of the most powerful unions in the United States, but not until the opening years of the twentieth century would miners' unions again appear in Washington's grim coal camps and towns.[19]

The Knights' struggles at Roslyn and Newcastle did have one notable positive result. The disturbing nature of the labor-management conflict influenced some of the delegates who met in Olympia in the summer of 1889 to frame a state constitution. Although only two members of the convention, Matt J. M'Elroy, a logger, and William L. Newton, a coal miner, ostensibly represented labor, the completed document contained not only a provision forbidding the use of convict labor but also one that forbade individuals or corporations to organize, maintain, or employ armed bodies of men. As organized labor soon learned, however, reform gained by political action was often poorly implemented and only weakly enforced. It was, in fact, the failure of the state government to restrain the Oregon Improvement Company's use of armed detectives that did much to spur the Knights of Labor into organizing Washington's Populist party in 1891.[20]

Coal mining on Vancouver Island antedated operations in Washington by at least twenty years. But like the mines of the Cascades, those on Vancouver Island typically employed a large number of workers. Like their counterparts in Washington, the Vancouver Island miners exhibited a class consciousness based on race. As early as 1867 when a few Chinese were hired as miners in the Nanaimo area, white miners had threatened to strike.

The most significant mining enterprise on the island was presided over by Robert Dunsmuir, an industrialist who regarded all labor unions with the combative instincts of a medieval baron. The anti-unionism of the Dunsmuir operations at Wellington and Extension contrasted vividly with the policies of the Vancouver Coal Company, which maintained industrial peace for twenty years by cooperating with the men at its Nanaimo mines. In time, the Dunsmuir miners became the most highly radicalized group of workers on the Pacific Coast. Labor radicalism on Vancouver Island and the peculiar evolution of socialism in British Columbia were, in large measure, direct responses to the intransigent attitude of Robert Dunsmuir and his son, James.

After Robert Dunsmuir opened the Wellington Colliery six miles northeast of Nanaimo in 1869, the mine yielded "more coal and more profit" than any other mining operation on the Pacific Coast. Even in its early days the company employed six hundred men, half of whom were Chinese working for wages that were 66 to 75 percent less than white miners received. Both Robert and James Dunsmuir thought that cheap labor was necessary to compete with Seattle coal. Not only did the Dunsmuir policy pose a threat to the jobs of white workers, but in the gaseous mines typical of the Vancouver Island field, Chinese miners allegedly added to the danger because they were usually unable to read the safety warnings posted in English. For whatever reason, the death toll from explosion and fire in the province's coal mines was among the highest in the British Empire.[21]

An observer noted in 1877 that Nanaimo had "none of that dried-up blackened appearance which colliery villages so often presented in the mining districts of England." At the time that observation was made, however, the Nanaimo area was already becoming an unpleasant habitation for miners. Strikes had been common there at least since 1855. A five-month strike in 1871 ended in failure, but new miners entering the field from the United Kingdom brought encouraging word of important legislative victories won by labor in Great Britain.

Miners at Wellington in 1877 formed a Mutual Protection Society and struck because of poor working conditions and a wage reduction. In typical fashion, Robert Dunsmuir imported strikebreakers and ordered strikers evicted from company-owned housing. When the strikers refused to move after peacefully convincing the scabs to leave the area, Dunsmuir persuaded the provincial government to send a force of militia to break up the miners' organization. After four months the strike was broken, and the Wellington managers then sought for years to root out the hated vestiges of unionism.

On Vancouver Island history often repeated itself. The expansion of the mining industry in the five years after 1877 attracted

new miners from Great Britain and Pennsylvania who helped rein-
vigorate the local union movement. But in 1883 Robert Dunsmuir
again intimidated his workers and smashed a three-month strike by
advertising for three hundred strikebreakers and allying himself
with the powerful American railroad barons, Crocker, Stanford,
and Huntington. The Knights bravely organized their first assembly in British Columbia in December 1883, a mixed local in
Nanaimo. But like their predecessors on Vancouver Island, the
Knights proved disappointingly weak in the face of determined
employers.

The Dunsmuir company in 1890 yet again refused to negotiate
with striking miners who demanded union recognition and an
eight-hour work day. A battery of artillery sent in by the provincial
government backed James Dunsmuir, who, after his father's death
the previous year, assumed full control over the company.[22]

THE LEGACY OF THE KNIGHTS OF LABOR

Faced with employer intransigence in most coal mines and a loss
of popular support in urban areas when anti-Chinese passions
calmed, the Knights tried to recapture a mass following by an
anti-liquor campaign, but by the early 1890s the Order had so
deteriorated that in most of the Pacific Northwest it was little more
than an agrarian reform body. A Yakima fruit grower represented
the Washington Knights at the 1891 national convention. James R.
Sovereign, an Iowa reform publisher, replaced Powderly as General Master Workman two years later. The depression of 1893 destroyed the remaining assemblies in western Washington and
British Columbia, but in isolated Spokane and the Inland Empire
the Order retained a following until at least 1900.[23]

Many a pre-World War I labor leader in Washington had been
introduced to the basic principles of trade unionism by the Knights
of Labor. Some leaders, notably those in Spokane and the Inland
Empire, continued to regard the labor egalitarianism and reform
politics of the mixed assembly as infallible principles well into the
twentieth century; others vigorously promoted the craft unionism
of the AFL because they were convinced by experience that the
concepts of the Knights of Labor were unworkable.

The Knights of Labor also influenced the course of reform in

Washington. M. P. Bulger, for example, a self-proclaimed socialist and a conspicuous anti-Chinese orator for the Knights in Tacoma and Seattle, was chairman of the state executive committee of the Populist party when it captured Washington's government in the election of 1896. The Order's reading rooms in Seattle, Spokane, and other communities helped to make reform literature available to workers. The Knights also established the first labor journals in Washington.[24]

In contrast to the ten-year hiatus that marked the union movement in the Washington coal fields, miners on Vancouver Island became the vanguard of the provincial labor movement during the 1890s. Although the Knights by 1890 had been virtually supplanted in the mines by the Miners' and Mine Laborers' Protective Association that dissident Nanaimo members had formed in 1886, the miners retained a basic faith in the Knights' argument that labor solidarity and political action were the best means of securing improved working conditions in the mines. Recent mine disasters and strikes helped unite the Nanaimo and Wellington miners in 1890, for the first time, in opposition to the Dunsmuir empire, and James Dunsmuir's unenlightened attitude did much to convert the Miners' and Mine Laborers' Protective Association into a bastion of radical unionism in the province. In its infancy, the organization advocated an eight-hour workday, union recognition, arbitration of industrial disputes, limitation of Chinese immigration, and a number of reform schemes popular with the middle class. Little more than ten years later, however, the Nanaimo branch of the Miners' and Mine Laborers' Protective Association embraced revolutionary socialism.[25]

Regional Unionism

The Knights were still a powerful force in much of the Pacific Northwest when trade unionists, disturbed by the structure and philosophy of the Knights, organized the American Federation of Labor (AFL) in 1886. Representing a federation of autonomous craft unions composed for the most part of skilled workers, the AFL preached a practical, conservative brand of "business unionism" that operated within the established order. Guiding the new federation for thirty-eight of the next thirty-nine years was Samuel Gompers, a British immigrant cigarmaker of Dutch-Jewish ancestry. It was Gompers who determined to dissociate the AFL from independent political action and utopian radicalism.

Eventually the Knights receded to a few isolated areas as the AFL established its dominance over Canadian and American labor. In the Pacific Northwest, however, recurrent Sinophobia and the class-conscious heritage left by the Knights became a part of the indigenous radicalism that frustrated an easy triumph by the AFL.

During the years prior to 1902, when the North Pacific region lay largely beyond the scope of AFL influence, a significant element in the local labor movement came to embrace concepts that were at odds with the principles espoused by Samuel Gompers during his long tenure as leader of the federation. Industrial unionism, a close link between labor and socialism, and labor political parties became hallmarks of Pacific Northwest labor.

The difficulty the AFL faced in attempting to establish its hegemony in the Pacific Northwest is attributable to geographic isolation, the attitude of workers in the region, the nature of the labor market, and the political and cultural framework within which unions operated. Geographic isolation, in particular, encouraged labor leaders on the Pacific Coast to develop a tenuous community of interest that posed a potential threat to the national aspirations of the AFL. By 1886, when the AFL took over the records and treasury of its moribund predecessor, the Federation of Organized Trades and Labor Unions of the United States and Canada, plans were already being formulated for a Representative Council of Federated Trades and Labor Organizations of the Pacific Coast. Little was done to implement such a plan until in 1891 the president of the central labor council in San Francisco traveled to Oregon, Washington, and British Columbia to rekindle interest in the idea of a "grand centralization" of labor organizations from San Diego to Alaska. Proponents of regional unionism were encouraged when delegates from the central labor councils in Portland and Seattle attended the first convention of the Pacific Coast Federation of Labor in San Francisco in 1891. Until the demise of the organization in 1895, Washington and British Columbia labor leaders were active participants in the movement.[26]

Although the new federation stated that it had no intention of establishing a rival to the AFL on the West Coast, Samuel Gompers was clearly worried. At the 1891 AFL convention Gompers complained that the Pacific Coast body had "practically established a 'Federation' outside of the American Federation of Labor." By the time of the 1892 convention, however, Gompers was able to report that the threat of dual unionism on the Pacific Coast had ended because the "previously isolated" unions of the Pacific slope had entered into fraternal bonds with those of the East. Gompers was being too optimistic. Delegates to the 1894 convention of the Pacific Coast Federation rather pointedly promised to promote the organization of unskilled workers, an idea that was not very highly regarded by some members of the AFL. And as long as the AFL ignored the concerns of Pacific Northwest labor, the potential for independent regional labor organizations continued to exist.[27]

Throughout the 1890s Pacific Northwest labor continued to think of itself as a movement largely separate from the new, insecure, and distant AFL. Reading the monthly report issued by the Pacific Coast Federation was a regular part of the meetings of Seattle's central labor council; and even after the federation ceased to exist, Seattle trade unionists continued to maintain strong bonds of kinship with other western labor leaders in Vancouver, San Francisco, and Butte. A synopsis of the proceedings of the weekly meetings of the San Francisco labor council was generally read at sessions of the Seattle central, as were reports from the Vancouver Trades and Labor Council. More than once, the Seattle central sent copies of Washington's proposed labor laws to its counterparts in other states and provinces.[28]

Labor journals that often doubled as reform organs helped reinforce the concept of a regional labor movement, and regional labor journalism remained viable long after the AFL moved to establish its hegemony in the region. In 1914, at the instigation of the Washington State Federation of Labor, editors of labor papers in Tacoma, Everett, Spokane, Seattle, Vancouver, B. C., and several other communities met in Tacoma to organize the Western Labor Press Association to share each week's news and labor cartoons. Workers were likely to get a left-wing slant in the materials exchanged by the new regional press association because three of the most influential editors, H. L. Hughes of Spokane, E. B. Ault of Seattle, and R. P. Pettipiece of Vancouver, were either socialists or had been socialists in the recent past. It is possible that the seeds planted by the regional left-wing journalists bore fruit in the labor disorders that shocked Pacific Northwesterners after World War. I.[29]

In the mid-1890s the AFL repeatedly adopted resolutions at its annual conventions urging organizational activity by the federation in the Far West, but little could be done to implement such proposals during the hard times that followed the Panic of 1893. The AFL was itself struggling to remain alive. With the return of prosperity in 1897 and the growing threat of a rival regional union movement posed by the Western Federation of Miners, the AFL leadership attempted to organize workers in the volatile Rocky Mountain region, but the task of appealing to labor in the Pacific Northwest remained less urgent. In Washington and British Columbia, a few unions affiliated with the AFL during the 1890s, but their members continued to be physically detached from the majority of AFL members. Before 1900, delegates representing the Pacific Northwest labor movement seldom attended AFL conventions, and AFL organizers usually ignored labor affairs in the northwest corner of the United States.

As a consequence of AFL neglect, the city centrals in the Pacific Northwest, aside from the conservative one in Portland, were slow to request AFL charters. While Portland joined the federation at the personal instigation of Samuel Gompers in 1889, Seattle did not affiliate with the AFL until March 1902, and Spokane trade unionists simultaneously formed three separate central bodies before the AFL triumphed in the city later in the decade.[30]

GOMPERS' CANADIAN DILEMMA

The inclination toward regional unionism was even stronger in British Columbia than in Washington because of the existence of a potential Canadian alternative to the AFL, the Trades and Labor Congress of Canada (TLC). Formed in 1886 by trade unionists and members of the Knights of Labor, the TLC had as its basic purpose the securing of legislation to help Canadian workers. But unlike the AFL, which had been created by trade unionists opposed to the structural and philosophical ideals of the Knights of Labor, the TLC was largely guided during its formative years by members of the Knights. The Knights constituted a majority of the delegates at all but three of the annual TLC conventions from 1886 to 1893; they also held the presidency of the body from 1888 to 1892.

There was, in fact, no significant AFL influence in the TLC until the late 1890s. By that time, however, the organization, which originated as an Ontario-Quebec body, had received a philosophical infusion from the industrially oriented trade unionists of British Columbia. The British Columbia influence became so strong that delegates to the 1896 session elected Ralph Smith, business agent of the Nanaimo Miners' and Mine Laborers' Protective Association, as vice-president. Smith soon became the "Gompers of Canada." At times during the years before World War I, British Columbians seemed to dominate the councils of the TLC.

Gompers and the AFL were anxious to organize Canadian labor, fearing that if Dominion labor were weak and poorly organized, American employers would take jobs into Canada in response to growing AFL power in the United States. The AFL chartered its first Canadian central in Montreal in 1897. Two years later it appointed a printer and a boilermaker as AFL organizers in British Columbia, and issued charters to central labor bodies in Revelstoke and Victoria and to the Nanaimo Miners' and Mine Laborers' Protective Association. AFL leaders, however, tended to ignore the fact that American labor methods, institutions, and objectives were not necessarily applicable in Canada. Gompers' concept of "pure and simple" unionism never had many strong supporters in the Dominion Congress. Furthermore, as the AFL began extending its influence into the Dominion, federation leaders did not quite know how to classify the TLC, since it did not correspond to any of the constituent units—such as international unions, city centrals, and state federations—that made up the AFL. Attempts by the AFL to force the TLC into a subordinate category resembling that of a state federation produced friction and ruffled Canadian feelings, which helped to limit AFL influence in British Columbia prior to World War I.[31]

In the 1890s the development of a regional labor movement in the Pacific Northwest was further encouraged by the results of labor-reform politics. By the time the AFL began extending its influence into the area, trade unionists in Washington and British Columbia had already forged two distinct patterns of political involvement in their respective regions. These patterns of political activity both drew upon and contributed to the region's radical heritage.

CHAPTER 3

Reform Panaceas and Pacific Northwest Labor

In the 1880s and 1890s an increasing number of Americans and Canadians became convinced that social and political development in their countries was not keeping pace with industrial progress. According to the conventional wisdom, however, Christianity offered the best solution to the problems of unemployment and poverty, vulgar displays of wealth, and labor violence. Concepts of collective regeneration were rejected by those who believed that a society is no better than its individual members.

Every man was supposed to be his own reformer according to the pious souls who held that the misery and impoverishment of the masses were due mainly to their "excesses and follies." Ironically, however, moral reformers did not hesitate to use the state to legislate prohibition when individual temperance failed to produce a sober society.

In that era of individualistic Protestantism, moral reform became an instrument of social control at a time of deteriorating community cohesion and apparent governmental impotence. In almost all the cities of the Pacific Northwest, the suppression of vice, the regulation of saloons, the banning of cigarettes, and Sunday legislation were advocated by the "best people" in an attempt to unite a society riven by profound economic, technological, and demographic changes.[1]

The most popular moral reform in the region was the regulation of the liquor traffic, which seemed so much a part of life in the

Pacific Northwest. British Columbians, by 1893, were imbibing almost one-and-a half times as much liquor as Canadians in any other province. Railroad, mining, and lumber camps were all noted for heavy drinking and the institutionalization of the saloon.

The saloon, more than anything else, symbolized the disturbing aspects of the liquor issue for the middle class. Reformers often saw it as an adjunct of prostitution; some saloons, indeed, featured private boxes complete with a couch. The saloon was also considered a center for gambling and drugs and a hangout for pimps and criminals. Frequently, the saloon was a power in local politics. Prior to the coming of the railroad, however, the difficulty of distributing unpasteurized and easily spoilable beer had confined the saloon almost entirely to the urban areas of the Pacific Northwest. Technological changes during the 1890s, though, resulted in a proliferation of saloons, many of which were open twenty-four hours a day, seven days a week.[2]

Moral reform fervor swept over the Pacific Northwest in waves. In such cities as Seattle, Vancouver, and Victoria white-slavery scares stirred up by ministers and journalists led to periodic and usually ineffectual campaigns to clean up notoriously wide-open red light districts. During spells of popular anti-liquor sentiment, evangelistic and moral uplift societies such as the Women's Christian Temperance Union and the Anti-Saloon League had been able to add numerous minor liquor laws to the statute books; but when a prohibition amendment to Washington's constitution was submitted to a popular vote in 1889, it was rejected.[3] The education of a recalcitrant populace had to continue for three more decades.

Despite their noble ideals the moral reformers were both offensive and naive. In Vancouver, the self-appointed guardians of moral purity played amateur detective shortly after the turn of the century to hound the city's prostitutes. When the Dominion Parliament, in 1906, passed a Sunday closing law, the Lord's Day Act, the common sentiment in British Columbia was, "We don't want any eastern code of morals thrust upon us." The provincial attorney general, consequently, did little to enforce the legislation. Prohibitionists directed an appeal to the working classes, but the obvious paternalism of the moral reformers offended many unionists. Many workers, furthermore, looked upon the saloon as a poor man's club. In British Columbia, organized labor began to cry that there was a need to reform the moral reformers because they wished to "do unto others things others do not wish to have done." The intellectual myopia of the moral reformers also appalled many labor leaders and socialists. For a socialist, drink was not the cause of poverty; poverty was the cause of drink. "The prohibitionists see the effect; the socialist would remove the cause." Prostitution, likewise, was supposedly caused by low wages that reduced the worker to a commodity.[4]

MORAL REFORM AND LABOR REFORM

In the mid-1880s moral reform appeared to be an inadequate solution to the ominous and growing problem of labor discontent, and disturbances such as occurred in Tacoma and Seattle caused some observers to challenge conventional wisdom. In an 1886 article on the labor question, E. V. Smalley, a Northern Pacific Railroad journalist and promoter, argued that the solution for labor discontent was more far-reaching than the restless working classes realized and was "beyond a remedy in any of the ways they are seeking it." Recognizing the difference between moral reform and labor reform, Smalley proposed that ministers "lay aside their outgrown theology to grapple with the real troubles of humanity which concern the ways of living decently and happily in this world and not how to get to Heaven." Society, said Smalley, must now heed the workers' cry that the "fruits of their labor are not equitably distributed."[5]

Unlike the well-meaning but often inept moral reformer, the labor reformer attempted both to educate workers regarding their condition in society and to convince them to improve that condition either by their own collective efforts or in conjunction with middle-class reform groups. Workers, according to the labor reformers, had too long been educated to hopelessness and depression by a press and pulpit that attempted to convince them that it was the "law of nature and the will of God" that they should remain poor and enslaved. Labor reformers argued that poverty and slavery were created not by God or nature but by bad laws, poor social organization, and the "meanness and greed of men." The solutions they offered ranged from women's suffrage and factory legislation to workmen's compensation and revolutionary socialism. Some labor reformers of a more conservative inclination, however, accused the socialists of failing to come to grips with the existing order by "building castles in the air or dreaming of the future golden age."[6]

The popular historian Frederick Lewis Allen once pictured reformers as "tree-surgeons" hacking away at "ugly and misshapen growths" while the tree continued to thrust out new shoots. In the 1880s and 1890s, however, a growing number of reformers became willing to root up the whole tree if necessary. In their search for solutions to society's ills, these reformers turned not to the moral tracts on prohibition and prostitution but to the more encompassing solutions that flowed from the pens of authors like Henry George, Edward Bellamy, and the various socialist writers. Their solutions may seem naive today, but to people living in the 1880s and 1890s, they offered a mind-stimulating opportunity to understand and cope with the momentous changes of that era.

So popular was Henry George's *Progress and Poverty* after it appeared in 1879 that economist Richard T. Ely claimed that the five-hundred-page study was read by tens of thousands of laborers who had "never before" looked between the covers of an economics book. Its concept of a single tax that would promote opportunity and equality by driving out the speculators and making more land available to all was incorporated into countless labor reform platforms. Likewise, Edward Bellamy's utopian novel *Looking Backward* enjoyed immense success after 1888 because many considered it a straw showing which way the winds of change were blowing. Even those critical of the book admitted that its vivid word pictures and appealing analogies "taught people to study questions they have never thought of before."[7]

Historian Eric Goldman has noted how the ideas of Henry George were influential in "dissolving the steel chain of ideas" used by Social Darwinists to sanction the status quo. The reason why the single tax solution so appealed to reformers, however, was probably best stated by ex-president Rutherford B. Hayes, who, despite his misgivings about the single tax itself, thought that Henry George had portrayed the "rottenness of the present system." The pervasive influence of *Progress and Poverty* is a tribute to its provocative quality.[8]

Henry George's single tax concept spread from the United States to New Zealand, Australia, Great Britain, and Canada, where most of the avid single taxers were members of the Knights of Labor. The Knights' organ, the *Palladium of Labor*, became the first Canadian labor journal to support George's scheme of "land nationalization." The single tax and other antimonopoly ideas also became articles of faith for the new Trades and Labor Congress (TLC).[9]

In British Columbia, the Knights commenced disseminating the ideas contained in *Progress and Poverty* around 1884. Soon, tax reform clubs dotted the province, making additional converts to reform as the ideas of Henry George found their most fertile intellectual soil in all North America. Labor in Washington was likewise active in the formation of the single tax clubs that served as clearing houses for reform ideas during the 1890s.[10]

In attempting to present their sweeping solutions to the problems of the new industrialism, the socialists and the single taxers, whom a socialist speaker in Spokane once referred to as "our little brothers," regularly debated one another. Although some people attended the meetings only to be entertained by the "fight" itself, many labor leaders pondered the choice seriously. In 1887 Henry George himself debated the issue of the single tax versus socialism with Serge Schevitch. The presiding officer of the debate was Samuel Gompers. In time, most socialists came to regard the single tax as simplistic and inadequate. "From the proletarian viewpoint," the *Western Clarion* declared, "Single Tax is an absurd piece of inconsequence." The single tax, nonetheless, helped convert many early reformers to socialism.[11]

The ideas of Karl Marx had little influence in America until Laurence Gronlund presented them in modified form. Realizing that no work existed in English to explain the principles of scientific socialism, the Danish-born Gronlund published *The Cooperative Commonwealth* in 1884 in an effort to adapt Marxian tenets to the American milieu. Gronlund believed that socialism had failed in the United States because its little band of adherents were making no attempt to understand it within the context of American society. In his book, Gronlund discarded Marx's idea of a class struggle and gave socialism a more moderate tone. Though Gronlund received no real financial reward for his book, his phrase "the Cooperative Commonwealth" became a shibboleth to designate all types of schemes proposed by all kinds of radicals in North America.[12]

How much influence *The Cooperative Commonwealth* had on Edward Bellamy is a matter of historical dispute; it is a fact, however, that Gronlund halted publication of his book when Bellamy published *Looking Backward* in 1888. Soon Bellamy's enthusiastic readers organized clubs to spread the gospel of "Nationalism." Although Gronlund and others equated Nationalism with socialism, the Nationalists were technically not socialists. Bellamy, in fact, has his leading character in *Looking Backward* blame the followers of the red flag for hindering the growth of Nationalism because "their talk so disgusted people as to deprive the best-considered projects for social reform of a hearing." [13]

Bellamy was well aware that the term "socialism" had become a very convenient malediction to pronounce on any person or idea that one opposed. Especially in America, as Michael Harrington has more recently noted, socialism is a bad word, and to call a man a socialist is to accuse him of being un-American.

Socialists were typically denounced for their class consciousness and their opposition to America's national faith in individualism, for allegedly promoting the confiscation of private property, opposing religion and morality, advocating free love, and pandering to the mob. Socialists were considered not only impractical dreamers but also unpatriotic and anarchistic.

The more rabid expressions of the non-socialist view of socialism were perhaps best summed up by Theodore Roosevelt. Describing socialistic notions of morality as "revolting," he went on to aver that socialists would replace the family and home life by a glorified state free-lunch counter and a state foundling asylum; they would deliberately enthrone self-indulgence as an ideal with the "absolute abandonment of all morality as between men and women. . . ." This emotional view of the supposed socialist threat no doubt caused Roosevelt and other conservatives to be more sympathetic to those reformers who could help preserve the system against both the plutocrats and the socialists. Roosevelt recognized, however, that there were different types of socialists, and he was willing to work with those "whose socialism is really only an advanced form of liberalism." [14]

The amorphous nature of the socialist movement in North America meant that one observer might accuse socialists of being opposed to Christianity, while another person described socialism as identical to Christianity. "We are all of us more or less socialists," the *Victoria Daily Colonist* declared in 1911, because the fundamental principles of true socialism and true Christianity "are so nearly alike. . . ." The concept of socialism was so variously construed by popular writers as to become almost meaningless. When indiscriminate observers noted solemnly that socialism was embodied in the first statute ever passed by a legislature or that "all public institutions in which people have a voice are socialistic," they did little to delineate the parameters of late nineteenth- and early twentieth-century socialism. No wonder a Populist in western Washington could gleefully declare that "Chehalis today is a socialistic town, for Chehalis very sensibly owns and controls her own electric plant." [15]

Because the Pacific Northwest socialists were unable to agree as to what constituted socialism, the regional socialist movement was wracked by an inordinately large number of schisms. In many ways, the only point of commonality for all socialists—"gas and water," utopian, scientific, or otherwise—was a devotion to that dream of a better society that each had indubitably fixed in his mind's eye. For Ernest Burns, treasurer of the Socialist Party of British Columbia in 1904, that dream was nothing less than the Cooperative Commonwealth "in which we shall behold a free man, grown to full physical and mental stature, no longer haunted by the fear of poverty in the life that is, or the idle terror of tortures in a life to come." [16]

Eugene V. Debs, the symbol of prewar socialism in North America, likened socialism to a movement that "awakens something of a religious enthusiasm among its adherents." Concerning that movement, a writer in the *Seattle Union Record* argued, "It is very evident to my mind that it [socialism] must be born of God or why is it that every power of evil there is in our midst today is against it and is opposing it with all their powers." This same writer viewed socialism as the "hope of the world." The chiliastic aspect of the dream is indeed noteworthy in the light of the pronounced schismatic tendency among socialists. Debs, in words almost reminiscent of William Miller's predicting the second coming of Christ in 1844, fervently claimed that the "coming of socialism is to them [socialists] not a debatable question. It is not a matter of doubt or conjecture but of scientific calculation." As in other millennialist movements, however, disappointment bred discontent and re-crimination among socialists, especially in the Pacific Northwest, where the followers of the "religion of economics," as Marxian socialists were sometimes called, were so absolutely fanatical in their devotion to the dream of the coming Cooperative Common-wealth.[17]

Long before the various socialist parties began contesting elections in Washington and British Columbia, workers had already been given a basic education in reform by regional labor organizations, which were dedicated purveyors of comprehensive root-and-branch economic schemes to improve society. In the Pacific Northwest, interest in popular reform schemes had increased as the more radical Knights turned from fomenting anti-Chinese hostility to developing a more enduring form of working-class consciousness. The Knights' reading rooms introduced workers to such literature as Gronlund's *Cooperative Commonwealth* and *Scientific Socialism*, and Bellamy's *Looking Backward*. Later, the more than one hundred labor-reform journals that were published in the Pacific Northwest for varying lengths of time in the pre-World War I era continued the workers' reform education. Any one of the labor or socialist weeklies might introduce workers to the ideas and activities of J. Keir Hardie and David Lloyd George in the United Kingdom, the novels of the socially conscious authors Upton Sinclair, Frank Norris, and Jack London, the many aspects of municipal owner-ship, and the more subtle dialectics of Karl Marx.

Probably the most popular of all the reform tracts promoted in the labor or socialist papers was "Merrie England," a pamphlet published in the mid-1890s by the British socialist Robert Blatch-ford. Representing a series of essays remarkable for their simplicity and directness of style, Blatchford's primer in socialism for the working class was widely disseminated in the United States and Canada at the modest price of five or ten cents.

It is impossible to measure accurately the specific influences of any one of the labor or socialist publications. The *Firebrand*, for example, was an iconoclastic publication from Portland that prom-ised to burn away the "Cobwebs of Ignorance and Superstition" by discussing frankly and openly a number of anarchistic concepts, including free love and nudity. Before the paper was suppressed and its publishers arrested for sending through the mail an allegedly obscene poem by Walt Whitman, the *Firebrand* had titillated radicals in as widely separated places as Victoria, British Columbia, and Silver City, Idaho. Historical evidence does not indicate whether the publication influenced any members of the Western Federation of Miners, specifically Bill Haywood, future leader of the anarcho-syndicalist Industrial Workers of the World, who was at that time a miner in Silver City. The historian, however, can observe the more general impact of the reform publications when, as a result of a disastrous economic crash in the 1890s, the populace of Washington and British Columbia suddenly became receptive to the strange nostrums that labor reformers had found so attractive in the 1880s.

In time, the Pacific Northwest became as well known for its reform proclivities as for its misty weather and seemingly endless forests. Washington, a socialist accurately declared in 1899 after surveying the bizarre succession of reforms that had appeared in the state during the decade, had "more 'isms' and 'osophies' than any other state in America." The encompassing schemes of single tax and socialism attained their fullest North American development in pre-World War British Columbia.[18]

CHAPTER 4

The Populist Revolt in Washington

Washington's labor movement had been interested in reform politics at least since 1884, when members of organized labor had joined with middle-class reformers in a Seattle municipal election to fight liquor, Chinese competition, and the business leaders associated with the city's notorious vice problem. Two years later the formation of a People's party (not to be confused with the People's party of the 1890s) in the Puget Sound region injected the notion of class consciousness into Seattle's municipal politics. The party in Seattle elected its entire slate, but in the aftermath of the Haymarket riot and trial in Chicago, its supporters were often lumped together in the public mind as a conglomeration of "anarchists, thieves and dynamiters." The next year the party failed to secure any offices in either Seattle or Tacoma, and by 1888 it had disappeared completely. Workers, however, did not completely abandon interest in reform politics.[1]

Helping sustain labor's political involvement were the new central labor councils that trade unionists formed to promote labor cooperation and harmony in the larger communities of the Pacific Northwest. The local political activities of trade unionists in the late 1880s and early 1890s were characterized by much diversity, as a comparison of the central bodies in Seattle and Tacoma reveals.

Otto F. Wegener, a one-time socialist and activist in the anti-Chinese campaign of the mid-1880s, organized Seattle's Western

Central Labor Union (WCLU) in 1888. Although he was a civil engineer, Wegener had identified with the labor movement after influential citizens stigmatized him for his blatant Sinophobia. He was president of the WCLU for fifteen months, a time when the nascent central body united both the craft locals and the Knights of Labor assemblies, including those in the nearby coal camps; each local, regardless of its size, had three representatives on the council.

The Knights predominated in the WCLU in 1888, but their influence waned when the building trades were strengthened by the construction boom that followed the great Seattle fire in June 1889. Although in 1890 the Knights participated in Seattle's third Labor Day parade, jurisdictional friction the following winter caused delegates from the ascendant craft unions to expel the Order from a council that now, at least temporarily, turned its back on reformist political schemes.[2]

In Tacoma, on 3 April 1890, delegates from the Cigarmakers, Carpenters, Bricklayers, Ironmolders, Cornice Makers, Stonecutters, and Longshoremen, Stevadores, and Riggers unions joined with representatives from the local assembly of the Knights of Labor to establish the Tacoma Trades Council. Charles Drees presided over a body that was far more a reform organization than Seattle's WCLU was. Sixty of the four hundred dues-paying members of the Trades Council as of September 1890 represented either the Knights of Labor or the local Nationalist club, and the meetings of the council were often attended by delegates from the Socialist Labor party and the Single Tax club as well. Although Samuel Gompers addressed members of the Tacoma Trades Council in early 1891 and presented his ideas on craft unionism, meetings were often laced with informal discussions of Nationalism, the single tax, or socialism.[3]

Whether a labor council devoted its time to discussing reform nostrums or business unionism made little difference after the Panic of 1893, however. Unemployment and the collapse of several trade unions during the depression decimated both the Trades Council and the WCLU. Of all the building trades in Seattle, only the Stonecutters and Bricklayers preserved their organizations between 1894 and 1898. There were no festive Labor Day parades during those bleak years.[4]

The Populist Revolt

In 1893, after more than a decade of rapid growth in Washington, adversity "stole in like a thief." The June financial panic that began on the East Coast so severely shook the state's vulnerable financial institutions that many collapsed like a house of cards in a hurricane. The spontaneous assault by panic-stricken depositors on the inadequate reserves maintained by several prominent Spokane banks contributed to the financial storm that brought insolvency and misery to the Inland Empire. In the Puget Sound area, the banking collapse was equally severe. In 1893 fourteen of the twenty-one banks in Tacoma closed; only nine of the twenty-three banks in the Seattle area survived the panic and depression. The failure of more than eight hundred banks in the United States between 1893 and 1897 compounded the anguish caused by rising unemployment.

The maverick Democratic governor of Oregon, Sylvester Pennoyer, advised President Cleveland that two-thirds of the workers in the state were without jobs. People with jobs often saw their wages reduced by 20 percent or more; prices also fell, but that was of little comfort to farmers. As the price of wheat fell to a new low, many Inland Empire farmers allegedly committed suicide when faced with collection demands from implement dealers, who were themselves often facing bankruptcy. Human distress caused by the Crash of 1893 became a fact of life even in British Columbia, where bank failures were virtually unknown and economic growth had been of a much less speculative nature than that south of the 49th parallel. Soup kitchens and kind citizens provided the meals that kept the unemployed in Vancouver from starving.[5]

The Panic of 1893 had been preceded throughout the United States by several years of real estate speculation and railroad over-expansion. Some people, consequently, saw hard times as "disciplinary" for the improvident: it was pointed out that the financial collapse had cured Puget Sound real estate fever and caused the financially ailing transcontinental railroads to work in harmony for the first time. Such sentiments, however, were obviously not popular among the victims of the crash. Businessmen and farmers who found it difficult or impossible to borrow and workingmen embittered by the loss of life savings wanted more than ever to change the system that ruined them. The economic collapse finally made obvious the disease that for years reformers had been offering to cure. Traditional solutions involving moral suasion were found inadequate by the increasing number of Americans who were determined to excise by radical means the more hideous outgrowths of unrestricted capitalism. In their hasty search for a simple solution, they swelled the membership rolls of exotic groups ranging from the anti-Catholic American Protective Association to the various single tax, Nationalist, and socialist clubs. The organization that attracted the largest following in both rural and urban Washington, however, was the Populist party, an amalgam of supporters of reform schemes.[6]

THE RISE OF POPULISM

The Populist movement constitutes a key element in the radical heritage of the Pacific Northwest. In the story of the rise and decline of the Washington Populist movement are contained many of the reasons for the absolutely fanatical desire of local socialists to avoid political expediency in their quest for the Cooperative Commonwealth. Organized labor, too, learned some valuable lessons from participation in the Populist movement.

The actual formation of the Populist party in Washington antedates the Panic of 1893 by more than two years and the party's first national gathering, the famous Omaha convention, by almost a year. Pursuant to a call issued in the spring of 1891 by the secretary of the Seattle District Assembly of the Knights of Labor, representatives from various farm and labor groups met as the "Confederation of Industrial Organizations" in North Yakima on 18 July 1891 to organize the People's party of Washington.

After rejecting proposals for temperance and women's suffrage, delegates adopted a platform that, with the exception of a plank endorsing the Cincinnati platform of the Populist movement, dealt entirely with issues affecting organized labor, particularly the Oregon Improvement Company's continuing practice of using black strikebreakers and armed guards at its mines in Franklin and Newcastle. The convention condemned the latest industrial disturbances and called for a removal of the militia and the "so-called Pinkerton detectives," who were thought to be trying to "provoke the white miners with some overt act as a pretext to murder them, as indeed they did."

The lopsided emphasis on labor issues reflects the composition of the convention: a few of the thirty-eight delegates represented agrarian and temperance organizations, but the bulk of them came from the ranks of organized labor. In addition to the reform-oriented trade councils in Tacoma and Spokane and at least fourteen local assemblies of the Knights of Labor, delegates hailed from the Brotherhood of Locomotive Machinists, Tacoma; Carpenters and Joiners, Tacoma; White Cooks' and Waiters' Union, Seattle; and the Hod-carriers Union, New Whatcom.[7]

Much to the disappointment of its sponsors, the North Yakima convention did not immediately result in any widespread interest in a farmer-labor reform coalition. While the Tacoma Trades Council voted to join the new Populist party, Seattle's WCLU rejected, for the time being, the idea of partisan politics. Farmers' organizations likewise divided on the idea of joining with labor to redress long-term grievances.[8]

The Populists continued to appeal to farmers and workers alike. When they met in convention at Ellensburg in 1892, Populists adopted a platform endorsing the national party's recent and much hallowed Omaha platform with its call for inflationary economic measures, government ownership and management of the railroads, direct legislation, shorter hours for workers, and elimination of the standing armies of Pinkerton detectives. The Washington document also added some suplemental demands, including government ownership and control of irrigation ditches and canals, liberalization of the delinquent tax law, reduction of railroad rates and fares, free employment agencies, an employer liability statute, and prohibition of Chinese immigration. Delegates also extended sympathy to the locked-out workers in the Coeur d'Alenes and at Homestead. Many of the planks had appeared previously in Democratic or Republican platforms, but to opponents the Populist platform was "unquestionably weak" because nearly every plank touched on comparatively "unimportant" details.[9]

The 1892 Populist campaign was far more subdued than subsequent attempts to capture the machinery of government, because a large number of Washingtonians had not yet been radicalized by economic hardship. For many Populists, the highlight of the campaign was probably the August tour by Civil War general James B. Weaver, the party's presidential candidate, and Mary Elizabeth Lease, the party's "hell-raising" female orator. More than five hundred people turned out in Seattle to hear them speak.

When Washington's voters spoke at the polls in November, their message was not altogether clear. Although eight Populists were sent to the state House of Representatives, where they held the balance of power in the forthcoming selection of a United States senator, election results revealed only a rudimentary pattern of Populist support. General Weaver failed to carry a single county; nonetheless, he received almost twenty thousand votes in the presidential contest won by the Republicans.

In the 1892 election the silver issue had not yet begun luring the party away from many of its original proposals and into the morass of political expediency. A few astute Populists must have noted, however, that silver producing Stevens County gave 32 percent of its vote to Weaver, one of the highest percentages that he received in the state. In general, the Washington electorate in 1892 was responding to local issues.[10]

Support for the Populist party increased in direct proportion to the magnitude of the economic distress and social disorder that followed the Panic of 1893. At last the concept of a farmer-labor reform coalition gained broad endorsement. Hard times forced even the most stubborn "pure and simple" trade unionist to reexamine his position on partisan politics. Soon, there were few farm, labor, or reform organizations not united under the umbrella of Populism. In the process, the People's party became an influential spokesman for Washington's growing number of radicalized farmers and workers.

THE EMERGENCE OF AGRARIAN RADICALISM

The conversion of farmers to Populism marked the culmination of a reform education that had begun as early as 1873 when the Grange swept into the Pacific Northwest from California. This nonpartisan fraternal organization first established itself in the southeastern corner of the territory and then extended its influence across the Cascades; until the early twentieth century, however, there were few Grange locals in the less affluent Palouse country, which was the center of Populist activity in the state. Wherever Grange halls were built, the previously isolated farmers came together to discuss the irksome issue of land and transportation monopolies. As elsewhere in the United States, farmers in Washington nursed a number of grievances related to railroad policies. After complaining for almost a decade about the allegedly ruinous shipping costs they were forced to bear so that the Northern Pacific Railroad could pay dividends to investors in the eastern United States and Europe, farmers hoped for a measure of relief from the Washington State Constitutional Convention.

Farmers were left disappointed and angry when the railroad lobby practically surrounded the Olympia gathering and beat back any attempt by delegates to include a constitutional provision for a railroad commission empowered to fix rates. When the proposed constitution was submitted to the voters, a bitter Grange urged them to reject a document that not only failed to deal adequately with the issue of rate grievances but also threatened to increase the cost of government. Although a majority voted against ratification in the agrarian Palouse and Walla Walla regions, the constitution was adopted. The failure of the Grange to secure a railroad commission was probably the single most important reason why the bulk of its members switched allegiance to the new Farmers' Alliances.[11]

The Southern Alliance, largely an organization of dirt farmers, competed for members with the Northern or Northwestern Alliance that also organized during the 1880s. Following an abortive unity session in St. Louis in 1890, during which the two alliances had been unable to compromise on such matters as secrecy, racial discrimination, and membership qualifications, both alliances launched intensive membership drives in Oregon and Washington. In no section of Washington did the alliances become stronger than in Whitman County, which soon dominated the state's Populist party. In many parts of the state the alliances had barely gotten established before third-party fever shattered the movement. Beginning in 1892, farmers turned to the new Populist party in their ever more desperate quest for redress of long-standing grievances.[12]

The grievances that converted Washington farmers to the Alliance movement and the Populist party can be summarized under three basic headings: discriminatory railway rates and monopolistic abuses, the lieu land controversy, and the mortgage problem. With each passing year these problems loomed larger in the minds of farmers.

Although some Washingtonians had been fighting arbitrary rate policies for years, railway abuses in eastern Washington only grew worse after the Grange failed to obtain a regulatory commission. Flour could be shipped from the Puget Sound region to St. Paul at a rate of 65 cents a barrel in 1891; the rate from Spokane, approximately 440 miles closer to St. Paul by rail, was $1.25 a barrel. Not until 1917 did Spokane receive the lower or terminal rate. In addition to rate discrimination, farmers in eastern Washington also suffered from an inability to sell wheat on the open market. In Whitman County, a Union Pacific subsidiary monopolized storage and market facilities. The wheat crop in 1890 was particularly abundant, but when railroads failed to provide enough cars to transport the wheat to market, the price went down and a wail of distress could be heard in the Palouse. Farmers angrily charged that the "wheat blockade" was the result of a conspiracy between the railroads and the elevator companies "to depress the price of grain and rob the farmers of the proceeds of their toil."

Monopoly and rate discrimination affected producer and consumer alike in eastern Washington, and in no part of the country was the call for public ownership of the railways more popular. As a result, Palouse farmers and Spokane laborers united with concerned businessmen and middle-class consumers as members of the Populist party; eventually some farmers embraced socialism as the only hope for remedying the economic problems that beset them.

At election time, railway regulation was such an appealing issue that even some Republican candidates could be heard denouncing railway abuses. Politicians, however, had a tendency to forget election promises once they got to Olympia. Railroads continued to exercise considerable control over the state legislature and the dominant Republican party until, in 1905, Washingtonians finally got their railway commission (as a result of internal conflict among Republicans). Meanwhile a generation had been radicalized by railway arrogance.[13]

The railroad was also the villain in the lieu land controversy. The Northern Pacific land grant compensated the railroad for any territory that had already been preempted by settlers; the company could claim lieu land from a ten- to thirty-mile-wide strip of territory extending along both sides of the primary grant. This provision not only locked up a great deal of land while the railroad seemingly inched its way across the continent but also raised the question of land ownership in an area of uncertain property titles. Settlers in eastern Washington were not inclined to surrender improved farms to the railway, but they were fearful that the Northern Pacific would dislodge them.

Although by 1890 some 44 percent of the Whitman County farmers were in debt, as compared to the national average of 23 percent, and interest rates reached as high as 14 percent a year, payable monthly, the mortgage problem was less irksome than freight rate "robbery" as long as the price of wheat remained between 60 and 80 cents a bushel. After 1891, however, wheat prices began to decline. The farmers' woes were compounded by drought followed by unseasonable rains and cool weather that caused a crop failure in the Palouse in the fall of 1893. A year later, the wheat that cost 32 cents a bushel to produce was selling for 23 cents. Many a mortgage had been contracted when the price of wheat was 50 to 75 percent higher than when the debt came due. No wonder Palouse farmers became fanatically interested in the money question—specifically, free and unlimited coinage of silver—as they sought a cure for ruinous deflation.[14]

Many of the complaints voiced by agrarians in eastern Washington were strikingly similar to the Populist litany of woes in Kansas and other Great Plains states. At the same time, Washington's Populist party continued to express the concerns of the state's growing number of working-class radicals.

THE NEW LABOR RADICALS

As trade unions languished as a result of the hard times that followed the Panic of 1893, many unemployed and desperate workers in the Puget Sound region joined protest organizations such as the Northwestern Industrial Army. Led by Tacoma prize fighter and saloon employee Frank T. ("Jumbo") Cantwell, the army constituted between seven hundred and fifteen hundred "Industrials" who had gathered in an unfinished and abandoned hotel in Puyallup, a town near Tacoma. There they rendezvoused with a contingent of Seattle's unemployed, published a newspaper, the *Industrial Army News*, and organized a ladies' auxiliary to provide a home for females left destitute by the economic disaster. Charitable donations of food, such as several sacks of bread from a Walla Walla bakery and twenty-six tins of salmon from an Alaskan supply house, helped keep the grim band from starving.

The Northwestern Industrial Army, which eventually included regiments from the major cities in the state, was one of the seventeen industrial armies that set out for Washington, D.C., in 1894 to demand jobs for the unemployed. Ohioan Jacob Coxey led the most publicized contingent, although the western armies were often far larger. In Oregon, Governor Sylvester Pennoyer refused to call out the militia to keep members of a local industrial army from stealing a train to take them to the nation's capital, but the Northwestern Industrial Army's plans to march east from Washington and join with Coxey's Army in a "petition in boots" were frustrated by Washington Governor John McGraw's threats to call out the militia and by the refusal of the receivers of the Northern Pacific to grant free transportation to the industrial army. A carload of Cantwell's men, nonetheless, attempted to leave Puyallup disguised as a load of hay; they were hauled several miles before the Northern Pacific discovered the true contents of the car.

At Roslyn, a group of striking miners attempted to join the crusade by capturing an empty coal car at nearby Cle Elum and letting gravity haul them down the twenty-five miles to Ellensburg in a little over two hours. Soon, industrial army recruits were beseiging Northern Pacific trains throughout the state. The railroad called in deputy marshals to help cope with the ragtag force, but it attempted to move freights out of Puyallup only during daylight hours. Although harassed by law enforcement officers on several occasions, a few hundred members of the brotherhood continued their pilgrimage east of the Rocky Mountains. Meanwhile, Coxey and two associates had been arrested for unlawfully parading their motley army on the Capitol grounds. The rude treatment of the unemployed further radicalized some members of the working class in Washington.[15]

Another new labor organization of a more conventional nature than the industrial armies was the American Railway Union (ARU), which Eugene V. Debs launched in Chicago in 1893 to bring all railway workers together in a single union. Interest in the organization spread westward along the trunk lines to the Pacific Northwest, where the first locals were formed among railway workers in Huntington and La Grande, Oregon, division points on the Oregon Railway and Navigation system, and in Tekoa, Washington, a junction town on the railway's lines linking Spokane and Portland to the violent and strife-prone Coeur d'Alene mining region. ARU locals appeared in most of the larger cities of the North Pacific region—especially after the successful Great Northern strike in 1894 popularized the new union.

At the time of the Great Northern strike, the Seattle central accepted the credentials of delegate William Blackman, president of the ARU local in Seattle, and the Vancouver Trades and Labor Council took similar action a year later when it seated a local ARU delegate. The Seattle council endorsed ARU strike action in the company town of Pullman, Illinois, but when local workers refused to haul Pullman's railway cars in the Seattle area, the WCLU would not support them. The Seattle central refused to become embroiled in the Pullman fight not necessarily because of a commitment to the conservative trade-union philosophy of the American Federation of Labor (AFL), but rather because of the perfectly rational desire to preserve its enfeebled existence during a period of economic hard times and the seemingly ominous threat posed by the milling armies of unemployed.

The powerful and united railway managers, with a helpful assist from the federal government, defeated the beleaguered ARU. The loss of the Pullman strike and the arrest of Debs cost the union most of the 150,000 members it claimed at the peak of its power, but the ARU left a legacy in the Pacific Northwest far more important than the several locals that had appeared among railway workers. Henry Demarest Lloyd perhaps overstated the matter when he told Clarence Darrow that the "radicalism of the fanatics of wealth" during the Pullman strike would unite reformers as the belligerent South did for the North in 1861, but Debs and many fellow members of the ARU became the vanguards of working-class socialism in the Pacific Northwest. The ARU was also a pillar of the Populist party in Washington, and several of its officials, including William Blackman, were appointed to significant state offices during the administration of John R. Rogers. Blackman remained active in the labor movement as president of the state Labor Congress and its successor, the Washington State Federation of Labor.[16]

THE EVOLUTION OF THE POPULIST MOVEMENT

In the tempestuous, topsy-turvy world of 1894 the Populist party appeared to be a real threat to the established order. Newspapers loudly warned that the "deluded beggars" from the industrial armies were infiltrating the party. Voters, however, were inclined to waste little sentiment on a discredited establishment, for in the fall elections of 1894 they sent twenty-three Populist legislators to Olympia and all but eliminated the Democratic party. The distribution of the Populist vote revealed a significant broadening of the party's support.[17]

Marked changes in the party platform resulted from the Populists' growing desire to woo the mass of Washington voters. After 1892 the party dropped some of its labor demands but added a new plank endorsing women's suffrage. Convinced that the inflationary silver issue had wider appeal than any other plank in their platform, many Populists began emphasizing monetary reform as an all-encompassing solution for society's ills.

As the party grew, two basic strains of thought emerged. For those Populists who saw as their goal political success and the simple restoration of prosperity, the party's ultimate achievement was supporting Democratic candidate William Jennings Bryan as the presidential standard-bearer for the united forces of silver in 1896. But Populists who hoped to use the party to make fundamental changes in America's governmental and social structure felt betrayed by the politics of expediency. They believed that the endorsement of Bryan had been engineered by an infamous silver conspiracy that captured the party's St. Louis convention.[18]

As important as the issue of free silver was in Washington, even more basic was the matter of fusion between Populists and other political parties in an effort to secure victory at the polls. Before the St. Louis convention of 1896, many of the state's Populists had voiced their opposition to fusion. Especially vocal were the ideological farmers from the Palouse region who saw fusion as a sacrifice of principles on the altar of expediency. Fusionists, mainly western Washington lawyers, editors, small businessmen, and opportunistic politicians, scored a major victory, however, when the party scheduled its statewide convention for August, during the middle of the wheat harvest.

Tri-party fusionist tickets had already been appearing in several locations when Populists, Democrats, and Silver Republicans staged what detractors labeled a "three-ring circus" in Ellensburg. Meeting in three separate conventions, each party nominated its own slate of candidates and wrote its own platform. After fighting bitterly over fusion, the Populists put together an agrarian document, conspicuously silent on local labor matters but incorporating most of the demands that farmers had been voicing since the early days of the Grange. The Silver Republican platform was similar, but less outspoken. Aside from adding another voice to the silver chorus, the Democratic party remained as noncommittal as good politics allowed.[19]

Perhaps the only notable candidate with any real labor credentials nominated in Ellensburg was Robert Bridges, former Knights of Labor leader and chairman of the Populists' founding convention in North Yakima. When he refused an offer of free railroad transportation and hiked the approximately 160 miles from Seattle to attend the convention, he inadvertently discovered a campaign technique that would later be widely used in the 1960s and 1970s. The newspaper publicity attending his walk through the rugged Cascade wilderness helped him secure the Populist nomination and subsequent election to a four-year term as state land commissioner. The experience he had gained as a coal miner in his native Scotland before emigrating to the United States at the age of twenty had led him to the mines of the Black Diamond area, where he worked for three years before moving to nearby Seattle in 1890. Like many of the state's Populists, he later became a Democrat, although he switched allegiance, not long before he died, to the new Farmer-Labor party that emerged just after World War I.[20]

In the fall election, the "Blight of Popocracy" swept across Washington with the fury of a Pacific storm. William Jennings Bryan easily carried the state, with a big assist from voters in the Spokane and Palouse regions; and fusionists put John R. Rogers, Populist journalist and pamphleteer par excellence, in the governor's chair and elected a reform majority to the state legislature. Both Bryan and Rogers received 55 percent of the vote; the few counties lost by the Populists were, with one exception, located in western Washington, and all were sparsely populated. Bryan easily carried the three urban, industrialized counties containing Seattle, Tacoma, and Spokane. Although free coinage of silver was indubitably the issue that helped Bryan capture approximately 68 percent of the presidential vote in Spokane County, where the economy was closely tied to silver production in the Coeur d'Alenes and Kootenays, and 81 percent of the vote in silver producing Stevens County, the high correlation between the distribution of the state's population and that of the Populist vote attests to the party's broad base of support. So elated were Washington's victorious Populists that they seemed almost to ignore that the Republican William McKinley and not Bryan would sit in the nation's White House for the next four years.[21]

GOVERNOR JOHN R. ROGERS

Voters, who had been warned that if John R. Rogers were elected governor, "ten shingle mills won't be worth a cent," quickly discovered that they had not elected a "dangerous sort of man." It was not his intention, as detractors claimed, to drive eastern capital from the state, neither was he committed to the "fantastic legislative measures" that made Kansas anathema for conservatives.[22]

John Rankin Rogers, the only gubernatorial candidate acceptable to the various factions of the Populist party as well as to the allied Silver Republicans and Democrats, was a tall, angular, and austere man. Part scholar and part eccentric, Rogers proudly identified with the kind of nostalgic agrarianism that historian Richard Hofstadter portrayed as Populist party ideology. His ideas were similar to those of the Locofoco Democrats of the Jacksonian era, and it is possible that he had encountered George Henry Evans' free land arguments as a boy in Brunswick, Maine, or as a young man in Illinois. Born in 1838, he founded the *Kansas Commoner* in Newton, forty-nine years later. His self-proclaimed "labor reform journal" soon took up the cause of the new Union Labor party. In fact, it was during his close association with the party that he became acquainted with Mary Elizabeth Lease and future Populist congressman "Sockless" Jerry Simpson, with whom he shared a bed at the Kansas Union Labor convention in 1888. Rogers moved to Puyallup, Washington, in 1890, and four years later won election as a Populist candidate for state representative. He built his reputation in the 1895 legislature by sponsoring the "Barefoot Schoolboy" law, a school finance measure that provided a state minimum allowance to guarantee the proper education of each child.[23]

Although the influential urban-labor element in the party thought him too conservative, Rogers, who considered himself a labor reformer, received strong labor support in the 1896 election because of his efforts to enact mine safety legislation and the endorsement given him by the labor-oriented *Seattle Call*. In his book *Free Land*, he warned that "labor is the turtle upon which Atlas stood to uphold the world. If the laborer is not provided for sooner or later something will drop." His antediluvian notions of labor reform, however, led him to urge workers to seek salvation on the land and not in the cities, which he denounced as "those sink holes of civilization." Rogers believed that the eight-hour workday was contrary to natural law.[24]

Rogers stated his views in a number of newspapers, books, and tracts. Curiously, after moving to Washington, he gradually abandoned interest in the money question that so animated the typical Populist. Only his tract "The Irrepressible Conflict" (1892) dealt directly with monetary reform. Unlike Governors Davis Waite of Colorado or Sylvester Pennoyer of Oregon, he showed little concern for the currency issue and still less for free silver. His overriding interest was always that of promoting his idealized society of self-sufficient small farmers. As a result of his antipathy to industrialism, he contributed little to real labor reform. He never understood socialism, and he was critical of Bellamy and George for ignoring the countryside. Rogers particularly irked George's many followers in the Seattle area by his strong opposition to the single tax.

For Rogers, single taxers were "cranks." In *Free Land*, he argued that "whenever the rabble of the cities voted a tax high enough," the homeowner would be dispossessed by the sheriff. He would hold title to his home only as allowed by "the fickle whim of a popular majority." The single tax, Rogers averred, was "some new fangled bottled nastiness." As much as his detractors might denounce his idyllic dream, though, they could hardly call Rogers insincere. An admirer of Jeffersonian simplicity, the governor-elect came to his own inauguration by public streetcar and on foot.[25]

FUSION AND CONFUSION

The membership of the 1897 legislature consisted of forty-five Populists, ten Democrats, eleven Silver Republicans, and twelve regular Republicans in the house, and twelve Populists, four Democrats, two Silver Republicans, and thirteen regular Republicans in the senate. Only one of the regular Republicans had been elected to the senate in 1896; the remainer were holdovers. Despite the seemingly overwhelming strength of the reformers, the legislature almost immediately bogged down in an attempt to elect a United States senator. After acrimonious infighting, the members selected Judge George Turner, a Silver Republican who had previously been a member of the Washington Supreme Court. Turner served only one term as senator and was never again elected to public office.

The fight between the fusionists over the senatorial selection in the 1897 session was a prelude to the future troubles that resulted when fusionists became unfused. The session passed measures establishing a bureau of labor, increased coal mine safety, provided a workers' lien, and exempted $100 in wages or salary from garnishment, but a direct legislation measure died in committee. Legislators referred the issue of women's suffrage to the voters and did little to lower railway rates significantly. An attempt to secure the long-demanded railway commission failed. Although a measure that promised to ease the financial burden on debtors finally made it to the governor's desk, the plan to provide free school books, like most other major items in Rogers' platform, got caught in the cross fire between erstwhile allies. In contrast to the subtle maneuvering of Olympia's entrenched lobbies, the much vaunted reform coalition had disintegrated into a state of thrashing disunity. The fusionists in the Populist party, in particular, had little of which to be proud, and when the session ended, Populists were fighting for their political lives.[26]

Never before in Washington history had there been a more abrupt and complete reversal of popular sentiment than occurred in the 1898 election. Fed up with fusion and Populist criticism of the Spanish-American War and intoxicated by the gold fever that revived the state's economy after the Klondike discoveries in 1897, voters returned to the Republican party with a vengeance. Even Spokane went Republican, as much of the electorate in eastern Washington returned to the two-party fold after almost a decade of wandering through the labyrinth of protest politics. The declining interest in reform, no doubt, contributed to the concomitant defeat of the single tax and women's suffrage amendments. Fusionists talked optimistically of making a comeback, but the subsequent demise of most of the Populists' thirty-seven local newspapers reflected the changing public mood. Voters finally buried the movement in 1900 under a quiet, but impressive Republican landslide.[27]

In a flourish of political independence that was to become typical of Washingtonians in subsequent decades, the electorate in 1900 chose John R. Rogers, now a Democrat, to serve another four-year term. A few months later, however, not long after the last Populist had vanished from the state legislature, pneumonia killed the state's popular governor. Not until 1912 would Republicans again lose a statewide race.

Because the Populists had sometimes seemed to be little more than a motley collection of dissidents, each of whom claimed to have a cure for the country's ills, the party found it harder to master the complicated machinery of the legislative process than to agitate and educate. The Populists provided two generations of Washingtonians with an agenda for reform, but it was the Republicans who finally enacted legislation to give the state the much sought railway commission as well as women's suffrage, the direct primary, the direct election of United States senators, and the initiative, referendum, and recall.

Although many of Washington's Populists subsequently joined the politically impotent Democratic party, their reformist activities in the mid-1890s encouraged workers to enter politics. At least 8 percent of the fusionists in the 1897 legislature were tradesmen at the time of their election or had been employed as laborers in the recent past, as compared with only 1 percent for the Democrats and Republicans. Blue collar workers comprised 9 percent of the leadership of the Populist party as compared with none for Washington's two major parties. Furthermore, the Populists and their reform allies secured enactment of some of the state's first meaningful labor legislation; they were responsible for the establishment of a bureau of labor, the first significant branch of the state bureaucracy to address itself exclusively to the concerns of the working class.[28]

As long as John R. Rogers was governor, he conscientiously appointed workingmen to government positions that directly related to labor. Inspector of coal mines, British-born R. H. Norton, had been a miner for twenty years. W. P. C. Adams had been head of the ARU locals in Spokane and Seattle before the governor appointed him to head the new Bureau of Labor. Adams' successor was William Blackman, Rogers' son-in-law and president of the state Labor Congress.'[29]

Despite organizational problems and undelivered promises, the Populist experience encouraged farm and labor leaders to work together. Soon after the Populist party died, the farmer-labor coalition reappeared as one of the state's most powerful pressure groups. In the Inland Empire, some of the anti-fusionist, "middle-of-the-road" Populist became supporters of a regional labor and socialist movement.

CHAPTER 5

The Unrest of the 1890s in British Columbia:

A Comparative Perspective

The Populist movement in Washington had no real counterpart in British Columbia. British Columbians, to be sure, suffered from the depression, but the response to economic hardship north of the 49th parallel was conditioned by a political, institutional, and philosophical framework notably different from that which existed in the United States. Reacting to these differences, organized labor in Washington and British Columbia forged during the 1890s two very different patterns of political involvement. The factors that help to account for the political divergence first apparent in the 1890s also provide insight into the subsequent rise of the Cooperative Commonwealth Federation and the New Democratic party in British Columbia and the lack of a significant labor-socialist party in Washington—and perhaps in other parts of the United States as well.

Populism in all its various guises was an attack on the laissez-faire order that was so highly developed in the United States. Populists were raising the question of whether the state should exercise superintendence to protect the individual from the ills of the new industrial society. In British Columbia, however, the reform argument in the 1890s was simply: how should that superintendence be applied? Because it was less an ideological struggle about the nature of the state than a pragmatic question of means, labor reformers in British Columbia did not have to fight the same fundamental philosophical battles as did their American counterparts. That is not to say, however, that the struggle for social and economic justice was won with less effort in British Columbia than in Washington.[1]

In Canada, an abiding fear of American expansionist tendencies had combined with a unique pattern of settlement to promote rejection of the laissez-faire philosophy. Geography tended to stress a natural north-south orientation of the various populated segments of the Dominion, which grew, in the words of J. M. S. Careless, like "separate melons" on one long vine. In isolated British Columbia, where a community of interest existed with the American West, the bonds of national unity were particularly tenuous. Typical American individualism would have had disastrous consequences on the Canadian frontier, where the American eagle seemed always willing to hatch annexationist schemes. Furthermore, since most Canadians lived within a hundred miles of the United States, the Dominion government had to encourage the development of a high standard of living or risk population loss by migration to the south.[2]

While a number of Americans waited confidently for part or all of Canada to drift into the Union as a result of the "inevitable law of gravitation," the Dominion government worked assiduously to counteract American influence by fashioning a strong, centralized economic and political structure. Although the roots of an intimate and open relationship between the state and business can be traced back to the fur-trading days, the rejection of laissez faire was formalized by Prime Minister John A. Macdonald when he introduced his plan for a "National Policy" in the election of 1878.

The National Policy promised something for everyone: immigration and settlement, the building of a Pacific railroad, and a tariff. While bearing a resemblance to the Republican party's program in the United States, the National Policy represented a kind of "capitalist socialism" through which the Canadian government actively sought to create a vigorous new nation. Gilded Age Republicanism, on the other hand, primarily regarded the federal government as an instrument to foster individual and corporate success and prosperity by offering opportunities to exploit and develop the nation's vast resources.

The Canadian businessman, as a consequence of the National Policy, never acquired quite the same awesome status as his American counterpart did. Also, most businessmen not philosophically committed to a rampant individualism were less inclined to regard labor as a threat than as an outgrowth of modern industrial conditions. When the National Association of Manufacturers later launched a campaign to hobble organized labor in the United States by vigorously proclaiming the virtues of the open shop, it drew little response from its Canadian counterpart.[3]

Although Canada's rejection of laissez faire did not prevent labor disputes in British Columbia, it did make depression life in Canada somewhat different from that in the United States. Even during the darkest days of 1893 and 1894, Canadians had more reason to fear being run down as the result of the new bicycle craze or succumbing to the psychosomatic ills conjured up by the omnipresent purveyors of patent medicine than the anarchy of an industrial army or the loss of life savings through the collapse of one of the country's chartered banks. When Americans wondered why Canada was experiencing less social tension and disorder during the troubled times, some Canadians simply pointed to the National Policy and contrasted it with the "wild-extravagance and over-speculation" typical of the American economic system. The *Colonist* averred that Canadians were "more conservative" and "sober minded" than Americans. Canadians, according to the *Colonist*, also had greater respect for the law; hence in the Dominion, there was no Coxeyism, Greenbackism, Populism, or lynching.[4]

The distressing economic events after the Panic of 1893 that led to the creation of a reform coalition in Washington were virtually nonexistent in British Columbia. The Canadian financial system, for example, was a source of institutional stability in the Dominion in contrast to the shaky banking and monetary system in the United States that contributed more than anything else to the fears and divisiveness that wracked society in the 1890s. The *Victoria Colonist*, after surveying the 715 bank failures that had taken place in the United States between January and September, 1893, smugly noted that only "one weak bank went down in Canada."[5]

Because the American national banking system was merely an aggregation of individual banks, any centralized control was at best only indirect and incidental. In Canada, by contrast, the banking system was under federal jurisdiction. Federal legislation allowed the Dominion's chartered banks to establish a nationwide network of branches in which the extension of credit would be backed by the formidable assets of the parent organization. As a result of the branch-banking system and the power of the chartered banks to issue their own notes, money was always available, even in the most inaccessible parts of the Dominion. The Canadian banking system was particularly well suited to serve the financial needs of the transient, often ephemeral mining population of British Columbia.[6]

Almost as disturbing to Americans in the 1890s as bank failures was the controversy that arose in the United States over the free and unlimited coinage of silver. The cry for free silver, which did so much to unite farmers, laborers, and businessmen in parts of the American West, represented a continuation of the conflict over the nature of the money supply that originated when Congress authorized the issuance of 450 million dollars in soft money or greenbacks to help finance the Civil War. Despite its compexity, the controvery over greenbacks and free coinage of silver could be boiled down to an ongoing struggle between debtors and creditors over inflation. The arcane "money question," however, troubled few Canadians not residing in the metal mining regions of British Columbia.[7]

In response to the stimulus provided by congressional passage of the Sherman Silver Purchase Act in 1890, an increasing number of American prospectors from Idaho, Washington, and Montana followed their dreams of wealth into the Kootenay region of British Columbia, where a silver boom soon developed. Repeal of the Sherman Act three years later, however, threatened the area's prosperity with a wave of bankruptcies. Many a Kootenay silver mine owner, as a result, became convinced that bimetallism would bolster the sagging price of the white metal. In the tiny community of Sandon, for example, feelings ran particularly high as the advocates of silver claimed that the gold standard offered bankers and large capitalists a financial advantage that had nothing to do with legitimate productivity and trade.

Soon, Colonel James Baker, who represented a constituency in the East Kootenay, was warning fellow legislators in Victoria of the appalling calamities that would result if spreading gold monometallism were not checked. Although the legislative assembly passed a resolution in 1894 supporting international bimetallism and sent it to the secretary of state for the colonies, it was difficult to generate much interest in the money question in most sections of the province because the elasticity of the currency prevented a money famine. Also, most Canadians were reluctant to do anything that might encourage formation of a Dominion counterpart to American Populism, which many Canadians considered reprehensible. Populists, the *Colonist* declared in 1896, "stand for everything that is wild and unsound in politics." A year earlier the paper had argued that Populism was "showing all men what a dangerous weapon political power is in the hands of men whose conceit and self-sufficiency are only equalled by their ignorance and their inexperience."[8]

Because the exceptionally high grade nature of Kootenay ore mitigated the impact of the general decline in the price of silver, silver agitation was far more subdued in the metal mining areas of British Columbia than in the Coeur d'Alene region south of the 49th parallel. As Spokane entrepreneur D. C. Corbin noted in early 1894, ore from the Slocan section of the Kootenay averaged 120 ounces of silver per ton, about double that of the ore mined in the Idaho panhandle. Furthermore, since Slocan ore was often 60 to 65 percent lead, a rise in the price of lead made it possible for some Kootenay lead-siver mining operations to make a profit despite the declining price of silver and the American tariff.[9]

Kootenay-area newspapers kept interest in the money question alive by faithfully reporting the Bryan-McKinley campaign battle. "This paper believes in Silver," the *Sandon Paystreak* declared in September 1896, "and will shout for Billy Bryan until frost strikes the infernal region and McKinley is sitting on ice." Throughout the province, British Columbians wondered what effect the outcome of the American election would have on Pacific Canada. Some feared another civil war in America if McKinley were elected; others believed Bryan's triumph would worsen the stormy financial climate in the United States. When the election results were announced, most British Columbians probably shared the *Colonist's* hope that Bryan's defeat had ended America's free-silver craze.[10]

Although the new industrialism resulted in problems common to both Canada and the United States, the preferred solutions of the two countries often reflected their differing attitudes toward the philosophy of laissez faire. On the question of monopoly, for example, the individualistic Americans adopted a trust-busting solution in the form of the Sherman Anti-Trust Act of 1890. The act attempted to minimize the federal government's role by limiting its involvement to prosecution of alleged trusts. Canadians, on the other hand, were at least willing in theory to use governmental power to regulate monopoly on an ongoing basis.[11]

Reforms that in the United States were ideological issues with mass appeal were frequently regarded in Canada as matters to be resolved by routine parliamentary action. There were, of course, Canadians who vigorously denounced monopoly, but, with the possible exception of the Progressive movement that swept the prairie provinces and parts of Ontario after World War I; Canadians were not likely to join together in a mass political crusade that promised to eradicate society's ills in a season.

Being citizens of a nation that represented, in a sense, the rejection of the claims of the American Revolution, Canadians were hardly likely to respond to the kind of idealistic appeals that moved Americans to attempt implementation of broad humanistic goals such as were emboided in the Declaration of Independence. Canadians, very simply, did not generally expect their politicians to legislate the millennium. Reform in Canada usually was achieved when a small band of reform-minded legislators mastered the machinery of parliamentary government and persuaded fellow members to respond pragmatically to a problem associated with industrial development. During the 1890s, legislators friendly to organized labor began assuming that role in British Columbia.[12]

EARLY LABOR POLITICS IN BRITISH COLUMBIA

Converting the ballot into a weapon to battle for social and economic justice was largely a trial-and-error process for British Columbia labor. Significant labor involvement in provincial politics began with formation of a Workingmen's party to contest the 1886 provincial election in Victoria and Nanaimo. Like the contemporaneous People's party in Washington, the Workingmen's party had a close kinship with the Knights of Labor, and its program, similarly, included demands for Asiatic exclusion, restruction of the liquor trade, a land tax, and adoption of the referendum and recall. In addition, the party on Vancouver Island called for mine safety legislation. All four of its candidates were defeated, but the idea of a political party to represent working-class interests continued to be encouraged by the gentle urging of Canada's Trades and Labor Congress, the prodding of local labor leaders, and the hostile attitude of industrialists like the Dunsmuirs, who refused to compromise their self-proclaimed prerogatives of management. Labor's interest in politics dramatically increased between 1889 and 1891 as central labor councils were formed in Victoria, Vancouver, New Westminster, and Nanaimo.[13]

In the fall of 1890, not many weeks after the government in Victoria had sent out a battery of artillery to help James Dunsmuir win a war with his striking Vancouver Island miners, labor leaders made an effort to unite all of British Columbia's unions into one province-wide organization that could effectively promote their growing political interest.

The Provincial Federated Labor Congress, which met in Nanaimo in late October selected as its president, Tully Boyce, the head of the Miners' and Mine Laborers' Protective Association, and adopted a typical labor reform platform. Little resulted from this effort, aside from the further encouragement it gave to labor's growing involvement in political affairs in the immediate Nanaimo area.

In Nanaimo, trade unionists had worked with farmers in the June 1890 provincial election to elect the first "labor" members of the legislative assembly: Thomas Forrster, a farmer with labor sympathies, and Thomas Keith, a miner. Forrster adopted a single tax platform, and Keith added the appeal for an income tax, a radical idea at that time. In the provincial parliament, they joined with Vancouver newspaper publisher F. Carter-Cotton to form a minuscule pro-labor bloc. Their accomplishments were few, however, because in the early 1890s there was no balance of political power for them to exploit.[14]

The political discouragements of the mid-1880s followed by the election of labor reformers to the legislative assembly in 1890 represented a recurring pattern of failure alternating with limited success. The Vancouver Trades and Labor Council, which raised the issue of a Canadian labor party in resolutions it sent to the Dominion Labor Congress in 1891 and 1892, repeatedly discussed political action and made forays into municipal politics. The Vancouver council also participated unofficially in the activities of the

Nationalist party, a local organization that formed to contest the provincial election of 1894. Espousing a collection of reform ideas that included direct legislation, the single tax, and public ownership of utilities, the Nationalist party sent Robert MacPherson, a carpenter, to the legislative assembly.

Although the Nationalist party has been called the province's first true labor party, it was more a middle-class reform organization closely linked to the personality of its leader, the Reverend G. R. Maxwell, who was elected to the Canadian Parliament on a broad reform ticket in 1896. Both MacPherson and Maxwell were soon absorbed by the Liberals, and the Nationalist party faded after two years. The organization never spread to Nanaimo, where the Miners' and Mine Laborers' Protective Association joined with other local groups to create a working-class reform club that nominated three candidates, Tully Boyce, Thomas Keith, and Ralph Smith, a recently arrived Northumberland miner, to contest the provincial elections of 1894. Their platform was similar to the one used earlier by Keith but was more oriented toward the single tax. All three labor candidates were defeated.[15]

Labor was more successful in the provincial election of 1898, after which a handful of pro-labor legislators held the balance of power in the legislative assembly. This motley group composed of Ralph Smith, Robert MacPherson, Dr. Robert McKechnie, R. F. Green, and F. Carter-Cotton, seemingly had little in common except a desire to help workingmen. McKechnie and Green both represented ridings containing a number of miners, but only Smith and MacPherson were blue collar workers. Carter-Cotton, a wealthy publisher, was characterized by the *Kaslo Kootenaian* as a man of ability but "reckless in his words and actions." The *Colonist* accused him of socialistic leanings, or even worse in the minds of Populist-loathing Canadians, of wanting to turn the province into a "Canadian Kansas."[16]

The pro-labor group was able to secure the enactment of several measures, including a controversial one that attempted to prohibit Orientals from working as placer miners. Sending shivers up the spine of many an entrepreneur was the statute giving metal miners an eight-hour workday. Naturally some observers were frightened by what was happening and portraying the province as a "seething cauldron of political unrest." On the other hand, labor leaders throughout Canada were inspired to involve themselves more fully in politics.[17]

Significantly, none of the reform legislation in British Columbia resulted from anything resembling the farmer-labor coalition that arose in neighboring Washington. Although the province's farmers were adversely affected by the economic troubles that followed the Panic of 1893, few common problems united them. The highly individualistic farmers were scattered through the province in pockets of settlement where they raised a number of different crops. They had no Grange heritage, and an attempt in early 1898 to establish farmers' alliances in the province quickly failed. Farmers preferred to act collectively through the Farmers' Institutes, a government-sponsored educational organization; and the legislators responded in the late 1890s by passing at least forty-two measures pertaining to such matters as cooperatives, drainage, and agricultural credit banks. Even when a farmers' reform movement swept the prairie provinces after 1917, the agrarians of British Columbia remained reluctant to support independent political action.[18]

A COMPARATIVE APPROACH TO LABOR POLITICS

Many of the reasons often cited to explain the lack of a labor party in the United States were inapplicable in pre-World War I British Columbia.[19] The province, for example, was far more riven by class division than by the ethnic division that supposedly helped keep immigrant voters in the United States from uniting politically. Furthermore, during the formative years of the British Columbia labor movement there was no major party heritage in the province. Aside from the possibility of a candidate losing his election deposit by a poor showing at the polls, neither law nor tradition militated against the formation of a labor party. Also, mounting pressure within the provincial labor movement to organize a separate party was not reduced by means of strong, competing parties appropriating labor's demands—as so often happened in the United States.

The political party, whether it represents narrow racial, religious, or economic interests or acts as an agency to resolve conflicts in a society, has traditionally been the favored American means of determining who shall operate the government. In Washington, for example, the first settlers seemingly brought the institution of the political party along with other portable heirlooms such as the family Bible. Whigs and Democrats were fighting one another in the territory as early as 1854, and the Republican party picked up the gauntlet in 1861. It was likely that even the lowliest county auditor would be elected on some kind of party ticket, as if there were a separate Republican or Democratic way to add and subtract.[20]

In post-confederation British Columbia, by contrast, political contests were seldom fought along party lines. In the legislative assembly, the loose political groups simply called themselves "Government," "Opposition," and, in the early 1890s, "Independents." The result has been described as a political aquarium filled with "loose fish" who were dashing from one side of the House to the other. As long as government was considered an analogue to a business corporation, to be managed or exploited as efficiently as possible by a group of professional politicians, political parties were viewed as an unnecessary nuisance.

Opponents of party lines in British Columbia regarded the introduction of Dominion party labels into provincial politics to be as "absurd" as the use of federal party labels in American municipal politics. The lack of a clear-cut division between Conservatives and Liberals, as a matter of fact, posed a problem for the majority party in Ottawa whenever it considered a British Columbian for a federal appointment. Growing political chaos in the province around the turn of the century, however, bolstered the arguments favoring the introduction of party lines, and Premier Richard McBride finally resolved the issue by simply announcing the formation of a Conservative government in 1903. Although it has been argued that the various shifting political groups in the legislative assembly performed the same function as political parties did, British Columbians did not come to regard party labels as something akin to a family inheritance. The province's trade union leaders, consequently, had all the more reason to contemplate formation of a labor-oriented party.

Canada's parliamentary form of government, furthermore, tended to favor formation of a labor party. Because of the strong discipline exercised by political parties over individual members in the Dominion Parliament and in the British Columbia legislative assembly after the introduction of party lines, the tactic of rewarding friends and punishing enemies, that basic political mechanism of labor as a pressure group in the United States, did not work well north of the border. In Canada, in addition, national and provincial leaders were not chosen directly by the electorate of the nation or the province as a whole. Canadian labor was thus less inclined than its American counterpart to build the kind of broad coalition necessary to elect a president or governor in the United States—a president or governor who wielded veto power over labor's legislative efforts.

Canada's parliamentary bodies also had an important constitutional function that they exercised far more frequently than their American counterparts. Aside from a few major constitutional issues decided by the Judicial Committee of the Privy Council in London (prior to 1949) or an infrequent move by the Ottawa government to disallow provincial legislation, Canadian parliamentary bodies tended to remain virtual courts of last appeal on most constitutional matters. Dominion trade unionists, therefore, had a far greater incentive to involve themselves in political matters than their American brothers did. Too often, the members of organized labor in the United States had seen the fruits of years of political agitation snatched from their grasp by nine old men in black robes, and only with herculean effort could Congress and the various states pass the necessary constitutional amendment to overrule the Supreme Court. No wonder Gompers preferred the use of collective bargaining to improve the lot of the workingman.[21]

"Americans alone of western peoples," Henry Steele Commager observed, "made constitutionalism a religion and the judiciary a religious order and surrounded both with an aura of piety." Canadians no doubt wondered why their egalitarian American neighbors submitted so willingly to the autocracy of a written constitution interpreted by a judicial elite. Since in Britain no court was above Parliament, some Canadians even asked whether the people of monarchical Britain had more power than the citizens of the American republic. Americans, who were so enthralled by their constitutional conception that they found it difficult to appreciate a contrary system, would probably have responded to questioning Canadians with surprise, shock, and an outpouring of declamatory statements on the virtue of living in America. Canadians, however, representing such divergent groups as Conservatives and Socialists, shared the feeling that the American Constitution and the inordinately large power of the Supreme Court helped the corporation to reign supreme in the United States. "We think it very fortunate for Canada," the *Colonist* declared in 1908, "that the development of her national institutions is not hampered by a written constitution as exists in the United States."[22]

"It was in the courts," labor historian Sidney Fine has noted, "that the idea of laissez faire won its greatest victory in the three and one-half decades after the Civil War." In the hands of the courts the due process clause of the Fourteenth Amendment was used as a weapon to attack social legislation and frustrate business regulation. In their battle for social justice, American trade unionists were further outraged by the labor injunction, described as a "Gatling gun on paper." Employed little before the early 1890s because of its doubtful legality, the labor injunction became a powerful anti-labor weapon after 1890 and earned the sanction of the Supreme Court in *In Re Debs* (1895).[23]

Remarking on the use of the labor injunction in the United States, the conservative *Victoria Colonist* declared in 1897, "Government by injunction is something new under the sun." In the opinion of the *Colonist*, courts were sanctioning the use of the injunction and instituting contempt proceedings to an intolerable extent. The labor unions of British Columbia, by contrast, had little to fear from the injunction during most of the pre-World War I era, particularly after the legislative assembly passed the Trade-unions Act in 1902 to protect unions from injunctions and their funds from liability.[24]

Few American labor leaders really believed that the United States Supreme Court was an impartial arbiter of justice, and they regarded the state courts in much the same way. Fortunately for labor and other pre-World War I proponents of reform in Washington, however, reform measures passed by the state legislature were not often invalidated by the state's fairly progressive supreme court. As a result, Washington was among the first states to restrict the working hours of women (then regarded as a desirable health measure), provide an eight-hour day for employees on public construction projects, set a minimum wage for women and children, and establish a compulsory system of workmen's compensation. In 1913 the Washington Supreme Court became the first in the United States to approve a minimum wage law.[25]

Elsewhere in the United States, two decades of bitter frustration had thoroughly convinced American labor leaders by the turn of the century that partisan political involvement, although it appeared to be a deceptively easy shortcut to power, inevitably dead-ended in the morass of constitutional interpretation if not political compromise. In British Columbia, however, the lessons learned during the 1890s led to the opposite conclusion. Without political power, organized labor could never force an economic individualist like James Dunsmuir to bargain collectively.

The Pacific Northwest's economic difficulties vanished in a day, or so it seemed, following arrival of the news of the Klondike gold discovery in 1897. The thousands of fortune seekers passing through Seattle and Vancouver brought prosperity in their wake. The inflation that accompanied the flood of gold destroyed the arguments for free and unlimited coinage of silver, and by 1900 the condition of the Seattle labor movement had so improved that trade unionists staged their first Labor Day parade in seven years. Membership in the Western Central Labor Union was greater than ever, and the strongest of the building trade unions won an eight-hour workday. Trade unionists, however, did not forget the political lessons learned during the formative decade of the 1890s.

Memories of organized labor's role in the Populist triumph in Washington and in balance-of-power reform politics in British Columbia encouraged regional trade union leaders to continue to seek political solutions to many of the problems that beset Pacific Northwest workers in the first decade of the twentieth century. When political involvement assumed the form of a labor party, however, trade unionists inevitably clashed with the rule-or-ruin policy of the local socialists, who seemed to spend so much time defending their utopian theories and criticizing workers who yielded to the temptation of a full dinner pail promised by politicans allegedly appealing to labor's stomach rather than its intelligence.

CHAPTER 6

Leftward Tilt on the Pacific Slope

As the American Federation of Labor (AFL) extended its sphere of operation into Washington and British Columbia, it encountered the regional peculiarities that characterized the Pacific Northwest labor movement. Of those local traits, the one most easily accommodated by the AFL was the continuing anti-Orientalism. When delegates from the Pacific Northwest and California pressured the federation to adopt an anti-Oriental posture, the AFL responded by calling for new legislation to halt Oriental immigration to the United States. The AFL confronted a much more difficult and complex problem in the tendency of some Pacific Northwest labor leaders to flirt with socialism and dual unionism.

The peculiarities of the labor movement in the Pacific Northwest were less a product of any overt campaign or conspiracy to thwart the AFL than a reflection of the lack of significant AFL influence in the area in the 1890s. Too often historians have looked at the growing power of the AFL from 1900 to 1916 and forgotten that in the 1880s and 1890s, as Melvyn Dubofsky has observed, the AFL was a "scared, uncertain, insecure infant." Shortly after the federation was founded, Samuel Gompers went without a salary for four months, and, in Dubofsky's words, "the family of the president of the AFL had to borrow money to buy groceries." Dubofsky further argues that most of the unions that had affiliated with the AFL by 1892 were "small and in parlous financial condition."[1] Most important, because the AFL did not penetrate the emerging mass production industries, a significant group of industrial workers in the Pacific Northwest were attracted to indigenous labor organizations that were built upon the ruins of the Knights of Labor and maintained close ties to local socialist bodies.

BLAZING A VERY NARROW TRAIL

Socialist organizations flourished in the expansive intellectual climate of the Pacific Northwest, but it is perhaps a paradox of history that the regional socialist movement eventually adopted such a narrow, sectarian ideology that it repelled more often that it attracted the rank and file workers eager to improve the new industrial society. Part of the explanation of that paradox lies in the heterogenous origins of the local movement.

Aside from the evanescent International Workingmen's Association, the first socialist organization of any importance in the Pacific Northwest was the Socialist Labor party (SLP). Unfortunately, the SLP exercised a blighting influence on the local socialist movement far out of proportion to its small membership. By the turn of the century, its activities had frequently enraged and antagonized moderate trade union leaders. The SLP also convinced many of the region's pioneer socialists that the Cooperative Commonwealth lay at the end of an exceedingly narrow, doctrinaire trail.

Ironically, when the SLP organized as a Marxist political party in New Jersey in 1877, its platform included demands for an eight-hour workday, employer liability, graduated income tax, government ownership of vital services, direct legislation, protective laws for women, and an end to child labor. The party's 1877 platform anticipated four decades of reform demands in America; the party itself fared less well. After a debilitating split with the anarchists and a concomitant drop in party membership, the SLP became a struggling little group of less than fifteen hundred socialists, the majority of whom were recruited from the immigrant German-American trade unions.

In 1890 the languishing SLP attracted the considerable talents of Daniel DeLeon, attorney and former professor of Latin American Diplomacy at Columbia University. A brilliant intellectual who developed an interest in Marxism following participation in the single tax and Nationalist movements, DeLeon used his power as editor of the party's English-language organ to direct fellow members into an ever more rigid, sectarian approach to the Cooperative Commonwealth.

After an infusion of DeLeon's dogmatism and invective, the SLP was characterized by an ever greater degree of philosophical "purification." The party degenerated into an ideologically rigid sect dominated by DeLeon, for whom, as Gompers caustically remarked, socialism had become a fetish. DeLeon's twin goals were to capture the state by political means and to create a class-conscious industrial union organization affiliated with the SLP by capturing the Knights of Labor or the AFL by infiltration ("boring from within").[2]

There was no SLP activity in the Pacific Northwest until mid-1890, when Charles Drees, president of the Tacoma Trades Council, established a section with nineteen members. Although the Tacoma section had strong ties to the growing Nationalist movement and was represented on the Trades Council, it did not survive the shock of electoral defeat in November 1890. The next year Daniel DeLeon visited the region to interest local radicals in the SLP. Despite some momentary successes, DeLeon must have been discouraged by the inability of the SLP to survive in the unsettled economic climate of the North Pacific. Only with the advent of prosperity in 1897 did the SLP attain a measure of permanence in Washington.[3]

The SLP in Washington held its first state convention in mid-1898. Of the several resolutions passed by the delegates, the statement condemning "fusion" was of greatest historical significance. Memories of the fate of Washington's Populist party touched off frequent and rancorous debates among local socialists on the question of their joining with other reform groups to change society. No other issue did more to split the pre-World War I socialist parties in Washington and British Columbia.[4]

The 1898 SLP convention nominated the first socialist candidates to contest a statewide election in Washington: Thomas Young and Thomas Lawry for judges of the state supreme court, and Walter Walker and M. A. Hamilton for the United States House of Representatives. Young and Walker, it should be noted, were former Populists alienated by fusion. In contrast to the aftermath of the 1890 campaign in Tacoma, the SLP survived inevitable electoral defeat in 1898 with only mild disappointment. The party's central committee in Seattle dismissed the results by suggesting that the SLP was not attractive to those reformers whose "heart oversways their judgment." By continuing to propagandize in the state, members of the SLP hoped to capture Washington as a first step on their way to assuming national power.[5]

The SLP established a toehold in British Columbia in 1896. Although the short-lived section in New Westminster published the *Pathfinder*, the province's first socialist newspaper, the SLP did not become firmly established in British Columbia until two years later. In December 1898, Arthur Spencer, a Canadian Pacific Railway employee who had recently moved to Vancouver from Hamilton, organized a vanguard of twenty-three persons into a section of the SLP. Schism wrecked the new organization before it could contest its first election.[6]

DeLeon's scheme to capture either the AFL or Knights by the tactic of "boring from within" fared no better than his plans to capture the state by political means. Rebuffed by leaders of both national labor organizations, DeLeon established the Socialist Trades and Labor Alliance (STLA) in 1895 as the industrial arm of the SLP.

The branches of the STLA that appeared in the Pacific Northwest before the end of the nineteenth century were spectacularly unsuccessful in everything except creating dissention in the labor movement. As a dual organization, the STLA was refused representation in the Seattle and Vancouver, British Columbia, labor councils. There was even a bitter conflict between the SLP and its offspring over the failure of the STLA to pay rent on a meeting hall. The STLA branches in the Pacific Northwest quickly withered and died, although elsewhere the STLA managed to linger on until DeLeon merged it with the Industrial Workers of the World in 1905.[7]

Ironically, the main achievement of the STLA seems to have been to convince Gompers that socialism and dual unionism were closely linked and that a political labor movement could ruin the trade unions. It had been common before the turn of the century for some labor leaders and socialists to picture trade unions and socialism as separate economic and political arms of the labor movement. Gompers, however, came to see socialists as men "whose minds have been warped by a great failure. . . ." He also believed that all the errors and faults of the trade unions, in the eyes of the socialists, fell within the limits of a single crime. "That crime," said Gompers, "is that the American Federation of Labor refuses to become the tail to the Socialist kite." At the 1903 convention of the AFL, Gompers delivered his most famous denunciation of socialism when he declared: "Economically, you are unsound; socially, you are wrong; industrially, you are an impossibility." The *Seattle Union Record* argued in 1900 that workers could believe in the general principles of socialism and not in a socialist party, but Gompers' attitude was an important factor that helped deprive American socialists of the support of the AFL leadership.[8]

AMERICANIZING SOCIALISM

Another reason for the stunted growth of the early socialist movement in the United States was given by Karl Marx's daughter, Eleanor Marx Aveling, who, during an 1886 trip to the United States, attributed the distrust of socialist platforms in America to the ignorance of workers and to the actions and attitudes of the German immigrant socialists. Socialism to be effective, she observed, "must be of native growth, even if the seeds are brought from other countries."[9] The Americanization of socialism in the late nineteenth century was not to be accomplished by academic theoreticians such as Daniel DeLeon, but by Laurence Gronlund, Edward Bellamy, J. A. Wayland, and Eugene V. Debs. Gronlund helped introduce English-speaking Americans to basic Marxian precepts, and Bellamy and Wayland popularized the socialist dream, a noble, humanistic ideal personified for millions of Americans and Canadians by Gene Debs.

Desiring to give plain answers to the problems confronting the common man, J. A. Wayland founded the *Coming Nation* in 1893 in the rural community of Greensburg, Indiana. After a series of misfortunes cost him control of the paper, he moved west and started the *Appeal to Reason* in 1895. Within five years, the *Appeal* had become the most widely read socialist journal in the United States and had made Girard, Kansas, a mecca for Wayland's subscribers. Wayland ignored the sharp distinctions made by Marxist theoreticians. His socialism was an eclectic blend that combined the emotional appeal of Populism and the dream of *Looking Backward*.

Dedicated to Wayland's brand of socialism, the *Appeal* attempted to educate and entertain its half-million subscribers by publishing parables, analogies, and short stories; it was in the *Appeal* that muckraker Upton Sinclair first published his stomach-churning exposé of the meat packing industry. Conservatives denounced the *Appeal* as the "squeal of treason" and attempted to keep it out of the United States mails. In Washington, the publication served as a rallying point for the agrarian socialists of the Inland Empire.[10]

DEBS

Eugene V. Debs was at one time more conservative than Samuel Gompers, denouncing the closed shop and the boycott as infringements of individual liberty. Before converting to socialism he had been elected city clerk in his home town of Terre Haute, Indiana, and had served in the Indiana legislature as a Democrat. He also became secretary-treasurer of the Brotherhood of Locomotive Firemen and edited the union's journal. Concern for the growing misery of labor in 1892 and 1893 led him to sever his ties with the brotherhood and to create the American Railway Union (ARU).

The ARU grew rapidly after winning a strike against James J. Hill's powerful Great Northern Railway but met disaster in the Pullman strike of 1894. As a result of that strike, the ARU withered, and Debs went to jail for contempt of court. When he launched the union, Debs had scarcely been aware of socialism. In 1894, *Railway Times*, the union's official newspaper, urged cooperation with Populists and promoted such reforms as direct legislation and the overhaul of the judicial system. The prison sentence, however, gave Debs the time to continue his education in radicalism. The writings of Gronlund, Blatchford, and Bellamy especially appealed to him, and he subscribed to the *Coming Nation*. As a celebrity, Debs also attracted a number of important visitors such as J. Keir Hardie, the British laborite, and Victor Berger, the Milwaukee socialist, who gave Debs a copy of Marx's *Capital*.[11]

Debs, however, did not emerge from prison a converted socialist; in the fall of 1896 he and the remnant of the ARU were still supporting William Jennings Bryan for president. Although Debs took his time digesting socialist principles, he immediately grasped one important lesson based on experience: he exhorted delegates at a

January 1896 meeting of the ARU to become involved in political matters. Speaking about direct legislation and abolishing the wage system, Debs warned that "laboring people, if they would make effective advances, must go into politics." Industrial strikes, he averred, were conducted against great odds because the government was in league with the corporations. "Labor," the *Railway Times* echoed, "has been cheated and robbed by a gang of brigands because it has 'kept out of politics.'" Members of the ARU, the paper continued, know by bitter experience "what it is to keep out of politics." [12]

To workingmen in Washington and British Columbia, Eugene Debs was a familiar figure; many could recognize his piercing eyes, balding head, aggressive chin, and forward-leaning posture. While awaiting the outcome of the contempt proceedings against him, Debs left Chicago on 28 February 1895 to tour the Great Northern system and talk to Pacific Northwest workers. After delivering speeches in Helena and Butte, he arrived at midnight in Spokane, where he was met at the depot by a large crowd unconcerned about the lateness of the hour. He was offered a carriage ride to the auditorium but preferred to walk the distance, accompanied by the admiring crowd.

In Spokane, where there was a close link between labor and Populism, Debs's speech struck a responsive chord in its praise of the Populist party and its denunciation of the Democrats and Republicans for being dominated by the "money power." Trade unionists, who had converged on Spokane from throughout the Inland Empire and the British Columbia Kootenay, heard Debs warn that because it was futile to strike against the money power, the ARU would carry its fight to the polls. He predicted the eventual formation of a railway corporation in which every citizen would be a stockholder. [13]

Debs must have been impressed by the enthusiastic crowds of workingmen that greeted him during his triumphful journey through the Pacific Northwest. He claimed to have recruited more than two thousand new members to the ARU during the trip, but the union was clearly on the decline. In mid-1897, less than six months after he had announced his formal conversion to socialism, Debs combined the remnant of his followers in the ARU with a group of SLP dissidents to form the Social Democrary of America (SDA). The

dream of the SDA was to establish a national Cooperative Commonwealth by first organizing a series of local communes; after acquir-
ing power in one state, the SDA hoped to make it a socialist model
for the remainder of the country. Debs specifically had Washington
in mind as the site for his first socialist colony.[14]

UTOPIAS OF PUGET SOUND

In the late nineteenth century the Puget Sound region became
known for its communitarian experiments. The first of these ventures was the Puget Sound Cooperative Colony, founded in Port
Angeles in 1887 by Seattle attorney George Venable Smith and
others. Smith was a leader in the local anti-Chinese movement, but
in the disillusioning aftermath of the disturbances, he turned to
communitarianism as a better solution to labor's growing discontent. He hoped to establish a colony that would enable a group of
workingmen to defy growing corporate power by producing and
distributing goods on a cooperative basis. For a few years the colony maintained close ties to the Knights of Labor, endorsing its
demands for government control of the means of communication
and transportation, the right to vote regardless of sex, temperance,
and the establishment of a monetary system to benefit the producer
rather than the speculator. The colony also advocated a potpourri
of reforms ranging from peace to the eight-hour workday and the
emancipation of women from the slavery of domestic drudgery.
Unlike some later communal ventures, however, the Puget Sound
Cooperative Colony eschewed free love and regarded good morals
and marriage as the foundation of the home. Attracting considerable outside interest, the Puget Sound Cooperative Colony soon
moved to establish subordinate branches throughout the United
States, especially in Illinois and Iowa, but like many of the colonies
that followed, it evolved into a joint-stock company seeking profits
for investors and gradually lost the vision of the Seattle labor reformers.[15]

The SDA's colonization scheme that so intrigued Debs had its
origins in Maine, where Norman Wallace Lermond organized the
Brotherhood of the Cooperative Commonwealth in 1895 to interest
people in the idea of developing cooperative colonies and industries
to socialize one state. After Lermond promoted his scheme among

the Populists meeting in St. Louis in 1896, the brotherhood elected the well-known reformer Henry Demarest Lloyd as its president. Although Lloyd had long been interested in communitarian experiments and believed that the cooperative movement was perpetuating the vision lost by the Populists in the morass of fusion, he declined the presidency of the brotherhood because he doubted the soundness of the scheme. Eugene Debs, by contrast, a new convert to socialism, dismayed some of his less utopian comrades by becoming an active colonizer. For Debs, according to Howard Quint, colonization offered the possibility of "providing a refuge for the unemployed, discouraged, and blacklisted American Railway Union men." A suitable site was found in western Washington, and in November 1897, Colony 1, "Equality," was founded. After this, the Brotherhood of the Cooperative Commonwealth led only a nominal existence, but the little settlement near Edison became an important addition to Washington's radical heritage.[16]

Equality was only one of several utopian communes that appeared in the Pacific Northwest in the late nineteenth and early twentieth centuries. Organizers of Equality, Freeland, Home, Burley, and several other cooperative colonies came to Washington not only because they believed that they had discovered the New Eden but also because they anticipated a hospitable social and political climate. G. E. Pelton of Edison observed in a letter describing the virtues of Washington for Henry Demarest Lloyd, "We find this state to be particularly adapted to the work on account of the fact that the people are, mostly, well disposed towards Socialism. . . ." When Governor John Rogers was told that the Social Democracy was considering the establishment of a colony in Washington, he welcomed the idea; in reply to an inquiry from the New York *Herald*, Rogers declared that he was in favor of any plan "consistent with our laws which promises to ameliorate the condition surrounding the poorer classes now enormously increasing in number." When he later enrolled as a supporter of the Burley Colony in order to participate in its insurance plan, Rogers probably became the first governor in the United States to "join" the colonization movement.[17]

Although Equality Colony failed in its twin goals of colonizing and socializing Washington, it nurtured a number of the state's early socialists. E. B. ("Harry") Ault moved to the colony with his parents in April 1898 and became editor of the colony's newspaper, *Industrial Freedom*, at the age of seventeen. He then worked for the labor-oriented *Seattle Call* before initiating the *Young Socialist*, a monthly publication that Ault aimed at the younger generation. He was associated with the *Seattle Socialist* for several years, and for a short time with the *New Time*, a Spokane socialist journal. All of this, however, was a prelude to his main contribution to Pacific Northwest labor history, the editing of the *Seattle Union Record* from 1912 to 1928. He not only transformed the *Union Record* into the only daily labor paper in the United States at that time but also played a key role in the Seattle General Strike of 1919.[18]

David Burgess and George Boomer, activists in the Socialist party of Washington, had also been members of Equality Colony. Burgess, formerly the editor of an Arkansas farm weekly, became the state party's first organizer, and Boomer, a popular columnist in the *Appeal to Reason*, was noted for his dedication to socialist journalism in Washington. Other colonies, likewise, helped give the state a leftward tilt by attracting people disposed to reform to the shores of Puget Sound. Although their direct contribution to the state's socialist vote was negligible, the various colonies served, in effect, as a socialist Chautauqua to educate dissident Populists and other reformers in socialist principles.

Equality Colony attracted a good deal of attention to the SDA, but Social Democrats also promoted a political program that emphasized the popular socialist reforms of the day. In late August 1897 the Social Democracy established its first branch in Washington in the farming community of Palouse; and later in the year additional branches appeared in Seattle, Tacoma, and Port Angeles. Growing antagonism developed between the colonizers and the political activists, and with proponents of these two fundamentally different approaches to the Cooperative Commonwealth warring within its bosom, the Social Democracy was doomed.

The Social Democracy's 1898 convention was marked by a major schism. A surviving remnant of the SDA proceeded to organize the Burley Colony, while the seceders, who were determined to cast off utopian colonization schemes and gain the support of trade unionists, formed the Social Democratic party (SDP). Debs, who renounced his earlier support for communitarianism, embraced the SDP and its platform, which advocated public ownership of utilities controlled by monopolies, trusts, and combines, abolition of discrimination against women, and direct legislation. The party generated a heated and ongoing controversy among socialists by including in its platform a set of demands apparently designed to appeal to farmers previously radicalized by Populism.[19]

From Populism to Socialism

Historians have often debated the connection between Populism and socialism. Both philosophies promised to destroy social privilege, and both placed a strong emphasis on the role of government as an active participant in economic affairs. Detractors often confused Populists and socialists; Bige Eddy, the Washingtonian who wrote the "Musings of a Mossback" column for Wayland's *Appeal to Reason*, noted in 1897, "when I was a Populist they called me a 'Socialist.'" The editor of the *Okanogan Record* probably articulated a commonly held view in eastern Washington when he called socialism "rampant popocracy" and warned that "from the unsavory garbage box of latter day populism has risen this lunacy which assumes a most menacing mien." Eugene Debs argued in 1900 that many of the citadels of socialism had once been Populist strongholds, and this, certainly, was true of Washington and several other states.[20]

Most Populists, to be sure, were more interested in reforming the capitalist system than in destroying it. The issue of fusion, however, revealed a basic difference of opinion among Populists, the party in 1896 being split into fusionists and middle-of-the-roaders, who were not, as the name implies, moderates. Henry Demarest Lloyd, after considering how to gather socialism out of the Populist fragments that remained after the ideological "explosion" at the party's 1896 convention, concluded that "the scene of ruin, confusion, and defeat" was hardly the place "to organize a really radical party," but socialism, in time, did recruit many middle-of-the-road Populists.[21]

At several Populist county conventions in Washington in 1896, middle-of-the-roaders rejected fusion, and during the next year the party was almost destroyed by the issue. In late 1897 one disgruntled group of middle-of-the-roaders met in Tacoma to repudiate fusion and consider impeaching Governor Rogers, who in his battle with the radical Populists had already isolated the middle-of-the-roaders by denying them state patronage. Among those present at the Tacoma meeting were W. P. C. Adams, the former ARU official who was the state's first commissioner of labor, Judge Richard Winsor of Seattle, who soon converted to socialism, Ernest Burns, destined to become a controversial figure in the British Columbia socialism movement, and Robert Bridges, one of the leaders of the urban wing of the Populist party. Bridges, who hoped to unite all labor unions, single taxers, Populists, and socialists, had previously published the *Socialist* in Seattle to promote his labor-reform program.[22]

Middle-of-the-roaders abandoned the idea of impeaching Governor Rogers, but the issue of fusion grew even more bitter in 1898. When fusionists were again victorious at the Populist convention in Ellensburg, many members argued that the old Populist party in Washington was dead. In Spokane, where there was a close link between middle-of-the-roaders and single taxers, *Freemen's Labor Journal* had long warned that fusion was destroying the Populist party in western Washington. After the 1898 election debacle, fusion became an epithet widely used by radical reformers in the Pacific Northwest.[23]

SOCIALISM'S MIDDLE-CLASS RECRUITS

The SDP gained urban recruits not only from among the middle-of-the-road Populists but also from among trade unionists, single taxers, Bellamy Nationalists, SLP dissidents, and adherents of the social gospel. Washington's first Nationalist club was formed in Tacoma in mid-1889 by Reverend W. E. Copeland, a Boston-born social gospeler, Christian Socialist, and Unitarian minister who lectured Sunday evenings on *Looking Backward*. Copeland, a typical eclectic middle-class reformer, later became associated with the Burley Colony, located fourteen miles northwest of Tacoma. Nationalist clubs also spread in 1892 to North Yakima, Spokane, and possibly Seattle. Although the Nationalist clubs attracted such radical reformers as Burnette Haskell, they remained basically non-Marxian, middle-class study groups.[24]

Another example of an organization that brought middle-class reformers together to study contemporary social ills is the Fabian

Society organized in Seattle by Laurence Gronlund. Among those present at the society's discussion of "Industrial Cooperation" in 1899 were clergymen, lawyers, doctors, school teachers, merchants, businessmen, and one professor, all representatives of middle-class groups that had "heretofore not been interested in socialism."[25]

Quite often, it was simply a naive interest in municipal reform or direct legislation rather than membership in a Nationalist club or a Fabian Society that led members of the urban middle class into the socialist movement. Beginning in the early 1890s municipal ownership of public utilities became an increasingly popular scheme. Advocates claimed that their proposals for public ownership of power and transportation facilities would mean a "square deal for all," fair wages and reasonable hours for labor, and large savings to the public because vital services would be provided at cost. For a time municipal ownership, sometimes described as "gas and water" socialism, appeared to be the most popular form of socialism in the United States.[26]

The "decided municipal unrest" in the Far West in the 1890s also led to the creation of a National Municipal League and to the proliferation of "good government" clubs. Spokane's Good Government Club hoped to purify local politics by getting a "better class" of citizens into public office, where they could pass and enforce good laws. Efficiency became one of the bywords of a movement that tried to cure the problems created by municipal disintegration and the corrupt interests that allegedly dominated urban politics.

Just how good-government reformers expected to alleviate unemployment and substandard housing by abolishing the ward system of electing municipal officials or instituting a commission form of government is unclear; Beatrice Webb, the British Fabian, was ahead of her time when she noted how shallow most American municipal reformers were. As members of the good-government movement progressed from a narrow concern with purely administrative matters to an interest in the social well-being of the entire community, however, a few embraced socialist solutions.[27]

Another of the popular nostrums that offered a cure for the ills besetting government in the late nineteenth century was direct legislation. Denounced by opponents as terribly radical, direct legislation schemes such as the initiative, referendum, recall, and direct primary promised to allow "the people" to seize the reins of government from corrupt political bosses and recalcitrant legislators. Like the single tax, direct legislation offered a way to correct social and economic abuses; it was a protean reform that united labor and the middle class in Washington and served as the seedbed of socialism in British Columbia.

One of the chief proponents of direct legislation in the United States was Samuel Gompers, who saw the scheme as a "first tool" that would enable the working class to counteract the "partisan prejudice" hampering its quest for economic justice. Although many Canadians thought that direct legislation was an undesirable novelty creeping into the British parliamentary tradition, the Dominion labor movement helped to import the reform into Canada in the hope of using this device to safeguard the interests of the working class. Until World War I, direct legislation had a strong following in the four western provinces. In Washington, direct legislation was one of several reforms that provided the basis for close cooperation between labor and farm groups in the early twentieth century.[28]

Although many trade unionists were convinced that middle-class reformers placed too much emphasis on individualism and idealistic solutions to society's problems, municipal reform and direct legislation campaigns, like the Populist crusade, often stimulated a greater appetite for fundamental social and economic change than they could satisfy. For the urban reformer left frustrated when the enthusiasm of a reform campaign began to ebb, socialism sometimes offered new hope.

The diversity of the elements that comprised American socialism was reflected in the factionalism that characterized the movement in the late nineteenth century. In Washington, the diverse origins of the socialist movement produced a highly volatile mixture.

"RIPEST FIELD IN THE WEST"

The Social Democrats made such impressive gains in Washington in 1898 and 1899 that Eugene Debs called the state the "ripest field in the West." Like other early branches of the SDP in Washington, the Seattle local that was formed in October 1898 apparently originated as a branch of the old Social Democracy. Party members in Seattle were led by W. W. Mallory and L. W. Kidd, a compositor, who, in addition to serving as the editor of the short-lived Seattle socialist journal, the *Clarion*, was a vice-president of the Western Central Labor Union. The party's first real show of strength at the polls occurred in Fairhaven (now a part of Bellingham), where the Social Democrats almost elected John Cloak as mayor in 1899. Emerging from the battle as the temporary hero of the SDP in the state, the thirty-nine-year-old Cloak typified a common pattern of conversion to socialism in the Pacific Northwest. Having once been a member of the Knights of Labor and the People's party in Ohio, Cloak turned to socialism as a result of the fusion effort in the Populist movement. In June 1898 he moved to Fairhaven, where he joined the SLP and later, when the local SLP section collapsed, the SDP.[29]

Leaders of the various SDP branches organized the Social Democratic party of Washington in April 1900. When the SDP held its first state convention in Seattle the following July, the delegates, most of whom were from western Washington, declared in favor of collective ownership of the means of production and distribution and also expressed support for such immediate reforms as direct legislation and municipal ownership. Although the party promised to support trade unions, the socialists expected to help the workers "complete their emancipation by united political action."[30]

The July SDP convention nominated a full slate of SDP candidates, who reflected the diversity of backgrounds of party members. Of the SDP candidates for statewide office in 1900, one had been a Nationalist, three had been active single taxers, two were former Republicans, one was an ex-member of the SLP, one had been a Populist, and one had marched in Coxey's Army. Herman Culver, the party's first statewide organizer, came from Equality Colony. James Ross and H. D. Jory, two socialist candidates for statewide office in subsequent elections, had both served as Populist legislators in the fifth Washington legislature.[31]

Probably the two most influential figures in the Washington socialist movement were George Boomer and Dr. Hermon Titus. The term "boomer" was an appellation often used to designate a real-estate promoter, and although George Boomer was hardly interested in selling town sites, his surname more than accurately describes his unstinting promotional activities in the cause of socialism.

Born in Maine in 1862, Boomer became a member of the SLP at the age of twenty-two, and was the SLP candidate for governor of Rhode Island in 1893. His ability to write copy directly from the printer's job case made him a formidable journalist. As the author of the popular "Uncle Sam" column, Boomer became an associate editor of the *Appeal to Reason* for six months; he later joined the Brotherhood of the Cooperative Commonwealth and came to Washington to edit *Industrial Freedom* at Equality. After six months at Equality he traveled to Tacoma, where he started the *Spirit of '76* to propagandize for the SLP.

After an additional period of toying with various Socialist schemes, Boomer became Washington socialism's knight-errant, battling the minions of capitalism armed with little more than printer's ink and moveable type. He edited an incredible number of socialist papers throughout the state before dying unexpectedly in Port Angeles in 1914 while working on his latest journalistic venture.[32]

Within the Washington Socialist party, no member, not even George Boomer, was more important than Dr. Hermon Titus. Although he seldom held a high position in the party, Titus used his position as editor of the *Seattle Socialist* to establish himself as a leading theoretician of left-wing socialism in the United States and the DeLeon of the Pacific Northwest socialist movement. Not even the British Columbia socialists, sheltered behind the 49th parallel, could escape the heresy-hunting gaze of Dr. Titus.

Born in Massachusetts in 1852, Titus spent seven years after college working as a Baptist theologian, but he resigned from the ministry because he concluded that churches did not truly represent Christ. This conviction, however, did not immediately lead him to socialism. After graduating from Harvard University Medical School in 1890, he practiced medicine for many years; it was as a company doctor for the Great Northern Railway that he made his way to Seattle in 1893. Toward the end of the decade Titus became associated with Laurence Gronlund as a member of the Fabian Society of Seattle and, along with other members of the community's middle class, developed an active interest in municipal reform. Titus played a prominent role in drafting a new charter for the city and helped create a Citizens' Non-Partisan League in 1900 to strike at the monopoly power of the Seattle Electric Company. Titus associated in the league with such labor reformers as George Cotterill, who later became mayor of Seattle. When the league fused with the Democrats, Titus and ex-Populist reformer Richard Winsor shifted their support to the socialist movement.

It was while he was doing social work on Seattle's skid road, a congregating place for lumber workers and other migratory laborers, that Titus first read *Das Kapital*. As a result the middle-class reformer soon became convinced that "reform was impractical and revolution necessary." Titus particularly came to detest the popular gas-and-water variety of municipal socialism, his position ultimately becoming as hard and rigid as cast iron. He agreed with DeLeon that a socialist party should reject all palliatives, but unlike DeLeon he opposed dual unionism, which probably explains his failure to join the SLP.[33]

The *Seattle Socialist* was born out of the frustrations that Titus encountered during his first unsuccessful foray into trade unionism. In attempting to organize striking telephone operators in Seattle, he petitioned the Western Central Labor Union (WCLU) for assistance. Titus wanted to call a general strike if all else failed, but the WCLU refused to support such bold action, and the strike collapsed. In the aftermath of the strike, Titus, on 12 August 1900, launched the *Socialist* to "Organize the Slaves of Capital to Vote their own Emancipation." Although the *Socialist* was not a party organ, Titus envisioned the paper as helping to complement his role as party organizer. There were, at that time, a number of indigenous socialist groups in Washington, and their members often wrote to him requesting information on the SDP and seeking his help in organizing local branches of the party.

In its drive to "organize the State for the Social Democratic party," the *Socialist* carried information and tips on organizing and holding meetings ("keep it lively") and suggestions for reading matter (Titus listed Blatchford's *Merrie England* as the first primer on socialism). Titus also made liberal use of instructional cartoons. The *Socialist* was a spirited if not always profitable newspaper; Titus sometimes practiced medicine on the side to pay the bills. After the Debs presidential campaign of 1900 the paper evolved into a forum for left-wing socialism, reflecting Titus' obsession with the SDP as the "Workingman's Ticket." Before the paper died in 1909, it had helped nurture several young radicals in the Pacific Northwest, including prominent Communist William Z. Foster, but the *Socialist* had also kept countless workers outside the local Socialist party.[34]

A writer in the *Seattle Union Record* described the difficulty the average worker faced when he wished to become a member of the local Socialist party. The prospective member, the writer averred, was forced to take an examination that was a cross between the Spanish Inquisition and the test given a candidate for a professorship at a Rockefeller college. The worker who somehow managed to become a member of the local found it "utterly impossible" to remain in the Socialist party in Seattle without yielding "a cheerful and subservient obedience" to the "dictates" of the "self-appointed despot," Dr. Hermon Titus.[35]

Hulet M. Wells, a Seattle activist in the cause of labor and socialism, once described Titus as a "dogmatic, dictatorial" person who possessed an incisive mind and considerable platform ability. It was these qualities that led Titus to attempt to merge the several sources of socialism in Washington into a single-minded, proletarian party, a goal that may have seemed feasible in the party's adolescent days in 1900. Although the party had failed to elect Debs president of the United States or even to capture the municipal government in Fairhaven, the Social Democrats in Washington were clearly growing stronger. During 1900 the state party grew from a collection of less than eighteen locals in the Puget Sound area to twenty-eight locals, and by November 1901 the Social Democrats were claiming forty locals scattered throughout the state. Many of the new locals, however, were formed in the agrarian communities of eastern Washington, and that fact threatened Titus' plans to proleterianize the party.[36]

PIONEER SOCIALISTS IN BRITISH COLUMBIA

The Socialist party in British Columbia, like that in Washington, was of heterogenous origin. A debate on socialism in Nelson's Presbyterian Church in 1893, lectures in the Rossland area by an organizer for Burley Colony, and performances in the Kootenay region in 1898 by Zeno, the contortionist, juggler, and socialist propagandist, were but some of the early means used in the interior of British Columbia to increase popular awareness of socialism. The Western Federation of Miners began to organize in the Kootenay mining camps in the late 1890s, but the union's influence on the development of socialism in the province was at best very indirect before 1902.[37]

In the coastal portion of British Columbia the early socialist movement was greatly influenced by middle-class organizations such as the Canadian Socialist League (CSL). The CSL owed much of its inspiration to George Wrigley, a reform journalist who began publishing *Citizen and Country* in 1898 as the official organ of the Canadian Direct Legislation League. The publication, which billed itself as a "Journal of Social, Moral and Economic Reform," carried news about single taxers and Christian Socialists, although Wrigley believed that direct legislation was the common denominator for all other reforms.

In the fall of 1898 Wrigley and his son, G. Weston Wrigley, attended a social reform convention in Toronto, where they no doubt encountered some socialist delegates from the United States. At that time, George Wrigley may already have been mulling over the idea of creating an alternative to the Canadian Socialist Labor Party, for a short time later he launched the CSL and attacked the SLP as "anti-Christian." The CSL, which characterized Christ as the first socialist, was for several years little more than an educational effort that blended the tenents of Methodism and Christian Socialism. Aided by the "ablest, brightest, most aggressive and popular paper published in the Dominion of Canada," as *Freemen's Labor Journal* described *Citizen and Country*, the CSL moved westward to the Pacific Coast shortly before the turn of the century.[38]

While the CSL equated socialism with middle-class respectability, another Ontario-based group, the Canadian Cooperative Commonwealth (CCC), equated it with colonization. The CCC established Ruskin Colony on the lower Fraser River in 1896. The Ruskin venture went bankrupt three years later, but the CCC left a legacy of reform education in the province. Some of its members in British Columbia subsequently joined other local socialist organizations.[39]

The CSL and the CCC are only two examples of the early socialist organizations that arose in turn-of-the-century British Columbia. In contrast to the more or less linear progression of the mainstream of the socialist movement in Washington—from the Social Democracy to the Socialist party—the Socialist party in British Columbia evolved from a confusing welter of splinter groups. A person almost needs a program or schematic diagram to follow the various combinations and permutations that characterized the British Columbia socialist movement.

It was this kind of intellectual ferment that caused George Wrigley to remark in late 1899 that in no part of Canada "has Independent Thought so firm a foot hold as in the West. Labor," he added, "controls British Columbia. . . ." The latter part of that statement was a particularly timely observation insofar as it applied to the Vancouver labor movement.[40]

Industrial relations in Vancouver and vicinity had not been especially turbulent before the 1890s. Because there was little primary industry and only a handful of businesses employing a large number of workmen, few major strikes had occurred in the Vancouver region. Major changes, however, accompanied the 1900 strike by Fraser River fishermen in nearby Steveston, the bitter culmination of a series of disputes between the cannery operators and fishermen. It would be several more decades before labor realized its dream of organizing all the fisheries on the West Coast of Canada, but the fishermen's strike, the first significant labor dispute in British Columbia outside the mining industry, marked the emergence of radical leadership in the Vancouver labor movement.[41]

The growing strength of both organized labor and socialism in British Columbia was evident in the provincial election of 1900, the first contested by a socialist candidate. At a joint convention in Vancouver, delegates from the CSL and the United Socialist Labor party—a group of moderates expelled from the local SLP—drew up a mildly ideological socialist platform and nominated Will MacClain to contest the next provincial election in the Vancouver riding.

MacClain, a member of the Machinists' Union and an organizer in the Fraser River fishermen's strike, was an Englishman who had jumped ship in British Columbia. He had given the first open-air socialist speech in Vancouver in 1899, lecturing for ninety minutes on the class struggle from a podium that consisted of two grocery boxes. MacClain allegedly resigned from the SLP because of its attacks on trade unions and other socialist groups, although the SLP accused him of being a "bogus socialist," remaining with the party only thirteen weeks, never paying any dues, and then leaving because the SLP did not give him a chance to gain notoriety.[42]

At the same time as the socialists nominated their first candidate, organized labor in British Columbia was becoming more interested in political activity. Three major options lay open to the trade unionists. They could support the candidate of the socialists, they could support reformers as they had generally done in previous elections, or they could organize a labor party. The United Socialist Labor party attempted to appeal to labor with a broad platform that included a demand for direct legislation and extensive government ownership, but many trade unionists were convinced that the socialists offered workingmen little that was realistic. Labor leaders were more interested in the labor parties that appeared in British Columbia before the provincial election of June 1900.

Prior to the provincial election, British Columbia labor leaders decided upon two different tactics to reach a common goal. Workers in the Kootenays were urged to support any candidate pledged to a general labor program that included the eight-hour workday, safety legislation, and restriction of Oriental immigration; on the coast, labor was encouraged to take independent political action. An Independent Labor party (ILP) was formed in May to coordinate labor's political activity, but the ILP remained less a political party than a loose coalition of people interested in the enactment of labor legislation. The ILP nominated several trade unionists to contest the election.

The moderate class consciousness that underlay labor's new political interest worried some British Columbians. They probably would have agreed with the *Colonist* when it argued that there would be no labor vote if only labor could see that its interests were bound up with those of business. Such an observation, however, meant little to the province's labor leaders, who saw growing evidence of labor's power as a distinct class. Unless the more than ninety candidates for the legislative assembly were lying, all promised something to labor.[43]

Labor in the interior of the province helped elect several pro-labor legislators, but of the five official labor and socialist candidates in coastal British Columbia, only Ralph Smith of Nanaimo won a seat in the legislative assembly. Industrial baron James Dunsmuir, having narrowly defeated laborite John Ratcliff in Nanaimo South, became premier of British Columbia.[44]

Perhaps encouraged by the election of Smith and the labor-leaning legislators, the Vancouver Trades and Labor Council urged formation of a province-wide labor party. The British Columbia labor movement, however, was divided on political matters, and coalitions that had been formed to contest the provincial election melted away in the heat of the Dominion election campaign that followed later in 1900. An Independent Labor Club in Rossland nominated Chris Foley to contest the Dominion election, but Foley, a hardrock miner and "the people's candidate," was defeated because he failed to generate a broad base of support. In Nanaimo, Ralph Smith, who had been persuaded to resign his newly won seat in the legislative assembly to become a candidate, was sent to Ottawa. Smith, variously called the "Gompers of Canada" and a "political juggler," was one of the first two labor members in the Dominion Parliament.[45]

During the course of its political activity in 1900, the labor movement of British Columbia took a subtle turn to the left. Most labor platforms urged the adoption of direct legislation, but the convention that nominated Chris Foley pointedly dropped the direct legislation demand because a number of Kootenay miners had come to realize that it was an inadequate solution to the everyday problems they encountered in the mines. Labor platforms still endorsed the single tax, but workers in 1900 were less enthusiastic about that reform than they had been a decade earlier. Socialism, on the other hand, began appealing to more workers about the same time as the socialists declared war on the labor parties. The socialists, who claimed that their party was organized labor's only legitimate political arm, had tried unsuccessfully to dissuade the Vancouver Trades and Labor Council from forming a labor party to contest the Dominion election of 1900; but when the Vancouver Labor party disappeared and labor MP's such as Ralph Smith joined the Liberal party, the Socialist party's *raison d'être* was more fully understood by politically conscious workers.

A generation enveloped in affluence and separated from the age of innocence by two world wars, atomic fission, and a Great Depression, no doubt has difficulty comprehending the earnestness

with which socialist pioneers pursued their dream of the Cooperative Commonwealth. They had no reason to doubt, however, that
with the right formula they might readily achieve their socialist
dream. The search for that elusive formula kept socialists in a state
of constant intellectual agitation and frequent disagreement.

CHAPTER 7

The Road to Revolution:

Left-wing Theoreticians and Working-class Rebels

Members of socialist organizations in the Pacific Northwest tended to be recruited from four somewhat overlapping groups: a small coterie of intellectuals, whose influence as left-wing theoreticians far exceeded their numbers; members of the working class, such as the miners who formed the backbone of the socialist movement on Vancouver Island and in the Kootenay region; farmers living mainly in the Inland Empire; and middle-class urbanites, who typically drifted into the movement as a result of some other reform campaign. Socialists recruited from the latter two groups almost invariably saw the Socialist party as little more than an extension of their favorite reform schemes, whereas the left-wing theoreticians and the more class-conscious workers believed that a genuinely revolutionary party dared not rely upon members who were more conscience stricken than class conscious or upon agrarian socialists who were more concerned about the price of wheat than the price of bread.

"'SOCIALISM' MAY NOT BE SOCIALISM"

Many socialist recruits were innocent of any knowledge of Marx, but they were eager to build a better society to replace the system they knew so well. No doubt more than one local socialist body in Washington had evolved out of a casual discussion of the condition of society by men lounging around the proverbial potbellied stove to escape the damp and chill of a Puget Sound winter afternoon. As a result, the early socialist movement was characterized by so much diffuseness of thought that disagreement among its adherents was inevitable. The *Colonist* had observed as early as 1893 that "uphold-ers of the established order need not be afraid that the socialists will turn the world upside down in their day." A century or two could be expected to elapse, the *Colonist* averred, "before any con-siderable number of them can agree upon any definite plan of ac-tion." Because phrases such as the "Cooperative Commonwealth" and "collective ownership" had many different connotations, the issue of what constituted socialism became so hopelessly confused that the Seattle *Socialist* quite properly warned that "'Socialism' may not be socialism."[1]

In discussing the problem of doctrinal purity in early 1898, F. J. Dean, the Socialist Labor party (SLP) organizer for Washington, caustically dismissed the members of the rival Social Democracy of America as "damd asses." He had spent a year trying to educate people but had discovered that "men will sign the application and come into the section and think they are Socialists but they bring in more fool ideas than would 'patch hell a mile,' all of which patches have to be raped [sic] off." Dean spoke of a man in Edmonds whom he regarded as the "most intense socialist you ever seen" but who "don't know any more about socialism than a Bull Frog knows of high glory." Dean often encountered such people in the Puget Sound area. After forcing himself to spend New Year's Day writing a letter to a confused socialist, "when I should have been drinking beer with the boys," he concluded that the only safe socialist was one who read the *People*, the SLP organ edited by Daniel DeLeon.[2]

The disunity that characterized the socialist movement in the Pacific Northwest was partly a reflection of the general disharmony that cursed the socialist movement throughout North America. A large segment of the American socialist movement in 1901 sub-scribed to Marxian ideology but disagreed on how best to apply the writings of Marx to America; other socialists derived their anti-capitalism more from the New Testament or *Looking Backward* than *Das Kapital*.

The formation in 1901 of the Socialist Party of America (SPA) by Social Democrats and members of several socialist splinter groups, excepting the SLP, brought only the illusion of unity to the movement. Although SPA delegates agreed not to attempt to dominate the politically neutral trade unions, the continuing controversy caused by the question of immediate demands and special platform planks for farmers threatened to tear the new party asunder and contribute new recruits to the uncompromising SLP, which still dominated the ultraradical fringe of the socialist movement.[3]

The question of whether or not such items as municipal ownership, direct legislation, and other immediate demands belonged in a socialist platform was directly related to the matter of party strategy. The SLP took the position at its 1900 national convention that immediate demands were "nonsense" and belonged to the infancy of the movement. By dropping such demands from the party's platform, the SLP proclaimed the incompatibility of social reform and revolutionary socialism, for as DeLeon had once declared, "Reform means a change of externals: Revolution . . . means a change from within."

Within the SPA, the question of immediate demands was not easily resolved. The revolutionary members of the party claimed that immediate demands such as municipal ownership and direct legislation were part of a "patch up" process that dulled the enthusiasm of the wage workers "who want revolution" and made laborers suspect the SPA of being merely another machine run by politicians. Other socialists regarded immediate demands as simply part of the evolutionary development of socialism, of serving the rather Machiavellian purpose of helping the party "catch votes." Later, in the era of Theodore Roosevelt's Progressive party, revolutionary opponents of such opportunism within the SPA noted how useless immediate demands had become as socialist "bait" for the middle class because the planks with the most appeal were being appropriated and used far more effectively by middle-class reform groups. As socialists pondered how best to reach the working class, however, they no doubt realized how fundamental was the matter of immediate demands; trade unions were by their very nature engaged in a day-to-day struggle for immediate gain.[4]

The years of wrangling that preceded the formation of the SPA allowed state organizations to win a high degree of autonomy. In Washington, the newly formed Socialist party was characterized by the ever-increasing influence of Dr. Hermon Titus, who, instead of encouraging the party to reach out to Washington's reform-conscious farmers and trade unionists, used his journalistic skill to enunciate more forcefully than ever his detestation of reform socialism in general and "Waylandism" in particular. Titus, who claimed that Wayland equated socialism and municipal ownership, wondered aloud in the *Socialist* what the *Appeal* would advise its readers to do when the Democratic party adopted a plank calling for public ownership of monopolies. The *Appeal* retorted by comparing Titus to DeLeon, a man for whom Titus had little use. As a result of a series of articles entitled "Revolutionary Socialism and Reform Socialism," Titus emerged as the leading theoretician of the left-wing of the SPA. A master of invective, much as DeLeon was, Titus condemned the SLP for its patronizing attitude toward trade unions and observed that the SLP was not growing "except in bitterness and intolerance toward all who do not acknowledge DeLeon." In Washington, however, "Titusism" was just as effective as DeLeon's dual unionism in antagonizing trade unionists.[5]

Perhaps Titus' fears that the SPA would become an ideologically diffuse middle-class reform organization were justified, for throughout Washington, socialist candidates in school board and municipal elections were equating the repeal of vagrancy statutes and municipal ownership of water works with socialism. The first Socialist elected to the Washington legislature, William Kingery, ran on a platform in 1912 that was little more than a mixture of homilies to the flag and a promise to "play peacefully the game of politics until a majority of the voters of this country are ready to swat capitalism hip and thigh." The Socialist platform in the Spokane suburb of Hillyard contained some sixty-three planks, running the gamut from "Peace" and the "Golden Rule" to concern for the "Nation's Youth." Revolutionary socialists were convinced that such platforms were likely to result in fusion and compromise. In their quest for ideological purity, however, Titus and his revolutionary socialist allies succeeded only in restricting the appeal of the Socialist party in Washington and reducing its political viability.[6]

AGRARIAN SOCIALISTS

Having idealized the proletariat, the revolutionary socialists regarded the farmer with unabashed scorn. "These little two-cows-and-a-lame-horse rangers," a western Washington reader observed in the *Weekly People*, "are digging out stumps with shovels and axe, and living more miserably than most workingmen without any property at all. But still, they belong to the 'great middle class,' the 'foundation of the nation.'" The Social Democrats had eliminated their special appeal to farmers by a referendum vote in 1899, but the Socialist party's unity convention in 1901 had been forced to review the matter. Many socialists were convinced that without the support of farmers, the socialist movement could never amount to much in the United States.[7]

The farmers of Whitman County were attracted to socialism in record numbers at the turn of the century. State organizer Joseph Gilbert (who was later a party in the landmark Supreme Court case, *Gilbert v. Minnesota*) was at that time setting up the numerous farmer locals in eastern Washington that Titus later claimed stood in the path of revolutionary principles. At the 1900 Whitman County Populist convention, C. B. Kegley, a former member of the Populist party State Central Committee and a Washington state delegate to the Populist party national convention in 1896, introduced a resolution urging the group to disband and reorganize itself as a local of the Social Democratic party (SDP). The matter was tabled, but in January 1901, Kegley arranged a meeting to provide SDP organizers an opportunity to recruit Whitman County farmers. Kegley, who soon became president of the State Grange and a prime mover in the powerful farmer-labor coalition in Washington, also worked closely with the socialist organizers to convert Whitman County's former Populists into socialists.[8]

The socialist movement in eastern Washington grew so rapidly that in mid-1901 the *Yakima Herald* began to include a special section for local socialists. The first columns were devoted largely to such innocuous subjects as direct legislation, but later columns sought to promote class consciousness and gain support for a socialist slate in the 1902 election in Yakima. Realizing that a full-fledged socialist journal was needed to speak for party locals in eastern Washington, state secretary Joseph Gilbert moved to Spokane and began publishing the *New Time*, a paper that soon evolved into the mouthpiece for the reform-wing of the Socialist party in Washington. By mid-1902, when Eugene Debs addressed an estimated two thousand persons in Colfax, the Whitman County seat, it was obvious that socialists had to regard the issue of special demands for farmers as something more than an academic question. The phenomenal growth of agrarian-oriented socialism in the Inland Empire led to the first major ideological confrontation between Washington's reform and revolutionary socialists.[9] The revolutionaries emerged victorious, but their triumph did not go unchallenged.

REVOLUTIONARY SOCIALISM IN BRITISH COLUMBIA

Although there were few if any farmer socialists in British Columbia, the young socialist movement, like that in Washington, split into revolutionary and reform wings. The reform wing was exemplified by the Canadian Socialist League (CSL), which claimed more than sixty branches scattered across Canada. The CSL contained many churchgoing members who were not interested in revolutionary politics, and its seventeen-plank platform omitted any reference to the class struggle.

Compared to the CSL, the revolutionary socialists in British Columbia appeared weak and fragmented. In the opening years of the twentieth century, however, socialism in the Pacific province entered a period of intense intellectual and organizational ferment that changed dramatically the character of the movement. Ultimately the cloak of moderation and Christian respectability was cast aside by the uncompromising revolutionaries who came to dominate British Columbia socialism.[10]

In the fall of 1901 the Vancouver branch of the CSL spearheaded a move that finally united almost all the socialist factions into the British Columbia Socialist party. At first, the moderates were in control. Ernest Burns, president of the Fishermen's Union in Vancouver, served the new party as secretary and organizer.

After writing to Seattle for a few copies of the Socialist party platform, Burns attempted to create a platform for the British Columbia Socialist party that would reflect American reform socialism and his own personal philosophy, which he once described as being of a "more elastic quality" than that of his ultraorthodox colleagues. Burns, who would later be responsible for a major schism in the British Columbia socialist movement, was the leader of the reform socialists in the province, and, like many other reform socialists in the Pacific Northwest, he had a Populist heritage.

Born in Birmingham, England, where he had been introduced to reform by *Progress and Poverty* and English socialist tracts, Burns was still a young man when he joined the Marxist Social Democratic Federation in the mid-1880s. Four years later he emigrated to Victoria, British Columbia. Moving on to Washington in 1890, Burns joined the Knights of Labor and subsequently the Populist party. The issue of fusion caused him to leave the Populist movement and to organize the Port Angeles local of the SDA. Just before the end of the nineteenth century, Burns returned to British Columbia, but he always maintained close ties with the reformers in Washington.[11]

By the end of 1901 the British Columbia Socialist party had seventeen locals, most of them in the Kootenay region. The growth of socialism in the Kootenays, however, was less the result of activity by a Vancouver-based organization than the natural product of discontent among metal miners of the interior.

The unofficial spokesman for the miners was the *Lardeau Eagle*, a mining-camp weekly edited by R. Parm Pettipiece. Pettipiece, who later became one of the leading socialist-laborites in British Columbia, moved to the metal mining region from Ontario. He organized a branch of the CSL in an isolated Kootenay village where he had begun publishing a newspaper in 1900. At first, his paper looked like a typical frontier booster rag, but Pettipiece soon gave the journal a major shove to the left.

In his weekly, Pettipiece boldly proclaimed that "The Masses Will Soon Rule" and published a list of reforms that the masses were supposedly demanding. When he took a vigorous stand supporting the eight-hour workday for miners, the British Columbia Socialist party selected the *Lardeau Eagle* as its official organ.

Pettipiece sold the *Lardeau Eagle* in 1902 and moved to Vancouver, where he made friends with another young and energetic propagandist for socialism, G. Weston Wrigley. The meeting of these two twenty-nine-year-olds may have helped convince Wrigley and his father to move their own journalistic venture to Vancouver. From this union of journalistic talents evolved the *Western Clarion*, for almost two decades the leading voice of revolutionary socialism in Canada.[12]

The socialist movement in British Columbia was influenced to a large degree by the widely circulating American socialist publications and by the American socialist lecturers who toured the province. The socialist parties of Washington and British Columbia exchanged fraternal delegates, and on at least one occasion the socialist leaders in British Columbia spent two days at a socialist "camp meeting" held just south of the 49th parallel, in Whatcom County. Ominously, perhaps, there was also much truth in the claim that Hermon Titus was exercising an increasingly large influence on the executive board of the British Columbia Socialist party.[13]

After touring British Columbia in June 1901 and visiting comrades on the lower mainland and Vancouver Island, Titus pronounced British Columbia the "most progressive" province in the Dominion. Because he had such high hopes for revolutionary socialism in so favorable an environment, Titus was enraged when he read the first platform drawn up by the British Columbia Socialist party since it omitted all reference to socialism as a working-class movement. Denouncing the document, Titus urged his comrades in British Columbia to fashion a "genuine Revolutionary Socialist program."

Although it is unclear how directly Titus influenced events in British Columbia, the Nanaimo Socialist Club, which had declined to join the British Columbia Socialist party, formed the Revolutionary Socialist party of Canada in April 1902. Convinced that reform socialism did not address itself to the problem of living in a society dominated by industrial autocrats, the long-suffering miners of the Nanaimo area drew up a document bristling with the rhetoric of class conflict. Billed as the political expression of the working class, the four-plank platform succinctly demanded collective ownership of the means of production and distribution, and industrial democracy.[14]

The revolutionary vanguard in Nanaimo had as their chief theoretician and spokesman, E. T. Kingsley, a man destined to acquire the same influence in British Columbia as Hermon Titus had in Washington. After working as a railway employee and a printer in California, where he had been a state organizer for the SLP, Kingsley moved to the Puget Sound area. There, in 1901, he became involved with the Revolutionary Socialist League, an organization composed of about sixty members expelled from a section of the SLP. The Revolutionary Socialist League had a low opinion of all labor unions, whether they were affiliated with the Socialist Trades and Labor Alliance or with the AFL. Kingsley believed that political action was the only weapon available to workers to improve their lot because the trade unions were too "feeble and insufficient" to confront capitalism.

Convinced that American socialists were confused, Kingsley moved to Nanaimo, where he successfully promoted his peculiar brand of socialism among the radicalized coal miners who formed the Revolutionary Socialist party of Canada. In 1903 he became editor of the *Western Clarion*, which he used to convince workers that there was an "irrepressible conflict of interests" between capital and labor and that revolution was consequently necessary. Embittered by the loss of both legs in a railroad accident, Kingsley became renowned in Vancouver for his vitriolic street-corner lectures on capitalism.[15]

The Nanaimo revolutionaries united with the reform socialists in November 1902 to create the Socialist Party of British Columbia. But the platform upon which the new party stood was fashioned entirely from planks drawn from the Revolutionary Socialist party. The next year the British Columbia socialists went even further and adopted a one-plank platform completely devoid of immediate demands. Writing in the *International Socialist Review*, G. Weston Wrigley called the document "probably the shortest and most uncompromising statement of the principles of revolutionary socialism that has ever been drafted in any country." After several years of wandering through the wilderness of reform socialism, the British Columbia movement thus committed itself to the narrow pathway of revolutionary socialism.[16]

REBELLION IN THE ROCKIES

No less significant than the routing of the reform socialists by the revolutionaries was the intellectual odyssey of hardrock miners in the northern Rocky Mountains. The miners' conversion to revolutionary socialism, however, was based less on cold logic or philosophical abstractions than on practical experience.

In 1890 some four thousand people lived in the half-dozen lead and silver mining towns nestled in the narrow canyons of the Coeur d'Alene river system. The Knights of Labor and several indigenous miners organizations had nominally existed in these towns for years, but the power of organized labor first became noticeable in the wake of the prosperity generated by the Sherman Silver Purchase Act. Workers revived the Miners' Union that had first been established at Wardner in the fall of 1887, and soon new or revived unions appeared in Gem, Burke, and Mullan. To strengthen their bargaining position, the unions consolidated on 1 January 1891 as the Coeur d'Alene Miners' Union.

When the union successfully pressed its demand for a $3.50 a day minimum wage for all men working underground, operators formed the Mine Owners' Protective Association of the Coeur d'Alene. The Mine Owners' Association alleged that the organization had been formed to represent mine owners in rate negotiations with the railroads, but it soon became evident that its real purpose was to destroy the Miners' Union.

A decline in the price of silver, combined with the decision by the Northern Pacific and Union Pacific railroads to increase the rate for shipping ore to Omaha and Denver smelters from $14 to $16 a ton, gave the Mine Owners' Association the long-sought excuse to destroy unionism in the Coeur d'Alene region. Rather than yield to the rate increase, the operators shut down the mines and mills in January 1892, idling some two thousand workers. A small number of family men regarded as "loyal" by the operators were retained for some mine development work, but as the bleak days of midwinter approached, many single miners trudged off looking for employment in other camps, such as those in the more prosperous Kootenays.

In March, when the railroads agreed to restore the old shipping rate, the operators announced both a reopening of the mines and a wage cut for miners. When the miners rejected the operators' wage offer, the two sides prepared for a fight. The Mine Owners' Association resorted to strikebreakers, court injunctions, mass arrests, hired gunmen, and Pinkerton spies, and finally secured the intervention of state and federal troops. When the miners resorted to violence, more than three hundred men were arrested by the military. Not just union men, notes Richard Lingenfelter, but justices of the peace, lawyers, merchants, saloon keepers — union sympathizers as well as innocent bystanders — were herded into two stockades, or "bull pens," at Wallace and Wardner. Confined like cattle for nearly two months, the men waited to be either charged or released. All the while, they suffered from the summer heat and intolerable sanitary conditions. Twenty-five of the union men were ultimately charged with contempt of court for violating a federal injunction and were taken to Boise for trial. Fourteen were found guilty and given sentences ranging from four to eight months in prison.[17]

The labor war in the Coeur d'Alene region prompted the Butte Miners' Union, the oldest and most powerful organization of hardrock miners in the northern Rockies, to issue an invitation to all other miners' unions in the West to attend a convention in Butte in May 1893. Although the Western Federation of Miners (WFM) was formally launched in Butte, the idea of a strong central organization uniting all metal miners in the West originated with the long-suffering miners imprisoned in Boise.

Among the miners who emerged from jail committed to the concept of a new mine labor organization was Ed Boyce. The twenty-nine-year-old Boyce had migrated to the United States from Ireland ten years earlier and settled in Wardner, in 1888, after first working in a number of western mining camps. The recognition Boyce gained from the martyrdom of the "bull pen" and the county jail helped him win a term as a Populist member of the Idaho senate. In 1894 he was also elected to the executive board of the WFM, and following a rebellion in the union against its Butte leadership, he was chosen to head the WFM. Though he was president of the WFM from 1896 to 1902, a time when the union moved progressively to the left, Boyce ironically struck it rich prospecting and retired from the labor movement to become an established member of the middle class.[18]

About half of the estimated ten thousand miners represented by the fourteen charter unions in the WFM came from Butte. The Panic of 1893 almost ruined the WFM, but by 1902 it had spread throughout the Rocky Mountain region and was claiming more than 165 affiliated unions of miners and smeltermen in the United States and Canada. Although the WFM acquired a reputation for radicalism, the delegates who attended its founding convention in 1893 were moderates interested in promoting "friendly relations" between miners and their employers. Their mild program of labor reforms, derived in part from an earlier association with the Knights of

Labor, was designed primarily to help members earn a living "fully compatible" with the dangers of their employment. The union's 1893 platform made no mention of the class struggle. A decade of encountering the almost total intransigence of the mine operators, however, radicalized the WFM.[19]

The WFM affiliated with the AFL in 1896, but Boyce and Gompers began quareling almost immediately over the alleged failure of the AFL to provide more than token support for striking miners in Leadville, Colorado. Additional conflicts over methods of organization and the idea of a regional labor movement caused a disappointed but ever more radical WFM to withdraw from the AFL in December 1897. Six months later the WFM spearheaded a regional labor movement to challenge the AFL in the West. The WFM continued moving left until in 1902 it officially endorsed the political program of the Socialist Party of America. In no part of the Pacific Northwest did the radicalized WFM and its regional progeny pose a greater problem for the AFL than in Spokane and its tributary areas.[20]

CHAPTER 8

Left-wing Unionism in the Inland Empire and the Kootenays:

The Spokane Connection

The coming of the Northern Pacific Railroad in 1881 and the development of the Coeur d'Alene mining district after 1885 set in motion the economic forces that made Spokane a nexus for transportation and commerce unequaled by any other community in the Inland Empire region. Spokane was a major distribution point for the mining camps, lumber mills, and wheat ranches of eastern Washington and northern Idaho. As a result of the activities of men like D. C. Corbin, who built a series of railway lines to drain the wealth of the Kootenays into the United States, Spokane was in closer touch with Canadian affairs than most American cities. Between Spokane and the British Columbia mining communities of Nelson and Rossland, the international boundary seemed to have lost all significance.[1]

Although Spokane was not a true mining town like Butte, it was an important focal point for hardrock miners and the international metalliferous mining industry. The lucrative mines of the Coeur d'Alenes and the Kootenays, as well as the marginal operations scattered throughout Washington's Colville region, were all tributary to Spokane, and until World War I miners and mine owners passing from one region to another had little choice but to travel through Spokane. Miners set out for the diggings from Spokane and spent most of their earnings there, and entrepreneurs such as F. Augustus Heinze and the Guggenheims channeled their activities

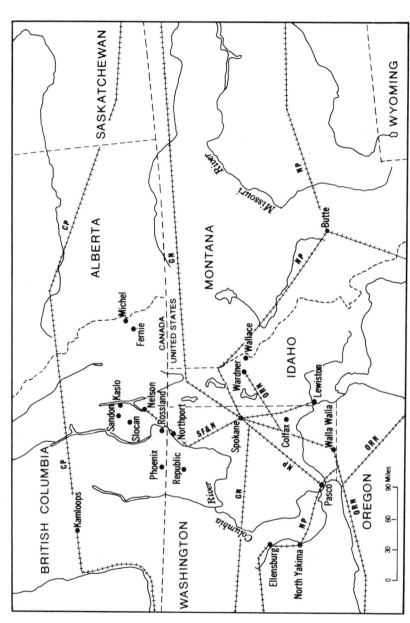

Map 3. The Spokane Connection: Major Railroads, 1893

in the formation of British Columbia mining syndicates through Spokane.[2]

In the 1890s the Spokane connection produced the anomalous situation of mining camps located on Canadian soil but peopled largely by Americans. An estimated seven-eighths of the population in the mining and smelting community of Grand Forks, for example, had originated in the United States. When the Venezuela boundary dispute raised the specter of an armed clash between the United States and the British Empire, Canadians expressed concern about defending the interior of British Columbia. Because they realized that the Kootenay mining towns would be at the mercy of the Americans in the event of war, Canadians organized militia companies in several communities in the Kootenay and Okanagan regions.[3]

The Kootenay region had experienced several brief mining rushes prior to the 1890s. A gold rush in the East Kootenay had generated several months of excitement in 1864, but, as often happened elsewhere, the flurry of placer mining was followed by years of placidity. The pick-and-pan prospector continued his lonely quest for precious metals, but developments beginning with the discovery of silver in the Nelson area in 1886 indicated that the era of individualism was passing. When experts described the "silvery Slocan" as the "best poor man's camp" in North America, they were not referring to the opportunities awaiting the lone prospector. When men began to talk of tunneling deep into the earth, building smelters, and laying railway track, the gold pan and the sluice box had to yield to the intricacies of high finance, mining syndicates, and international politics.[4]

As large corporations absorbed the smaller, less efficient, and less well capitalized firms, mining communities discovered themselves subjected to the vicissitudes of a world market and almost totally dependent upon outside sources of capital. When the economy faltered, as during the Panic of 1893, the price of silver slumped, and mines throughout the Pacific Northwest closed. Misery was widespread in the mining camps. The advent of the large mining corporation also meant that American capital accompanied the northward migration of American miners. American miners and American money dominated much of the Kootenay until, in 1898,

British and Canadian investors began to reclaim the area economically.[5]

No one organization did more to counteract the influence of Spokane and the Americans in the Kootenay than the Canadian Pacific Railway. For years the British Columbia government had provided generous land grants and cash subsidies to aid the construction of railways and public works in the province, but few Canadian railway companies had materialized in the Kootenay region by the turn of the century. Instead, D. C. Corbin's Spokane Falls and Northern line had made the area less than nine hours distant from Spokane by rail. In 1898 James J. Hill acquired Corbin's line and used it as a feeder for his expanding Great Northern system. Soon, the Canadian-born Hill, who had once been a director of the Canadian Pacific, threatened to use the Great Northern to increase American influence along the entire southern boundary of British Columbia.

The Canadian Pacific, which saw itself as part of an imperial transportation system and was determined to prevent an "invasion" of the Kootenay region by "foreign lines," engaged in a literal battle with the Great Northern forces at Sandon. Although the Canadian Pacific lost a depot in the skirmish, it ultimately won the war. An ever-increasing volume of trade and commerce flowed between the Kootenay and Vancouver, but so rugged were the mountaing separating the coast and the interior portions of the province that not until well after World War I was the Canadian Pacific's system of rail and steamship service in southern British Columbia replaced by an all-rail route. Meanwhile, ideas and people continued to enter the Kootenay region from Spokane.[6]

SPOKANE'S LABOR MOVEMENT

Spokane was characterized at an early date as a community where reformism and radicalism commingled freely with conservatism. Depending more heavily upon commerce than manufacturing for their economic well-being, otherwise stolid businessmen committed themselves to political reformism when the price of silver fell or the railroads failed to provide the community with the lower or terminal freight rates available in coastal cities like Seattle. The Spokane labor movement was likewise a mixture of conservative tradesmen, who were proud of their stake in a growing metropolis, and rootless and often volatile day laborers and migratory workers, whose memories of Spokane focused on the "employment leeches," the bogus or marginally legitimate employment agencies that flourished by fleecing the casual laborer who drifted into the city in search of a job in one of the region's extractive industries.

Although the anger produced by paying for a nonexistent job was the main source of the storm of protest stirred up in Spokane by the Industrial Workers of the World (iww), labor radicalism in the city manifested itself long before the free-speech fight of 1909. Spokane's early labor movement was far more influenced by the Knights of Labor and regional labor unions than by the American Federation of Labor (afl). Only after the Western Federation of Miners (wfm) and its regional offspring, the Western Labor Union (wlu), began to enjoy marked success did the afl send organizers to the city. The Spokane Trades Council, unaffiliated with either the wlu or the afl, developed into a strong, independent body in the early twentieth century.[7]

During the 1880s the labor movement in Spokane differed in no appreciable way from that in western Washington and British Columbia. By 1893, however, an informal farmer-labor reform alliance had developed in Spokane. Even more remarkable was the continuing influence of the Knights of Labor. Spokane District Assembly 249 had been organized in August 1888, and the following November members of the Knights of Labor and the various trade unions met to lay the foundation of a trades council. The meeting, presided over by Spokane's mayor, devoted considerable time to examining the relationship between organized labor and political activity. Led by William Galvani, a Knights of Labor organizer and promoter, the Spokane Trades Council was from the beginning a hybrid body that united structurally diverse labor organizations, served as a focus for reformist ideas in the community, and encouraged labor's political involvement.[8]

Although a few of Spokane's craft unions, especially those in the building trades, had affiliated with the afl by 1893, the Knights of Labor remained ascendant in the Inland Empire. The continued strength of the Knights in the Spokane area can be partially attributed to the tireless organizational activity of Galvani and to his position as leader of the Trades Council during the late 1880s. A civil engineer with a penchant for reform schemes, Galvani also published the *Northern Light* to propagandize for the Knights in Washington. Galvani left Spokane shortly after 1890 to become a national organizer for the Southern Alliance in Oregon, but the Knights in the Inland Empire retained a following that later became the backbone in the region of the WLU and its successor in 1902, the American Labor Union (ALU).[9]

The Spokane Trades Council and the Knights of Labor maintained a close relationship throughout the 1890s. As a political reform body, the Trades Council frequently served as a forum for learned discussions of municipal ownership as well as for diatribes directed at monopoly and the landed aristocracy. *Freemen's Labor Journal*, the official organ of the Council, helped the Spokane labor movement extend its influence as far east as Butte and north into the Kootenay region. The paper not only helped sustain interest in the Knights of Labor and the American Railway Union but also encouraged readers to develop a broad interest in reform. For $2.50 a year, any person could purchase a combined subscription to *Freemen's Labor Journal*, the *National Single Taxer*, and the *Social Democrat*. Not all readers of *Freemen's Labor Journal* were laborers, however, since the paper also offered reduced rates on combined purchases of socialist and poultry and livestock-raising journals. The paper's motto, "For the Masses Against the Classes," was more a reflection of its Populist heritage than a statement of commitment to labor radicalism.[10]

When, on Labor Day, 1891, members of the Knights of Labor assemblies and the trade union locals staged a parade in Spokane under the auspices of the Trades Council, members of the farmers' alliances joined the workers in their festivities. Following the march, which was led by the head of the Knights of Labor in Spokane, the crowd was addressed by Ahira Manring, chief organizer and soon to become president of the Southern Alliance in Washington. Manring was followed by other speakers who praised the alliance movement as well as Greenbackism and the Knights of Labor. With the growth of the Populist party, the farmer-labor alliance in the Inland Empire became ever noticeable.[11]

The depression of 1893, the sinking price of silver, and a controversy involving a local utility company caused the growth of the

Populist party in Spokane. Metallic leagues and silver societies appeared all over the state, but nowhere else in Washington was interest in the money question greater than in Spokane. Since business interests in the city depended on the healthy condition of metal mining in the Coeur d'Alenes and the Kootenays, the fall in the price of silver affected the economy of Spokane more adversely than it did any other major urban center in the Pacific Northwest.

Spokane's leading newspapers and businessmen joined with organized labor and the Populists to endorse William Jennings Bryan and free coinage of silver in the election of 1896. Although Bryan and the silver interests failed to capture the citadel of national power, Populist successes in the Inland Empire benefited the local labor movement, which enjoyed a significant influence in the ruling circles of the Spokane Populist party. In the summer of 1896, Thomas R. Lawler, an organizer for the Trades Council, was president of the Spokane Populist Club, and John Coffeen, vice-president of the Trades Council, was a member of the Populist party State Central Committee. Horatio N. Belt, the Populist mayor of Spokane from 1894 to 1897, was sympathetic to organized labor.[12]

The issue of fusion caused consternation in the Spokane labor movement. For a short time a few members considered forming a separate labor party; others, no doubt, became middle-of-the-road Populists and eventually converted to socialism. A majority of the trade unionists in Spokane, however, were ultimately convinced that organized labor could best continue its commitment to reform as a political pressure group.[13]

Although Populism gave some members of organized labor in Spokane an interest in reform that continued long after the demise of the Populist party, it also contributed to local labor radicalism. As John H. M. Laslett has observed, the unions most committed to Populism were typically those in which the socialists later exercised a considerable influence. One of those unions was the WFM.[14]

FROM THE KNIGHTS TO THE WESTERN FEDERATION OF MINERS

The single most important source of labor radicalism in the Inland Empire and the Kootenays was the WFM, an organization that espoused the more advanced ideas of the Knights of Labor and Populism long before it officially embraced socialism. In the Inland Empire and the Kootenays, the Knights and the WFM remained officially separate until the last local assemblies vanished in the spring of 1900. In the late 1890s the Knights had retained a following in the Idaho panhandle, where former General Master Workman James R. Sovereign edited and published the *Idaho State Tribune*, the official publication of the Coeur d'Alene miners. The coexistence of the WFM and the Knights of Labor in a single mining camp sometimes produced mutual antagonism resulting from a fear of dual unionism, but the Knights ultimately provided numerous recruits for the WFM. Bill Haywood, the Miners' secretary-treasurer, had been introduced to unionism by a member of the Knights of Labor; others moved directly from membership in the Knights to the WFM. A miner in British Columbia's Slocan district noted in 1902 that there were "thousands" of former members of the Knights of Labor in the WFM.[15]

W. J. Walker, the influential editor of *Freemen's Labor Journal*, and Ed Boyce, president of the WFM, embarked on a joint crusade in mid-1897 ostensibly to organize eastern Washington, Idaho, and Montana for the Knights of Labor. After forming local assemblies in each of the larger towns in the Spokane area, the two men transferred their activities to Rossland, British Columbia, where two years earlier Boyce had organized the first WFM local outside the United States. Walker returned to Spokane following the establishment of a Knights' assembly in Rossland in July, but Boyce remained in the province for several more days to visit with miners in the hardrock mining camps. Later in the year the Rossland Knights decided to boycott a Canadian Pacific subsidiary because it allegedly degraded workers in isolated construction camps by forcing them to eat with their hands and to sleep packed together like cattle. The Rossland Knights never matched the growing power of the Miners' Union, however. By 1899 Rossland had become the site of the largest WFM local outside the United States.[16]

When Ed Boyce visited the Kootenay miners in 1895, he no doubt discovered the preexisting sentiment favoring unionization. In March and April, 1892, the Slocan district had been a favorite destination for unemployed and blacklisted miners from the Coeur d'Alenes. There were no representatives from British Columbia at the founding convention of the WFM in Butte, but Kootenay miners could follow the news of the convention by studying a copy of the local newspaper, the Nelson *Miner*. Sentiment favoring unionization existed in almost every British Columbia hardrock mining camp, but many miners, recalling the battles of the Coeur d'Alenes, were understandably reluctant to join any labor organization until circumstances made it either safe or necessary to do so. Shortly after the formation of the WFM, union representatives discovered some weak AFL affiliates in the Trail area but were unable to convert them into locals of the WFM. Similarly, after formation of the Rossland local in 1895, the WFM languished in the Kootenays until 1899.[17]

A major milestone in the evolution of the WFM in British Columbia occurred when labor sympathizers in the 1899 session of the legislative assembly secured the passage of an eight-hour law for metal miners. Denounced by its opponents as "Populist legislation" that would possibly paralyze the silver mining industry, the Mines Regulation Act probably had a more far-reaching effect than either its sponsors or detractors imagined possible. As a direct result of this legislation, WFM organizers accelerated their activities in the Kootenays, and the union soon became a major political force in British Columbia.[18]

When the Kootenay miners later in 1899 began demanding $3.50 for an eight-hour day underground or, in effect, ten hours pay for eight hours work, the mine operators closed their mines and formed the Mine Owners' Association rather than comply with the new law. Accused of "sulking like a bunch of children," the mine operators decided to reopen the mines using scab labor. The importation of scabs from Washington and Minnesota raised the possibility of violence in British Columbia, and members of the Silverton Miners' Union warned operators that this might occur in the Kootenays just as it had in the Coeur d'Alenes. Sanity prevailed, however; the miners won their battle, and the WFM solidified its position in western Canada. Representatives from thirteen miners' locals in British Columbia and one in Alberta met in Rossland on 13 December 1899 to form District 6 of the WFM. They also agreed to establish a library and a lecture series to educate local miners politically. The wfm soon acquired a Rossland newspaper, the *Industrial World*, which agitated for the eight-hour day and served as the official organ for District 6 and the Rossland Trades and Labor Council. By 1901 the wfm had established sixteen locals among the hardrock miners of British Columbia.[19]

MINING CAMP RADICALS

Mining camps and mining towns, no matter whether they were hidden among the aspen and pine of British Columbia's Kootenays, stretched along the narrow valleys of the Coeur d'Alene, or standing in the shadow of Pikes Peak, all exhibited common characteristics that influenced development of a particular form of union organization. In the Pacific Northwest, the mining communities were often urban islands isolated by terrain and distance and dependent on a single industry. The prime concern of an adult as he opened his morning paper was the current price of lead, silver, zinc, copper, or gold. In a sense, the miners of the remote Kootenay region were more at the mercy of financiers and speculators than the citizens of New York or Boston were.[20]

Despite their physical isolation and dependence on one industry, the mining communities were microcosms of urban life in eastern America or Canada. No matter how small a community might be it still exuded municipal pretensions. The mining camp of Sandon was established in 1896, and within a year its citizens could boast of a water system, electric lights, a fire department, public school, theater, lodges, and two important institutions of life in any mining camp, churches and saloons. Nelson, the self-proclaimed capital of the Kootenays, backed its 1904 boast of being the largest city between Winnipeg and Vancouver by construction of a complete streetcar system.

Churches, schools, libraries, and debating societies followed the miners and brought culture to the wilderness. A culture of sorts also arrived with the saloon, dance hall, and theater. With the coming of the hardrock miners, a theatrical boom hit the Kootenays, and soon entertainment companies from eastern Washington were providing variety shows and musicals in the remotest mining camps. Theaters became symbols of municipal development, but they were also sources of trouble because of their sometime raucous entertainment. Soon, however, the desire to maintain a sense of decorum in these vigorous and often crude mining towns led to the policing of theaters.[21]

The violence in the Coeur d'Alenes and a lynching in Georgia prompted a mining town newspaper in British Columbia to observe: "It is fortunate that on this side of the line the people have a supreme confidence in a rigid enforcement of the law." The province, indeed, had gone to great effort to establish a strong, centralized system of law and order and to advertise that fact to potential settlers. Mining camps in the United States, by contrast, were generally lawless places that could expect little or no outside help in law enforcement. As Daniel Boorstin observes, American frontier communities typically existed before there were governments to care for public needs or to enforce public duties. As a result of the notoriously inefficient and loose-knit structure of frontier government in the United States, the six-shooter and the hanging rope were frequently arbiters of justice. Even those who professed a dislike for lynch law were often pragmatic about the end product. "Lynching is wrong; but necessity makes it right," editorialized Washington's *Okanogan Record* in 1905. "Judges may juggle with justice but when Judge Lynch closes the docket the verdict is writ so that all may read."[22]

Labor organizers in Washington and Idaho, especially those operating in logging and mining camps, discovered that where government was weak, anti-union employers were apt to take the law into their own hands and employ mob violence against labor unions. The *Coeur d'Alene Barbarian* of Wallace, for example, urged mine owners in 1892 to "assert the prerogative given them by the laws of the land and be aggressive." When the mine operators in British Columbia waged a losing battle against the eight-hour law at the turn of the century, the *Miners' Magazine* sarcastically noted that they were to be "pitied when they look across the line and see how easily their associates can defeat any law passed in the interest of labor, by a judicious distribution of a few thousand dollars in legislative halls and court chambers." In British Columbia, the system of law and justice and the institutions of culture and learning militated against violence, and thus Rossland could at once be a "hustling" town, the scene of financial battles between mineral king F. Augustus Heinze and his Spokane rival D. C. Corbin, and yet remain "as quiet and orderly as an English village on Sunday."[23]

Rossland in 1894 was still mainly wilderness, but two years later the "Johannesburg of British Columbia" was a thriving community of four thousand persons. Rossland's prosperity, however, still rested almost wholly on the precious metals dislodged from the fastness of the earth by employees of the various mining companies. These men were still called miners, but they had more in common with the urban proletariat of Pittsburgh or Chicago than with the placer miners so typical of an earlier era. In Rossland, as in other western mining communities where labor solidarity was promoted by relative isolation and the intransigence of the mine operators, class consciousness and union organization developed simultaneously. Between 1896 and 1899 the Rossland local of the WFM increased from two hundred to twelve hundred members; in addition to the miners' organization and a local assembly of the Knights of Labor, carpenters, typographical workers, tailors, cooks, and waiters all organized into craft union locals.[24]

Even after the enactment of protective legislation, the miners of Rossland and other Kootenay mining communities were sometimes required to work ten hours a day, seven days a week for wages that they considered inadequate. Lack of safety was also a part of life for both coal and metalliferous miners. A flaw in the machinery, poor ventilation, coal dust, a gas explosion, a kick in the head by a mule, a cave-in caused by rotten timber supports, a careless, unthinking comrade—any one of these could reduce a miner to a statistic in the annual reports compiled by mine inspectors. These reports are grisly reminders of the dangers inherent in mining.[25]

During the early years of coal mining in Washington, mine inspection was largely a farce. Not only were there few inspectors, but for a time they depended for their salaries on the mine operators themselves. In British Columbia, inspectors did little to prevent mine operators from violating the eight-hour law for metal miners. Although labor reformers were often able to secure the passage of mine and factory safety legislation, inspection techniques and poor enforcement rendered the legislation virtually inoperative. In Washington, many fatal accidents occurred in logging camps, but the lethargic labor commissioner, Charles Hubbard, shrugged off the mishaps by arguing that they were of such a nature that "inspection would not prevent them." It is no wonder that miners as well as loggers described their miserable condition in bitter, mocking songs such as "Dump the Bosses Off Your Back" or "Nearer, Oh Gold, To Thee."[26]

A miner's life was not all hardship, however. Miners celebrated such holidays as the Queen's Birthday, the Fourth of July, and Labor Day with brass bands, horse races, and mucking and drilling contests, and many of them enjoyed the solace of reading in the union hall or drinking in the saloon. The saloon was in the eyes of most workingmen a place where they could meet and talk in a "democratic way." The idea of prohibition, consequently, especially disturbed miners. It was feared that a mining camp without a saloon would have little to offer except monotony.[27]

As important as the saloon might be for many miners, the union was still more important in some camps. In the minuscule mining community of Sandon the union was the center of life for the five hundred members of the WFM. The city hospital, established in 1899, was cooperatively owned and operated by the miners, and the union hall doubled as an opera house. Miners, as Bill Haywood noted, were avid, even voracious readers, and many a union hall contained a reading room stocked with magazines, newspapers, and books. According to Haywood's romanticized account, Darwin, Voltaire, Byron, Shakespeare, Burns, and Milton were the miners' favorite authors, but many miners also undoubtedly enjoyed reading the latest dime novels.[28]

Miners' unions and their publications helped workers to become more keenly aware of their class status. In many areas in the nineteenth century, miners formed the vanguard of the labor movement because of their intense solidarity and their militancy. The miners of Vancouver Island and the northern Rocky Mountains earned a reputation for radicalism, but their radicalism was derived from the same bread-and-butter issues that appealed to members of the AFL. The AFL and the WFM were structurally and philosophically at variance, but each represented a successful, pragmatic response to particular industrial conditions. Miners turned to the state to legislate on matters of safety, wages, and hours only because employers used spies, scabs, and blacklists to defeat organized labor. Only when conventional reform politics failed did the WFM turn to socialism.[29]

ROSSLAND AND NORTHPORT

In May 1901, labor turmoil halted operations at the Le Roi Mining Company's smelter in Northport, Washington. Located 130 miles northwest of Spokane and 17 miles from Rossland, Northport was a mere hamlet on the east bank of the Columbia River when it was chosen in 1893 as the site for a new smelter to handle the increased output of the Rossland mines. In March 1901, smelter workers persuaded James Wilks, a vice-president of the WFM, to come down from Nelson to help organize a local of the affiliated Mine and Smeltermen's Union. When management shut down the smelter operations rather than tolerate unionization, the members of Local 115 of the Mine and Smeltermen's Union unanimously declared a strike. During the long and bitter conflict, marked by the importation of scabs, riots, shootings, and bloodshed, it became apparent that the mine owners were hoping to smash the hated Rossland Miners' Union by breaking its affiliate at Northport.[30]

Beginning in July, sympathetic miners in Rossland closed not only the two Le Roi mines but also the Centre Star, the War Eagle, and several other mines in the community. More than a thousand members of the WFM remained on strike in Rossland until November, demanding a wage increase and an end to discrimination against the union. The Le Roi Mining Company refused to accede to strikers' demands, and the mine operators, in an effort to stop the union miners from picketing, obtained an injunction. Also, the recently concluded Taff Vale Case in Great Britain, which resulted in a union's having to pay for damages suffered by an employer in a labor dispute, no doubt prompted the Centre Star and the War Eagle companies to sue the Rossland Miners' Union for damages.

Shortly after the Rossland case went to trial, legislation was introduced in Victoria to protect unions against injunctions and their funds from liability. The Trade-unions Act, approved in June

1902, was the first such statute enacted in either Canada or Great Britain. It was, however, the only gain for the miners in what was otherwise a disastrous strike. Not only was the strike broken, but the union also lost the civil suit. After two years of litigation, damages were set at $12,000 and the Rossland Miners' Union Hall was seized along with the union's funds. Paul Phillips has estimated that as a result of the blacklisting fewer than 20 percent of the striking miners remained in Rossland. In 1903 the WFM recorded approximately three hundred members in Rossland as compared with twelve hundred in 1899. Although the membership increased slightly after 1905, the union never regained the following it had before the Rossland strike of 1901.[31]

The failure of strikes in Rossland and Northport increased labor's interest in political activity in both British Columbia and the Inland Empire. As a result of the smeltermen's strike, Northport became divided. Each side in the dispute had its own newspaper and its own political party. In the December 1901 municipal election, a local Socialist party, organized by the workers and their allies, triumphed over the management-dominated Citizen's Ticket and elected a mayor, several councilmen, and other city officials. Dr. Hermon Titus warned that these recent converts to socialism might not be "well instructed in socialism themselves," and later worked to expel the Northport socialists from the state party; nonetheless, the first socialist electoral triumph in Washington, so lauded in the pages of the *Miners' Magazine*, was no doubt one of the factors encouraging the WFM and ALU to officially embrace socialism at their Denver conventions in 1902.[32]

The collapse of Populism, growing disillusionment with the AFL, and bitter labor disputes in the Coeur d'Alenes, the Colorado Rockies, and the Rossland area helped convince the leaders of the WFM that the union must adopt new tactics if it were to win for its members the traditional goals of shorter hours and higher wages. To secure justice in the mining camps and towns of the intermountain west, where the struggles between capital and labor tended to divide the entire community into two mutually antagonistic, class-conscious groups, the WFM leaders became convinced that the union had to overthrow the capitalist system itself. Delegates to the WFM's 1902 convention reinforced the union's growing reputation as a radical body when they voted to support the tenets of socialism, but it was local conditions that gave meaning to the Denver convention's endorsement.[33]

THE EVOLUTION OF WORKING-CLASS SOCIALISM

Although socialism did not accompany the initial appearance of the WFM in British Columbia, the miners' organization, nonetheless, introduced hardrock miners to the producer-conscious radicalism peculiar to the Spokane area. And after Eugene Debs addressed two mass meetings sponsored by the Rossland Miners' Union in 1899, socialism and trade unionism grew ever more entwined in the Kootenay mining camps.[34]

The strike-sick metal miners of British Columbia became convinced of the necessity of political action as a result of the Rossland strike, but many of them would not give wholehearted support to a Socialist party until they had first tested and found wanting a more conventional form of labor-reform politics, the Provincial Progessive party. Sixty-three delegates, largely representing the forces of organized labor, socialism, and the single tax, converged on Kamloops in April 1902 to create a new organization designed to harmonize the political interests of labor and reform bodies in the province. The convention itself, however, was far from united. Members of the WFM, comprising the largest single group of delegates, were factionalized, as the socialists and the single taxers argued about the substance of a party appeal to the workers, artisans, small farmers, and farm laborers of the province. The single taxers, who had a following in the Trades and Labor Council of the host community of Kamloops, devoted much attention to the platform, but only quick action prevented a socialist victory. The final platform reflected the heterogenous nature of the Provincial Progressive party in its inclusion of planks calling for restriction of Oriental immigration, implementation of the single tax, and a number of immediate demands popular with reform socialists at that time.[35]

Chris Foley, a miner who had moved to Rossland after the depression of 1893 ruined his contracting business in Vancouver, was chosen to head the Provincial Progressive party. An executive officer of the WFM, Foley had previously gained political experience as an Independent Labor party candidate in the Dominion election of 1900. Branches of the Provincial Progressive party appeared throughout British Columbia, but workingmen were only marginally interested in Foley's emphasis on moderate reforms or his argument that Henry George was a great benefactor of the people and that land monopoly was a "curse."[36]

Eugene Debs, who visited the province shortly after the Kamloops convention, expressed fear that the Provincial Progressive party would retard the development of a true socialist movement, and he denounced the new party as a "jar of mixed pickles," a middle-class movement that proposed to take a shortcut to power. Debs's utterances, Foley's defeat in a 1902 by-election, and the official support given to socialism by the WFM after mid-1902 sealed the fate of the Provincial Progressive party. Not only was the way cleared for the emergence of an uncompromisingly radical party, but the socialist ascendency in the metalliferous regions of southeastern British Columbia was seemingly confirmed when socialist James Baker succeeded the more conservative James Wilks as president of WFM District 6.[37]

When Hermon Titus argued that the chief danger to socialism in Canada lay in the formation of a labor party composed of one part trade union, one part municipal ownership, and one part church, he was speaking for all the revolutionary socialists in the Pacific Northwest who were convinced that the Socialist party alone should constitute the political arm of the labor movement. Many revolutionary socialists, unfortunately, adopted a condescending attitude toward the complementary economic arm, and this alienated trade unionists.[38]

In Spokane and its tributary areas, however, where a majority of the local socialists could probably trace their radical heritage to the Knights of Labor of the Populist movement, the economic and political arms of the labor movement were working in admirable harmony at the turn of the century. Shortly after sixteen members of the Socialist Labor party (SLP) organized a Spokane section in January 1899, *Freemen's Labor Journal* almost facetiously warned the local labor movement to be prepared to hear a great deal of talk about "class consciousness," "proletarians," and "surplus values." The "fakirs," "skates," labor politicians, and "pure and simple" trade unionists were told to prepare themselves for the "rich brown roasts" of verbal abuse. In truth, the vocabulary used by DeLeon's followers in Spokane turned out to be surprisingly restrained; members of the SLP had no desire to jeopardize their close ties to the local labor movement by torrents of invective.[39]

Socialism in Spokane continued to evolve with the formation of a branch of the Social Democratic party in March 1900 and an infusion of middle-of-the-road Populism after the state and national conventions of the Populist party refused to support the 1900 presidential candidacy of Eugene V. Debs. In contrast to the movement in Seattle, which was influenced by a bourgeois theoretician renowned for his polemical feats, the socialists in Spokane were guided by David C. Coates and H. L. Hughes, two men active in local labor affairs.

David C. Coates was a prominent member of the International Typographical Union, a labor editor, and a successful politican. While living in Colorado, Coates served a term as president of the state Federation of Labor. In 1900, at the age of thirty-two, he was elected lieutenant governor of Colorado on a Democratic-Populist-Fusionist ticket. One of the most thoroughly practical trade unionists to join the IWW, Coates moved to Spokane in 1906 and severed his ties with that radical body. Nonetheless, he remained a prime mover in the local socialist movement until Puget Sound revolutionaries precipitated trouble in the party following his election as a city commissioner on a nonpartisan ticket in 1911.[40]

The career of H. L. Hughes resembled that of his business partner, David Coates. Before moving to Spokane around the turn of the century, Hughes had been a member of the International Typographical Union in Butte, Montana, and a labor editor and an active Populist in the Coeur d'Alene region. In the election of 1894, Ed Boyce and he campaigned together successfully as Populist candidates for the Idaho legislature; at the age of twenty-three, Hughes took his seat as the youngest member of that body.

Hughes converted from Populism to socialism shortly before moving to Spokane. He often ran as a socialist candidate for public office but was never able to win election. A prime supporter of left-wing unionism in the Inland Empire, he announced in early 1905 that he would attend the next convention of the Washington State Federation of Labor to do some "boring from within." And he did just that. So amazingly successful was he that by 1914 Hughes and another former socialist represented the influential farmer-labor coalition in Olympia. Hughes by then had been driven from the Socialist party by revolutionary theoreticians seeking to cleanse the movement of all taint of reformism, but there is reason to believe that he remained a socialist at heart.[41]

Helping to extend the influence of labor-oriented socialism throughout the Inland Empire and the Kootenays was Joseph Gilbert and his newspaper, the *New Time*, which appeared in 1902. Gilbert, who was a member of the ALU in Spokane and who had helped to organize farmers and miners for socialism in eastern Washington and southeastern British Columbia, believed that the interests of the farmer and laborer were identical. Such an opinion made the *New Time* suspect in Titus' eyes even after Gilbert retired and Hughes became editor. Titus also disliked the paper because it appealed to Pacific Northwest socialists who enjoyed the Wayland-esque musings and other theoretically diffuse instructions on socialism written by such men as Ernest Burns of British Columbia and Walter Thomas Mills, a ubiquitous and popular orator whom Titus regarded as the incarnation of intellectual depravity. Titus apparently encouraged E. B. Ault to take a job with Gilbert so that the young journalist might spy on the reform socialists of Spokane.[42]

Because of geographical isolation and the powerful influence of left-wing unionism, a large portion of organized labor in the Inland Empire and the Kootenays at the turn of the century remained opposed to the traditional principles of the AFL. The later emergence of the IWW in the Inland Empire was thus no abberation. The essence of the Spokane connection was the radical element that it injected into the developing Pacific Northwest labor movement. This proved to be an important factor in preventing the AFL from gaining an easy victory in the region during the crucial years from 1900 to 1905.

CHAPTER 9

The Struggle to Prevent AFL Hegemony in the Pacific Northwest

In the opening years of the twentieth century, the American Federation of Labor's (AFL) sporadic organizational efforts in the Inland Empire contrasted sharply with the vigorous activities of the Western Labor Union (WLU). Created by the Western Federation of Miners (WFM) in mid-1898 to organize all workers west of the Missouri River into industrial unions, the WLU claimed more than sixty-five affiliated labor organizations in October 1899. The WLU, however, remained closely linked to the hardrock mining industry in the northern Rockies. Dan McDonald of Butte was the union's president, and David Coates' *Pueblo Courier* was its official organ. Following incursions into the West by the AFL, the WLU retaliated by reconstituting itself as the American Labor Union (ALU) in 1902 and directly challenged the AFL by extending the scope of its organizational activities to include all of North America.[1]

In Spokane, the WLU and the ALU organized such diverse groups as brewers, teamsters, beer drivers, expressmen, butchers, retail clerks, steamfitters and plumbers, gas makers, and shingle weavers. The powerful position of the WLU and ALU in the Spokane labor movement is in part attributable to the close proximity of the Coeur d'Alene mining area and to the heritage of the Knights of Labor and middle-of-the-road Populism. W. J. Walker used his *Freemen's Labor Journal* to promote both the Knights of Labor and the WLU as organizations that could successfully cope with the working conditions peculiar to the Inland Empire.[2]

The WLU and the ALU had considerably more difficulty organizing workers in the Puget Sound region than in Spokane. Central labor unions in Seattle, Tacoma, and Spokane had all been formed as the result of the joint efforts of the Knights of Labor and members of the various craft unions, but in Seattle and Tacoma in the early 1890s the number of craft unions affiliated with central labor bodies had increased markedly as the Knights of Labor assemblies declined or were expelled. Although the depression that followed the Panic of 1893 almost destroyed organized labor on Puget Sound, the revival of trade unionism that accompanied the return of prosperity in 1897 seemingly confirmed the triumph of the craft union in Seattle and Tacoma. On Puget Sound the WLU thus appeared as a reincarnation of an old threat to craft unionism, while in Spokane the WLU benefited from the heritage of close cooperation between the craft unions and the Knights of Labor.[3]

As a result of increased organizational activity by the AFL, the bakers, icemen, upholsterers, and laundry workers in Seattle returned their WLU charters in early 1900. Coal miners at Leary organized under a WLU charter, went on strike, lost, and returned the charter. Although the federation's organizer, W. Gwin Armstrong, confidently predicted that he would eliminate the WLU in both western Washington and Spokane, a crucial affiliation battle had yet to be fought in Washington's central labor body.[4]

The Washington State Labor Congress had originated shortly after the election of 1896, when William Blackman, a railway engineer and the leader of the American Railway Union (ARU) in Seattle, urged fellow trade unionists to form a temporary alliance to pressure the Populist-dominated legislature into enacting reform legislation. On 25 January 1897, representatives from nine trade unions and several farmers' organizations met in Olympia and created the Pacific Northwest Labor Congress. Like its predecessors, the Pacific Coast Federation and a short-lived State Labor Congress in 1893, the Pacific Northwest Labor Congress was a lobbying body. It also hoped to bring together all "urban and rural labor unions" in the northwestern part of the United States and British Columbia into one "grand central union."[5]

The new reform organization met in Spokane in 1898 under the more modest title of the Washington State Labor Congress but retained its goal of promoting the interests of the producing class and securing legislative benefits for the nonunionized. Aside from a statement supporting the eight-hour workday and several labor-oriented planks, such as the condemnation of the labor injunction and the issuance of "truck" or scrip by employers in isolated lumber and mining camps, the platform drawn up by the State Labor Congress might just as well have been issued by a farmers' organization. Although the convention contained delegates from craft unions and city centrals, several unions that were elsewhere declining or supposedly defunct were well represented. President William Blackman was one of several delegates from the ARU, and Secretary-Treasurer W. J. Walker was probably the best known of the many Knights of Labor representatives present.[6]

The eclecticism that characterized the State Labor Congress frustrated AFL organizers until shortly after the turn of the century, when the state central organization was markedly transformed. The labor lobby in Olympia had not been very successful—aside from the creation of a labor bureau and the passage of an unsatisfactory lien law, almost none of the reforms endorsed by the State Labor Congress had become law. When the fifth convention of the State Labor Congress convened in Tacoma in January 1902 a majority of the delegates voted to reorganize as the Washington State Federation of Labor. William Blackman was retained as president, but unlike the State Labor Congress, which had been interested merely in the passage of labor legislation, the new State Federation of Labor proposed to organize workers in the state in an active manner.

When the Tacoma convention began debating the question of affiliation, delegates representing seventy-seven local unions and central bodies in Seattle, Spokane, Tacoma, New Whatcom, and Northport split into three factions representing the AFL, WLU, and WFM (mainly members of the Mill and Smeltermen's Union at Northport). Supporters of affiliation with the AFL were at first in the minority, but after three days of rancorous debate they won a significant victory when the convention approved a plan to seek membership in the AFL pending a favorable vote on the issue by the member unions of the State Federation of Labor.[7]

A "Stage Coach Gait" versus "Automobile Speed"

When the State Federation of Labor's affiliation referendum was announced, both the AFL and the WLU engaged in what the *Seattle Union Record* described as a "healthy rivalry." Since its inception in 1900, the *Union Record* had been a frequent critic of AFL leadership. In December 1901, Gordon Rice had editorialized that Samuel Gompers and some of his ideas were "getting a little aged and must soon get out of the way of more progressive men and measures." Editorials in the *Union Record* a year earlier had described Dan McDonald and Ed Boyce as "humanitarians" and called upon them to send organizers to help resolve the chaos on Puget Sound that resulted from AFL neglect and a lack of recognized leadership in the local labor movement. During the referendum battle in 1902, the *Union Record* referred to the WLU as "that young giant of Western unionism." The AFL was criticized for its "cumbersome red-tapeism and New England parsimoniousness, while the Western Labor Union," the *Union Record* averred, "acts quickly and supplies funds when they are needed; Sam Gompers travels toward organization along well-known roads at a stage coach gait; Dan McDonald cuts across country at automobile speed." Despite the anti-Gompers tone of his remarks, the editor of the *Union Record* was not urging workers in western Washington to affiliate with the WLU but rather prodding the AFL leadership to awaken to the importance of the affiliation battle in Washington.[8]

Dan McDonald and several lieutenants in the WLU actively campaigned in Washington to keep the State Federation of Labor from affiliating with the AFL. Because the structure of the referendum made it possible for several small unions to outvote one union with a large membership, WLU organizers hoped to control the outcome of the affiliation vote by organizing a large number of unions among miners and mill workers. The referendum campaign, however, ended in an AFL victory. Although Seattle's Western Central Labor Union (WCLU) also affiliated with the AFL, the contest between the AFL and the WLU for "survival of the fittest" in the Pacific Northwest had not yet been finally resolved.[9]

The Washington State Federation of Labor aroused only minimal interest in Spokane; as of 1903 only fourteen of Spokane's forty-seven local unions had joined the state federation. Many workers in the Inland Empire were convinced that the AFL was interested in organizing labor only in western Washington. The ALU, on the other hand, became so successful in appealing to Spokane workers that it even considered organizing two hitherto unorganizable groups, janitors and schoolteachers. The largest union in Spokane in 1904 was the ALU's Federal Labor Union 222.[10]

As a result of AFL pressure on affiliates to discourage locals from retaining membership in central bodies not chartered by the AFL, a number of trade unions began withdrawing from the Spokane Trades Council. The ALU fought back, but the growing prestige of the AFL in other parts of the state and nation and dissatisfaction with the socialist orientation of the ALU caused a majority of the members of the Trades Council in 1904 to consider affiliation with the State Federation of Labor and to apply for an AFL charter. Then, irritated by the continued lack of AFL activity in Spokane, the Trades Council reversed itself and requested that the AFL return its $5 charter fee.[11]

The AFL dispatched organizer C. O. Young to Spokane to battle for the federation. Young, the fifty-four-year-old leader of the International Union of Steam Engineers in Tacoma, had been appointed an AFL organizer only shortly before his trip to the Inland Empire. He soon became one of the AFL's most tireless advocates in the Pacific Northwest.

Young had earlier joined the Knights of Labor after moving from Missouri to Seattle in 1883. A few years later, he spent a short time in jail for participating in Seattle's anti-Chinese riot. This experience coupled with the decline of the Knights on Puget Sound caused him gradually to reject the organizational philosophy of the Knights and become a staunch supporter of craft autonomy.

In Spokane, Young urged fellow trade unionists to be "cautious and conservative" and to conduct their affairs along "strict business lines." Young had the aggressiveness of a new convert, but he was at first unable to curb the tendency toward dual unionism in the Inland Empire. His efforts to win the six hundred members of ALU Federal Labor Union 222 to the AFL resulted in the existence of separate AFL and ALU federal labor unions in Spokane. His organizational activity also led to the formation of several central labor bodies.[12]

Young and the AFL finally won a nominal victory in 1905 when out of the confusion emerged a single central body affiliated with the AFL. Dual unionism in the Inland Empire was by no means eliminated, however. A number of unions in Spokane remained unaffiliated with any central council, and considerable opposition to the AFL continued to center in former ALU Federal Labor Union 222, which maintained the heritage of industrial unionism as an affiliate of the Industrial Workers of the World (IWW).[13]

Spokane was for a time the center of IWW strength in the Pacific Northwest. At the same time, Spokane's central labor body grew ever more conservative. The IWW and the Spokane Labor Council, nonetheless, remained capable of joining forces to fight injustice to the working class, such as when they launched a joint crusade in 1908 to battle the city's corrupt employment agencies.

In contrast to the protracted struggle in Spokane, the AFL victory in western Washington was deceptively easy. During their 1902 battle with the AFL in the Puget Sound region, the WLU and the ALU had handicapped themselves by their adherence to economic and political radicalism. After the electoral triumph of the Northport socialists, the *Miners' Magazine* had incautiously declared "socialism is unionism and unionism is socialism . . . ," but in Seattle socialism was "Titusism." Thus a person like Gordon Rice might admire the organizational zeal of the WLU but find an endorsement of the Socialist party by its successor most distasteful.

Although the *Union Record* had supported Eugene Debs in the election of 1900, the rise of "Titusism" in Seattle led the paper to declare in 1901 that socialists were dynamiters and utopians and that the local party was dominated by nonunion, nonlaboring men. The editor of the *Union Record* came to believe that one "full-fledged 'scientific' socialist" could do more toward breaking up a labor union than a dozen strikes.

The ALU's declaration of support for socialism, the *Union Record* averred, had given the AFL "another chance to become popular among the unionists of the West." After its affiliation with the AFL, the Washington State Federation of Labor was determined to keep the discussion of socialism out of its deliberations. Even in such areas as the Inland Empire and the Kootenays, involvement in socialist politics did little to help the ALU or WFM. Support for socialism not only disrupted the Spokane Trades Council but also caused smeltermen in Grand Forks, British Columbia, to quit the

ALU in 1903 and join a new Smeltermen's Federal Union affiliated with the AFL.[14]

The affiliation of Seattle's WCLU with the AFL in March 1902 did not necessarily mean full commitment to Samuel Gompers and his ideals, however. The Seattle central contained a growing coterie of trade-union socialists. The WCLU also nurtured a strain of labor radicalism derived from the continuing desire of workers to protect their jobs from the encroachments of Oriental labor and to defend themselves against the anti-union, wage-cutting activities of certain employer groups. Ominously, the *Seattle Union Record* warned the Eastern-oriented trade unionists in the AFL not to rely on past accomplishments as a guarantee of future success in western Washington.[15]

The WCLU passed into history in May 1905 when it reconstituted itself as the Central Labor Council of Seattle and Vicinity (CLC). Although it remained a member of the AFL, the CLC adopted an organizational structure that helped sustain the intense localism that Robert L. Friedheim has described as "unique." Seattle locals of craft unions gave their loyalty to several semi-autonomous trade councils and to the CLC. A worker was thus conscious of being a member of a Seattle labor organization no matter to what union he belonged. Seattle's Labor Council was also a prime supporter of industrial unionism in the AFL.[16]

An Important AFL Victory in Canada

The leadership of the labor movement on the mainland of British Columbia at the turn of the century was almost evenly divided between the WFM and the Vancouver Trades and Labor Council. The WFM remained firmly entrenched among the metalliferous miners of the Kootenays, but it had also begun to organize coal miners in the Rocky Mountains, and it would soon absorb the Miners' and Mine Laborers' Protective Association on Vancouver Island.

Events in 1901 on Vancouver Island constituted another chapter in the island's dreary chronicle of strikes, lockouts, and mine disasters. James Dunsmuir decreed that miners living at the site of his Extension mines must move their houses to the nearby community of Ladysmith or lose their jobs. He argued that this was necessary because there was a lack of good drinking water at Extension, but miners who were forced to pay $150 to $200 to rebuild their houses in a company town saw the edict as the further unfolding of a plan to give Dunsmuir total control over their lives.[17]

Because conventional forms of union organization failed to deter Dunsmuir on Vancouver Island or to win the Rossland Miners' Strike in 1901, the socialist message attracted converts among the workers, and the socialists acquired greater power in the councils of organized labor. Trade-union socialists captured the Miners' and Mine Laborers' Protective Association in the spring of 1902 while the Miners' long-term secretary, Ralph Smith, was visiting in England. Smith, who was also the president of the Trades and Labor Congress of Canada (TLC), was further humiliated by his home union when it decided by a referendum vote of 264 to 260 to withdraw from the Dominion Congress.[18]

Smith ran into yet another storm of trouble created by the socialists of British Columbia at the 1902 Berlin, Ontario, convention of the TLC. Much of Smith's presidential address was devoted to answering the diverse charges leveled at him in a letter circulated by officers of the Phoenix, British Columbia, Trades and Labor Council to TLC delegates of known socialist sympathies. Possessed of a radical fervor derived from ties to the Phoenix Miners' Union, one of the largest and most radical WFM locals in the Kootenays, officers of the Phoenix Labor Council claimed that Smith was a "henchman of a capitalist party," carried a pass issued by the Canadian Pacific Railway, and was James Dunsmuir's son-in-law. The socialist allegation of kinship was a blatant untruth. Smith, in fact, had run as the nominee of the Nanaimo Reform Club against Dunsmuir's son-in-law in the provincial election of 1894. Although a special TLC investigating committee soon cleared him of all the socialist charges, Smith stepped down from the office he had held since 1898 rather than continue the fight with the radicals from his home province. A majority of the delegates to the 1902 convention then chose John Flett as president of the TLC. Flett was a carpenter from Hamilton, Ontario, and had been an AFL organizer for Canada since 1900.[19]

The Berlin convention resulted in more than a change in leadership for the TLC. As Robert H. Babcock has observed in his study *Gompers in Canada*, it was a pivotal event in the history of AFL involvement in Canadian labor affairs. By reversing the traditional TLC position on compulsory arbitration, labor political parties, and the Knights of Labor, delegates voted to alter the course of organized labor in Canada. Two years earlier the TLC convention had refused to seat a representative from the Canadian Socialist League but had accepted delegates from the Knights of Labor. In 1902, however, the TLC convention voted not only to drop its endorsement of compulsory arbitration but also to expel the Knights of Labor. Henceforth, the most powerful labor federation in Canada would represent only craft unionism. For an investment of a mere 7 percent of its total organizational budget in 1902, the AFL had gained a significant enlargement of its influence in Canada.[20]

The success of the AFL in 1902 is partly attributable to the tremendous growth of international craft unionism in Canada during the four years prior to the Berlin convention. Although AFL organizers became ever more visible in Canada around the turn of the century, it is significant that local workers in a particular craft or industry were themselves often responsible for organizing a number of the new locals that appeared in the Dominion between 1898 and 1902. Frequently, they sent a request for a charter directly to the headquarters of an international union. Thus workers could acquire a charter from a union affiliated with the AFL and yet not subscribe to the philosophy of the AFL leadership.

Although the AFL victory in Canada in 1902 was impressive, it was not total, since dual unionism and labor radicalism remained endemic in certain parts of the Dominion. As of 1902 there were no less than seven organizations in Canada with which a local union could affiliate for its protection and benefit. The AFL's competitors were particularly strong in British Columbia.[21]

THE UNITED BROTHERHOOD OF RAILWAY EMPLOYEES

In no twelve-month period prior to World War I was life in British Columbia more wracked by labor disorder than in 1903. Working-class discontent that for years had been smoldering in the tinderbox atmosphere that marked labor-management relations in certain basic industries blazed up into class-conscious action as the result of the United Brotherhood of Railway Employees (UBRE) strike that began in Vancouver on 27 February 1903.[22]

The UBRE owed much of its original inspiration to George Estes, a young station agent employed by the Southern Pacific System in Grants Pass, Oregon. Estes had joined the Order of Railroad Telegraphers in 1898 and was elected general chairman of the Telegraphers' San Francisco Division in early 1899. When he became general chairman of the union for the entire Southern Pacific System a few months later, Estes was hailed as a charismatic leader, a "Moses" who was leading the telegraphers out of the "wilderness."[23]

Many employees on the Southern Pacific discovered to their dismay in 1900 that they were required to contribute to the railroad's newly established Relief Department. Some workers saw this as a scheme to make it difficult for them to afford union dues. President Collis P. Huntington agreed to abolish the Relief Department because of worker opposition, but he died soon after taking this step, and his successor reinstituted the scheme on a supposedly voluntary basis for unorganized employees only. During the time of the controversy surrounding the Southern Pacific's Relief Department, the Order of Railroad Telegraphers struck the Atchison, Topeka, and Santa Fe. Other railway brotherhoods on the Santa Fe refused to support the strikers, many of whom lost their jobs as a result of the abortive strike. Both of these events convinced the railroad workers, led by George Estes, that they must create a new railway union to protect themselves from the twin perils of oppressive management and craft autonomy.[24]

On 27 January 1901, eight men met in Roseburg, Oregon, a Southern Pacific passenger and freight division point approximately two hundred miles south of Portland, and created the UBRE. The UBRE was an industrial union modeled after the Amalgamated Society of Engineers and the United Mine Workers of America. With a core of some three hundred members in Roseburg and with Estes as president and organizer, the UBRE spread along the lines of the Southern Pacific.[25]

As Estes and his associates proceeded to organize in the West, they discovered a similar organization in San Francisco, the Railway Employees' Amalgamated Association, and an indigenous United Brotherhood of Railway Employees that had been eking out an existence in Winnipeg since its founding in 1898. The three organizations united after they had discovered one another. In search of both legitimacy and converts, the expanding UBRE became the self-proclaimed reincarnation of the old American Railway Union (ARU); the labor movement was encouraged to think of the UBRE and the ARU as the "same thing" under a different name. The association of the UBRE with the ARU, however, was at best a double-edged sword: many railway brotherhoods, mindful of the bitter clash with the ARU during the Great Northern Strike eight years earlier, were determined to destroy the UBRE before it could assume the role of a powerful dual union in the West.[26]

The Order of Railroad Telegraphers, which believed that the UBRE was a new ARU conceived by disgruntled telegraphers who had failed to realize their ambition to hold office in the brotherhood, expelled Estes and his associates in June 1901 for allegedly attempting to wreck the Telegraphers on the Southern Pacific. Until called upon to scab against members of the UBRE, the brotherhoods fought the new union with the weapons of ridicule and calumny. The official organ of the Telegraphers in 1902 called the UBRE a "house built on the sand," and the *Railway Trainmen's Journal* described Estes as "The Able-Bodied Liar."[27]

In attempting to establish a common identity with former members of the ARU, UBRE organizers apparently were willing to risk negative reaction from the railway brotherhoods in the hope of attracting those followers of Eugene Debs who had not forgotten their union heritage. Whether their love for Eugene Debs or the proletarian consciousness sometimes manifested by former members of the ARU ever really translated into active membership in the UBRE is unclear, however. Although the new organization struck a sensitive nerve among former members of the ARU, it is likely that most remained convinced by previous experience that industrial unionism could not survive the combined onslaught of conservative railway brotherhoods, ruthless and determined management, and hostile government. If anything, many must have remained convinced that political socialism offered more hope for industrial justice than industrial unionism did. Although Philip Foner argues that the founders of the UBRE at Roseburg were past members of the ARU, the *Railroad Telegrapher* was closer to the mark when it reasoned that the UBRE had been born out of Estes' lack of union experience. It is probable that Estes dedicated himself so fully to the millennial promise of the UBRE because he had never tasted the bitter defeat of the Pullman strike.[28]

The UBRE applied for an AFL charter in July 1902, but the Executive Council rejected the application by arguing that, although the railway brotherhoods were not affiliated with the AFL, the UBRE was inimical to the interests of all working people. Rebuffed, the UBRE voted to join the ALU. The headquarters of the thirty-eight-thousand-member union was moved to Denver, and Estes became a member of the ALU Executive Board.[29]

Clerks on the Canadian Pacific Railway in Vancouver organized a division of the UBRE in June 1902, and local divisions also appeared within the next year in the Pacific Northwest communities of Seattle, Tacoma, Everett, Revelstoke, and Nelson. The UBRE won its first big strike in January 1903, when employees on the Canadian Northern Railway gained union recognition, increased wages, and an eight-hour workday.[30]

In Vancouver, the UBRE gained members from among the trainmen, maintenance-of-way men, clerks, freight handlers, machinists, and sailors. The Canadian Pacific, however, replied to agitation for union recognition by suspending or dismissing known members of the UBRE, harassing the union's officers, and using spies. These provocations caused the Vancouver division of the UBRE to launch a protest strike against the Canadian Pacific in late February 1903. Soon the walkout spread eastward along the Canadian Pacific to railway workers in Revelstoke, Calgary, and Winnipeg.[31]

LEFT-WING UNIONISM IN TRIUMPH AND DEFEAT

The UBRE walkout developed into the first great sympathy strike in British Columbia history. In Revelstoke, machinists, clerks, and freight handlers walked off the job. The navigation arm of the Canadian Pacific was threatened when longshoremen and seamen joined the growing work stoppage. Labor demonstrations were held in Vancouver to voice support for the UBRE strikers, and even the telegraph messenger boys staged a sympathy strike; but with the weight of the Canadian Pacific, the government, and many trade unions pitted against the fledgling UBRE, early euphoria gave way to disappointment. The Canadian Pacific violated the Alien Labor Law by importing dozens of strikebreakers from Seattle. Estes' appeal for a sympathy strike evoked a favorable response from the building and iron trades, the bakers, and the Vancouver Trades and Labor Council; but because the UBRE was considered a dual union, many of the AFL-chartered internationals pressured their Vancouver members back into line.

Frank Rogers, a coast labor leader formerly associated with the Fraser River Fishermen's strike, was shot and killed by Canadian Pacific constables while he picketed the railway tracks in Vancouver. Estes was arrested in Vancouver for allegedly delaying the delivery of His Majesty's Mail, but after a two-week trial the charges were dropped. The increasingly bewildered leaders of the UBRE strike also discovered that Organizer General Harold V. Poore had sold his allegiance to the Canadian Pacific. Although the UBRE lost its strike against the Canadian Pacific, the sixteen-week-long confrontation contributed to the growing concern about industrial relations in British Columbia.[32]

The UBRE strike was accompanied by a series of disputes in British Columbia's major coal fields. During its battle with the Canadian Pacific, the UBRE had been promised help by the leadership of the WFM, which had begun to organize coal miners in British Columbia. The WFM established its first coal local in Canada in April 1899, at Fernie, in the Crowsnest Pass region of the northern Rockies. In December 1902, the influential Miners' and Mine Laborers' Protective Association in Nanaimo had affiliated with the WFM as Local 177. However, the local's most prominent member, Ralph Smith, resigned rather than become associated with an American organization.[33]

Just before the UBRE strike began, fifteen hundred miners in the three Rocky Mountain coal camps of Fernie, Michel, and Morrissey struck for recognition as members of the WFM, and aggrieved coal miners on Vancouver Island were encouraged to take similar action. The WFM wanted desperately to aid the UBRE, its sister organization in the ALU, by shutting off coal to the Canadian Pacific, but it was unable to do so. In February 1903, the Nanaimo local of the WFM won a strike in the mines recently purchased by a California capitalist, but that company had no contract to supply coal for the

Canadian Pacific. In the two other major coal camps on Vancouver Island, the WFM faced a determined James Dunsmuir.

Dunsmuir's removal of miners' homes from Extension to Ladysmith was but one of the grievances that encouraged miners at the Dunsmuir operations to form a union in early March 1903 and to seek help in the resulting strike-lockout from James Baker, a member of the WFM executive board from British Columbia. More than eight hundred miners joined the new WFM local before Dunsmuir ordered the strikers discharged. He threatened to keep his operations shut down for two years to rid the mines of the hated WFM, which he believed was dedicated to the importation of foreign agitators. "I object to all unions, federated or local or any other kind," Dunsmuir declared at a government inquiry a few months later. He explained that he wanted the management of his own enterprises, but "if I recognize the union I cannot have that." [34]

While Ladysmith was in turmoil, WFM organizer James Baker was able to form a local among miners at another Dunsmuir operation, the Union Colliery at Cumberland. A mass dismissal of union members presaged yet another strike in British Columbia's coal fields. More than twelve hundred coal miners were out on Vancouver Island by May 2, and labor newspapers were warning workers to stay away from the Vancouver Island mines. The Dunsmuir mines used Chinese labor to dig coal; when an explosion killed twenty Orientals, the mine manager was simply fined $25 for illegally giving the Chinese mining permits. "Coal Baron Dunsmuir of British Columbia," the *Seattle Union Record* remarked, "seems to have even more stubbornness in his makeup than the average Britisher—who has enough." Dunsmuir perservered, however, and the WFM was defeated at Ladysmith and Cumberland. [35]

The turmoil that enveloped the British Columbia labor movement in 1903 resulted in part from an attempt by the ALU to regain some of the momentum that it had lost the previous year as a result of the struggle with the AFL on Puget Sound. The ALU concentrated its organizing activities in areas of peripheral AFL influence, such as southern Oregon, eastern Washington, and British Columbia. In Spokane, under the expert leadership of H. L. Hughes, the ALU appealed to skilled and unskilled workers alike. In the Inland Empire some of the lumber workers who later joined the IWW were first converted to the principle of industrial unionism by the ALU. In British Columbia, the ALU organized cooks and waiters in Phoenix; engineers, electrical workers, and culinary workers in Nelson; bartenders in Fernie; millworkers in Vancouver; and the less skilled workers into general labor unions in a number of Kootenay communities.

In early 1903, at a time when two to three hundred unemployed workers a month were arriving in British Columbia from New Zealand and Australia and when the AFL and the railway brotherhoods were encouraging members to scab against the UBRE, it was easy for ALU organizers to reaffirm the need for a labor organization especially attuned to the needs of western workers. The UBRE strike convinced many ALU organizers that the "old simple trade unionism of a Samuel Gompers type" would soon be a thing of the past.[36]

The ALU stimulated within the British Columbia labor movement a growing interest in the twin questions of socialism and industrial unionism. In 1903, the proponents of industrial unionism won a significant victory in the Vancouver Trades and Labor Council. When its attempts to secure a Trades and Labor Congress endorsement of industrial unionism failed, the Vancouver Council withdrew from the TLC and associated with the ALU. Although the Vancouver Council reaffiliated with the TLC in 1905, it remained committed to the idea of "boring from within" to promote industrial unionism in the Dominion Labor Congress.[37]

The Phoenix Trades and Labor Council withdrew from the TLC because of the issue of socialism, whereas the Victoria Trades and Labor Council, disgusted by the failure of eastern trade unions to come to the aid of the UBRE strikers, apparently left the TLC briefly and endorsed the ALU. As the number of local unions affiliated with the AFL declined, both the TLC and the AFL conceded that they were losing ground in British Columbia as a result of the combined assault by the UBRE, the ALU, and the WFM. Conservative trade unionists, according to the British Columbia Executive Committee of the TLC, had "temporarily stepped aside and allowed the political socialists to run their course."[38]

As a result of the unsettling labor turmoil in far western Canada in early 1903, a Royal Commission on Industrial Disputes in British Columbia was established to study the causes of the ever more bitter confrontation between labor and management in the province. The Commission hearings, which proved to be more of an inquisition than an inquiry, sustained the conviction of many Canadian entrepreneurs that the disorder in British Columbia was the result of an American-directed conspiracy rather than the product of real labor grievances. Because America's bloody record of industrial disputes in the 1890s contrasted so vividly with the more peaceful labor-management relations in Canada, Canadians associated the American labor movement with violence and viewed the extensive disorder in British Columbia in 1903 as having a decidedly American character.

The Royal Commission attempted to tie the unrest in British Columbia to American funds and agitators, specifically the ALU and the WFM. The commission alleged that the strikes were part of a socialist conspiracy to sweep all Canadian Pacific employees into the UBRE and all coal miners into the WFM. It also accused the WFM of "dictating" provincial labor matters from Denver in an attempt to defeat James Dunsmuir. Although it is true that Butte and Denver played some part in the strikes, there is no evidence to support the fears of some observers that the UBRE strike was part of a concerted American plan to bring about the economic annexation of Canada.[39]

By ignoring the real grievances of the workers and unfairly characterizing the UBRE, ALU, and WFM as political organizations rather than legitimate trade unions, the Royal Commission report only added to the misunderstanding about the true cause of industrial disputes in British Columbia. The one meaningful commission recommendation, that employers should not be allowed to discriminate against union workers, was ignored by employers and government alike. Since the government was unwilling to address itself to the concerns of workingmen and since the unions had been weakened as a result of Dunsmuir's victory over the WFM and the collapse of the UBRE strike, workers in British Columbia turned to socialism in record numbers.

Severely crippled as a result of the UBRE strike, the ALU retreated to its redoubt in the Kootenays, where it continued to draw strength from its ties to organized labor in Spokane and Butte and from the WFM. The UBRE never recovered from its strike, and its remaining locals—they were really paper locals—joined the IWW in 1905. When Estes later wrote a book on railway unionism, he did not mention the UBRE or his own part in the union debacle in western Canada.[40]

The collapse of the UBRE strike was only one of the problems besetting the WFM in British Columbia. Almost a year earlier, the United Mine Workers of America (UMW) had begun to challenge WFM hegemony in the Rocky Mountain coal fields. The WFM lost the confidence of the miners in the region when the union lost a series of local strikes, perhaps because of a lack of funds. Miners at Fernie left the WFM and joined the UMW in May 1902, following which the UMW grew rapidly in western Canada. In November 1903, former WFM coal miners' locals in Fernie, Michel, and Carborado joined with four locals on the Alberta side of the continental divide to form District 18 of the UMW. The WFM retained a mere eighty-three members in Nanaimo in mid-1903, a number that continued to decline after UMW organizers reappeared in the Vancouver Island fields. The beleaguered WFM accused the "Ralph Smith crowd" of scheming to switch the allegiance of the WFM local in Nanaimo. Dual unions existed among the Nanaimo miners for several years after 1904, but the combined influence of both the WFM and the UMW on Vancouver Island was negligible. The WFM suffered a further setback when the hardrock-mining industry in the Kootenays began to slump after 1906.[41]

The WFM and the UMW were remarkably similar in many ways. Both organizations were organized along industrial lines, both claimed a heritage from the Knights of Labor, and both were interested in political activity. After its founding in 1890, the UMW had taken a greater interest in politics than most American unions, and several of its members had been elected to legislative bodies. Of the eleven principal planks in the UMW constitution of 1890, more than half were demands for legislation.

One of the major differences between the WFM and the UMW was that the socialists were never able to capture the national leadership of the UMW, although they were active on the local level. The 300,000 member UMW was the largest AFL affiliate in 1905, but the UMW's presence in the increasingly class-conscious coal fields of Vancouver Island did little to alter the local heritage of labor radicalism and socialist politics—as developments on the eve of World War I demonstrated.[42]

The Challenge of the IWW

Labor radicalism in the Pacific Northwest entered a new phase when delegates from such organizations as the WFM, the ALU, the UBRE, the Brewery Workers, the Socialist Trades and Labor Alliance, and the Socialist Labor party met in Chicago in mid-1905 and formed the Industrial Workers of the World. Proposing to eliminate trade divisions and emphasizing class lines, members of the IWW, or Wobblies, epitomized the kind of idealistic radicalism that flourished in Washington and British Columbia. Wobblies not only built on an inheritance stemming from the Knights of Labor but also continued to promote the inclusive organizational philosophy of the ALU by announcing as their guiding principle, "Injury to One is the Concern of All." The Knights, the ALU, and the IWW successively nurtured a belief in "perfect working class harmony."[43]

David C. Coates, who had succeeded Dan McDonald as president of the moribund ALU in April 1905, was nominated by McDonald to be the chairman of the IWW's founding convention. Coates withdrew as a candidate for the position of permanent chairman in favor of WFM secretary-treasurer William D. Haywood but remained very active in the proceedings. In addition to Haywood and Coates, Pacific Northwest workers were represented at the convention by John Riordan, the ALU organizer from Phoenix, British Columbia. Delegates elected Riordan to serve on the IWW's Provisional Executive Council, but he was dismissed a few months later on what some considered to be a trumped-up charge.[44]

The proceedings of the IWW's founding convention, which Haywood characterized as "the Continental Congress of the working class," were marked from the beginning by a division between bona fide trade unionists and utopians. The first group, composed largely of industrial unionists, was unofficially led by David Coates, whom labor historian Philip Taft called the "most adroit" delegate to the convention. Coates wanted to form a practical organization that would align the forces of labor in North America into the industrial groupings into which modern industry was evolving. The chief obstacle to the realization of the Coates scheme was the group of delegates led by theoreticians such as Daniel

DeLeon, who still bore the stigma of his terribly unsuccessful Socialist Trades and Labor Alliance, and Thomas J. Hagerty of the Industrial Workers' Club of Chicago. At one point Coates referred to Hagerty's fanciful organizational chart for the proposed body as "Hagerty's Wheel of Fortune," a description Gompers was subsequently to use.[45]

It took less than a year for the ideological differences within the IWW to produce a schism in the organization. A rift between the WFM and the IWW that led the Miners to secede in early 1907 contributed to the growing instability of the IWW. The Wobblies' first and only president, Charles Sherman, who was deposed by the "revolutionaries" in 1906, blamed the IWW's difficulties on DeLeon, a "millstone around our necks." DeLeon was himself ousted by delegates at the 1908 convention, who then proceeded to delete references to political action from the IWW preamble.[46]

Political socialists in the IWW were understandably upset by its decision to shun politics; many socialists had left the AFL to join the IWW, and they now felt betrayed. Disappointed socialists in British Columbia warned that by rejecting socialist politics the IWW had become a valuable asset to the capitalist state. A number of Wobblies probably continued to use the ballot where possible, but western migratory workers were seldom in one place long enough to acquire the vote, which, in any event, seemed only to sustain the oppressive capitalist state.[47]

Because of its low initiation fee, interchangeable membership cards, and rank-and-file rule, the IWW appealed to the migratory workers who drifted into such communities as Seattle and Spokane. The IWW was particularly active in the timber and forest industries of the Pacific Northwest. Many of the loggers were migrants who hiked from job to job carrying all their worldly possessions in their blanket rolls or bindles. When the "bindle stiff" arrived at an isolated logging camp, he worked a ten-hour day, and as of 1910 he earned between seventeen and twenty cents an hour. A dollar a month was sometimes deducted from his pay for the rudimentary medical care available in some camps. In the bunkhouse, he slept in a vermin-infested bed that was often little more than a wooden box filled with straw (a mattress was sometimes available for fifty cents a month). In some camps workers slept two to a bunk. Rain of between four and five inches a day was common in some localities, but work generally continued as long as nothing vital washed out. At night a stove at either end of the bunkhouse sent up clouds of steam from the wet clothes that hung from wall to wall. When the lumberjack emerged from the woods, social leeches in the nearby towns helped relieve him of any earnings he might have accumulated. Because of the low wages, long hours, unhealthful conditions, and lack of normal family and community life, the labor turnover in logging camps was high. The lumberjack, or "timber beast," was a natural candidate for unionization and radical political action, but his life style as well as the isolated, feudal nature of the camps made organization difficult.[48]

Life in a sawmill town was frequently no better than in a logging camp. The typical mill town, whether in Washington or British Columbia, had many of the characteristics associated with industrial feudalism. Sawmill workers, sometimes called "sawdust savages," lived in company housing, purchased supplies from the company store, and sent their children to company schools. A worker went to the company hospital in the event of accident or sickness, and he was buried in the company cemetery. In the eyes of some workers, their souls were also saved by a company preacher. Work in a sawmill was monotonous and uninteresting; it was also dangerous, since a sawyer had to spend ten hours a day fighting with his machine.[49]

Although Pacific Coast lumbermen organized as early as 1891 and became a powerful force in the Washington legislature by 1905, trade unionists were unable to organize the loggers and had little better success among sawmill workers. The first lumber workers on the West Coast to organize were the shingle weavers (sawyers and others who worked as a crew in a shingle mill). According to Norman Clark, a skilled packer worked so rapidly as he stacked slices of cedar into overlapping bundles that he appeared to be "weaving" the shingles together. The West Coast Shingle Weavers' Union established several locals in western Washington in the early 1890s, but the loss of a strike in 1893 and a depressed economy destroyed the union. In early 1903 representatives from the shingle weavers' unions that began reappearing after the turn of the century met in Everett and organized the International Shingle Weavers' Union. The shingle weavers soon became the most militant members of the Everett Trades Council.[50]

Because of the natural solidarity resulting from the lack of craft divisions in the logging camps and sawmills, the lumber industry attracted the attention of the IWW. After a strike in a Portland mill in the spring of 1907, Wobblies made a determined effort to organize sawmills in the Pacific Northwest. In Aberdeen, for example, two hundred Wobblies swarmed into a mill in early 1912 and persuaded workers to leave their jobs. They then marched on to the next mill with the same request. Because of the poor economic climate in the lumber industry at that time, however, mill owners did not have to operate their mills at full capacity, and so the IWW lost the strike. Wobblies discovered that hard as it was to organize the mills, it was even more difficult to organize the logging camps. After seven years of activity, the IWW had little to show for its efforts other than the less than a thousand members scattered throughout Washington's almost numberless logging camps. Detractors claimed that Wobblies had been unable to raise wages a cent or decrease the work day by a minute and that their activities had helped to taint the whole Pacific Northwest labor movement. By maintaining an indomitable spirit in the face of overwhelming adversity, the Wobblies nonetheless demonstrated that even the most ruthlessly exploited workers partook of the region's utopian dreams.[51]

THE ESTABLISHMENT OF AFL HEGEMONY

Until the outbreak of World War I, the Wobblies continued to challenge the AFL in the forests and fields of the Pacific Northwest. Despite this activity, the federation gained an ever increasing influence over organized labor in Washington and, to a lesser degree, in British Columbia.

The eventual triumph of the AFL in the Pacific Northwest was not necessarily the inevitable corollary of the rise of the national or international trade union in North America. The same international trade unions established locals on both sides of the 49th parallel, but in British Columbia the local labor movement remained far more independent of AFL leadership than that in neighboring Washington did. Gompers' "Voluntarism," for example, never attracted a large following in British Columbia because of the province's political and governmental heritage.

The establishment of AFL hegemony in Washington was largely a consequence of the economic integration of the state into the remainder of the nation. Had Washington remained physically or economically isolated, it is probable that given the generally tolerant and frequently innovative climate of political and judicial opinion that prevailed in the state during the twenty years preceding World War I, Washington labor would have evolved toward industrial unionism two or three decades prior to the rise of the Congress of Industrial Organizations in the 1930s. But Washington contained a mere .68 percent of the nation's population in 1900. (At the same time, Washington, Oregon, Idaho, and California combined contained only 3.4 percent of America's population.) The growing strength of the AFL among conservative tradesmen in many of the major commercial and industrial centers of the East and Midwest after 1900 placed the federation in a position to thwart the development of indigenous industrial unionism in most parts of America's hinterland. When radical members of Seattle's CLC came to the realization in 1919 that workers holding cards from Washington State industrial unions would find it difficult to find employment outside the state, they had arrived at an insight similar to that reached by men like AFL organizer C. O. Young some twenty years earlier.[52]

CHAPTER 10

Labor, Socialism, and the Quest for Political Power

Shortly after the turn of the century both example and necessity encouraged trade union leaders in Washington to reassess the political lessons learned during the formative decade of the 1890s. In San Francisco, Eugene E. Schmitz, president of the Musicians' Union, was elected mayor in 1901, and workingmen in British Columbia had recently obtained several labor reforms by political means. In Washington, by contrast, labor's political fortunes had declined steadily since the heyday of the Populist party.

After the 1901 legislature adjourned, the *Seattle Union Record* called upon workers to elect their own members to office because "labor never got a more complete ignoring by any session of the Washington State Legislature than the last." Some trade unionists in Seattle appeared ready to form a labor party but dropped the idea not long after Dr. Hermon Titus began wondering aloud what the proposed party could do that the Socialist party was not already doing. "It would have to be Capitalist or Socialist, would it not? If it was Capitalist it wouldn't help labor any, and if it was Socialist why not call it Socialist?" The Western Central Labor Union, however, abandoned its long-standing policy of political neutrality in 1902 and promised to give its support exclusively to workingmen in the forthcoming municipal election.[1]

Statewide, the labor movement was politically handicapped by the deep philosophical divisions separating trade union leaders. Not only did they disagree on such matters as craft versus industrial unionism and affiliation with the American Federation of Labor (AFL) but they also supported opposing political parties. Whereas the leaders of the Republican and Democratic parties encouraged trade unionists to act as a pressure group, the *Union Record* advised the local labor movement to abandon its policy of "rewarding friends" and put forth its own legislative ticket.[2]

The growing interest in independent political action manifested by some trade union leaders coincided with the threat posed to organized labor by a new wave of Oriental immigration to the Pacific Northwest. Although the Exclusion Act of 1882 and subsequent measures had restricted Chinese immigration to the United States, immigrants from other Far Eastern countries as well as some Chinese continued to arrive on the West coast. Their numbers became so noticeable after 1900 that anti-Orientalism again began to stir while workingmen, notably the Norwegians and Swedes who had so recently migrated to Washington.

The Pacific Northwest needed a Denis Kearney to awaken the people to the "dangers of Japanese immigration," the *Union Record* editorialized in 1901. A year earlier the paper had observed that Everett was "fast coming to the front as a union town. The anti-jap agitation is the chief incentive, and it is a powerful one." In their use of anti-Oriental demogoguery to promote labor solidarity, the editors of the *Union Record* yielded little to the Sinophobic journalists of the 1870s and 1880s. "We Must Halt the Little Brown Horde," the paper warned workers in 1900, and seven years later it hinted of an impending "Mongolian Invasion" of the United States. "Does a Chinaman do your washing?" the *Union Record* asked. "If so, you are not carrying out the principles of unionism."[3]

Samuel Gompers, who favored the restriction of Oriental immigration to the United States, spoke at length at the 1901 AFL convention in Scranton about the Chinese menace on the West Coast and the necessity to continue the exclusion principle. "Every incoming coolie," Gompers averred, "means the displacement of an American and a lowering of the American standard of living." The AFL's famous "Bill of Grievances" in 1906 called for a law to prevent violation of the Chinese Exclusion Act.[4]

Anti-Orientalism was even more pronounced in British Columbia than in Washington in the first decade of the twentieth century. After the anti-Chinese riots of the mid-1880s, the Chinese population in Washington had declined to less than 1 percent of the total; in British Columbia, by contrast, the number of Chinese climbed to 9 percent of the population shortly after the turn of the century before dropping to approximately 5 percent in 1911. In addition, more than 2 percent of the population in 1911 was of Japanese origin. The festering issue of Oriental immigration so poisoned British Columbia's body politic that in September 1907 an embarrassing race riot shook Vancouver.[5]

The Russo-Japanese War in 1905 had intensified racial feelings in the province. The *Colonist* began a new series of editorials on the "yellow peril" and criticized eastern Canadians for failing to understand the plight of British Columbia. In 1907, when it was officially estimated that one in four adult males in the province was of Asiatic origin, many white British Columbians feared that a majority of the working people in the province would soon be Oriental. Some British Columbians were further convinced that the Japanese government was plotting to secure an enclave on Canada's Pacific Coast. Worry about a "Hindu invasion" from the Indian subcontinent also stirred racial consciousness in the province.[6]

The British Columbia legislative assembly passed several measures early in the twentieth century to exclude Japanese from a wide range of occupations, but Prime Minister Sir Wilfrid Laurier used his constitutional powers to disallow these bills. The prime minister did not seem to understand that in British Columbia, Oriental restriction was more important than the cultivation of good relations between Great Britain and Japan. By its actions, the Dominion government helped to create an ugly mood in British Columbia.[7]

During the course of the Vancouver riot, the mob "sent a message" to Ottawa by burning in effigy Lieutenant Governor James Dunsmuir, the representative of the Dominion government in British Columbia. The outraged citizens of Vancouver also sought to drive the Japanese from the city. Unlike the Chinese in the Tacoma and Seattle riots of the 1880s, however, the Japanese fought back. Most Canadians were surprised and shocked by the Vancouver riot, and because they did not understand the true cause of the outbreak they tended to blame it on labor agitators from Washington. The Japanese government likewise believed that the violence had been caused by a mob of irresponsible ruffians. Many

British Columbians, by contrast, feared that the riots gave the false impression that "exclusion is desired only by the mob element."[8]

At the same time as organized labor perceived a threat from Oriental immigration it was assailed by an increasingly aggressive group of employer associations. First established in the United States on a national basis during the 1880s, these associations provided their members a powerful voice in many state legislatures as well as serving as a united front in opposition to labor demands. Twenty-six employers' associations had been formed in British Columbia by 1905. Although exact figures are not available for Washington, a significant number of employers' associations were also formed in that state after the turn of the century.

The employers' associations in the United States aroused the concern of American labor organizations when they began to unite with such patently anti-labor groups as the American Anti-Boycott Association to oppose unionism. The National Association of Manufacturers, which had been established in 1895 to lobby for small and medium-size manufacturers, spearheaded the drive against organized labor after 1903.[9]

WASHINGTON'S FARMER-LABOR ALLIANCE

Speaking to the 1906 AFL convention, Gompers, as he had on several previous occasions, warned that labor had yet to form a political party that had not been "wheedled" out of its control by "faddists, theorists, and self-seekers." Gompers, however, had come to believe that positive political action was required to free the trade unions to bargain collectively, and he now pointedly urged central bodies and local unions to nominate labor candidates.[10]

Gompers' admonition, the threat of competition from Oriental labor, and the growing aggressiveness of employers' associations caused trade union leaders in Washington to cast about for an effective political response to industrialism. During the years 1906–10 they were torn between partisan political efforts, such as labor and reform parties, and the nonpartisan tactic of joining with farmers and reformers to influence legislators in Olympia. For several years the pendulum of sentiment swung back and forth between partisan politics and pressure politics.

In 1906, for example, the Seattle Central Labor Council supported formation of a Municipal Ownership party and worked to elect Judge William H. Moore mayor on a platform calling for public ownership of basic utilities. Trade union leaders were generally pleased by the performance of Seattle's "labor mayor," but rank-and-file apathy contributed to Moore's defeat two years later.[11]

Moore's defeat and fears of socialist infiltration if labor attempted to establish a political party discouraged partisan political activity by labor leaders. In 1909, however, Titus and his revolutionary allies appeared to have lost their grip on the Socialist party in Washington. With socialists in turmoil the time seemed right to form a statewide labor party.

At the urging of the Bricklayers' Union, labor leaders in February 1910 formulated plans that resulted in the launching on 4 July of the Washington State Labor party. The charter convention, composed of delegates representing almost fifty unions, endorsed the slate of union members and drew up a platform that not only demanded the standard items of labor reform but explicitly set forth the notion of a class struggle. Although a chastened Titus had high hopes for this supposedly class-conscious proletarian movement, many labor leaders were as skeptical about the party as the rank and file was apathetic. The result was that the Labor party fell apart before the fall election.

A number of union leaders in Washington continued to be fascinated by examples of successful labor politics in such diverse places as Australia and Milwaukee, Wisconsin, but efforts to resurrect the idea of a statewide labor party always foundered on the rock of rank-and-file apathy. By way of contrast, the farmer-labor lobby was becoming more influential each year.[12]

The farmer-labor lobby had begun to take shape in 1906. Unable to secure any meaningful labor legislation because of the growing power of employers' associations and divisions within the ranks of organized labor, the State Federation of Labor resolved at its 1906 convention to seek support from other reform-minded organizations. The Washington State Grange, presided over by ex-socialist C. B. Kegley, quickly endorsed the idea of farmer-labor cooperation.[13]

As a result of a large increase in membership after the turn of the century, the center of Grange influence had shifted from the conservative farming areas of western Washington to the Palouse country, the former stronghold of middle-of-the-road Populism. In 1905 retiring Grand Master J. O. Wing called for cooperation between the Grange and other agricultural organizations to secure direct legislation, but the newly elected Kegley urged cooperation with all reform groups and proposed the establishment of a committee to work with the Washington State Federation of Labor to secure legislation of mutual interest. Under Kegley's leadership the Washington Grange not only became the fastest growing branch of the Patrons of Husbandry but also, according to a reporter from the *Arena*, one of the most progressive organizations in the state. Kegley, who believed that reform measures could help "the people" regain their "lost sovereignty," used his persuasive talents to keep the Washington Grange in the vanguard of the Progressive movement.[14]

Shortly after Kegley became leader of the state Grange, branches of another agrarian organization, the Farmers' Union, began appearing in eastern Washington. The Farmers' Educational and Cooperative Union, founded in Texas in 1902, originally addressed a vigorous Populist-style appeal to those Southern farmers allegedly ignored by the more conservative Farm Bureau and the Grange. Farmers in the Waitsburg, Washington, area read about the Farmers' Union in 1907 and persuaded President C. S. Barrett to organize several branches in the state. Representatives from the various local branches met in Pullman a year later and organized the first statewide Farmers' Union west of the Rocky Mountains. Although contemporaries identified the Farmers' Union with the "dirt farmer," the organization in Washington appealed largely to the more prosperous farmers. The Farmers' Union never adopted a reform program as vigorous as that of the state Grange, but it did augment the growing strength of the farmer-labor coalition in Washington.[15]

President Blackman of the Federation of Labor and Grand Master Kegley of the Grange met in late 1906 to launch a formal program to secure reform legislation in Washington. Cooperation between city centrals and Grange locals was to complement joint activity in Olympia. Many farmers, however, were apprehensive about working with organized labor. Grange delegates to the 1907 convention of the State Federation of Labor tried to explain these fears by reminding workingmen that they would find it "almost impossible to understand how utterly and absolutely ignorant the average farmer is as to the principles of unionism." The farmer, the representatives from the Grange explained, was an independent operator; he was inclined to look at such matters as strikes from the employer's point of view. The Grange delegates averred that the farmer was willing enough to strike a blow at monopoly but rarely considered such questions as wages and hours. They emphasized the point by citing the painful example of farmers in British Columbia who allegedly wanted more Chinese labor to help pick the apple crop. During the next several years state and national farm and labor leaders attempted to reduce apprehensions among their constituents by frequently exchanging convention appearances and pledging mutual cooperation.[16]

The State Federation of Labor, the Grange, and the Farmers' Union were joined in their reform coalition by the Direct Legislation League. Although the socialists characterized this united front as an "unholy alliance," the Joint Legislative Committee established by these groups was so successful in its effort to secure reform measures that in 1913 the British Columbia Federation of Labor sent a circular letter to farmers' organizations in the province urging them to cooperate with the local labor movement in political matters.[17]

Washington's Joint Legislative Committee was one of the most influential of the several committees of the same type that were formed in the United States in the pre-World War I era. Because party lines were so weak in Washington, pressure politics worked well in Olympia. As reform clubs proliferated in Washington after 1909, the farmer-labor coalition benefited from the increasing popular interest in reform. The platforms drawn up by the Federation of Labor, the Grange, and the Farmers' Union usually wrapped demands for such items as public ownership, good roads, employers' liability, and eight-hour work laws in a reform package of broad appeal. Leaders of the coalition managed for several years to keep controversial issues such as prohibition from dividing the members of the Joint Legislative Committee.[18]

The Quest for Political Power

A SOCIALIST VERSUS LABOR PARTY IN BRITISH COLUMBIA

In British Columbia, the parliamentary system of government, labor's high degree of class consciousness in mining camps and towns, the perceived threat posed by Oriental immigration, and the inability of labor to cooperate politically with the province's small and diversified agrarian community combined to encourage the formation of a labor party. Labor-reform parties, however, tended to run afoul of an increasingly powerful socialist movement. Just as experience clearly convinced trade union leaders in Washington to adopt the tactics of pressure politics, experience reinforced by success at least temporarily assured the ascendancy of the revolutionary socialists in British Columbia labor politics.

In a manner reminiscent of Eugene Debs following the collapse of the Pullman strike, American Labor Union (ALU) organizer and socialist leader G. Weston Wrigley began exhorting workers in British Columbia after the 1903 UBRE strike to conduct a "political strike" by their votes. The Socialist Party of British Columbia emerged from the UBRE strike stronger than ever, and while the provincial labor movement factionalized, the socialists were able to achieve an unusual degree of unity.[19]

It was with a measure of confidence that the Socialist party fielded eleven candidates in the 1903 provincial election since, at that time, a candidate for the legislative assembly in British Columbia was required to put up a deposit of $200, which he forfeited if he failed to secure one-half as many votes as the winning candidate. The *Boundary Creek Times* no doubt spoke for many a British Columbian when it expressed the hope that the Socialists would not hold the balance of power in the next session of the legislative assembly. "What the province needs," the paper concluded, "is stable government." It was no time for voters to experiment with "dangerous fads." The election, nonetheless, gave the balance of power in the legislative assembly to William Davidson, a labor member from the Kootenay riding of Slocan, and two Socialists from Vancouver Island ridings, Parker Williams and James Hawthornthwaite. The *International Socialist Review* described the growing power of revolutionary socialism and the concomitant increase in labor radicalism in British Columbia as "remarkable." A few North American radicals may even have regarded developments in British Columbia in 1903 with the same feeling of expectancy that was later engendered by the Bolshevik ascendancy in Russia in 1917.[20]

Paradoxically, the electoral triumph that seemingly confirmed the theoretical correctness of the province's revolutionary socialists also forced party members to confront common sense. Particularly when they had the power to correct long-standing abuses, socialists found it difficult to abjure immediate reforms for the sake of revolution by and by. Thus the pioneer Socialist legislators of British Columbia worked together with Premier Richard McBride in what some observers described as a "Socialist-Conservative" government.

There was no politician in British Columbia during the first decade of the twentieth century more skillful than Richard McBride. Having once served briefly as the minister of mines in the government of James Dunsmuir, the bold and energetic McBride presided over the province during the years from 1903 to 1915, a time generally characterized by unprecedented growth and prosperity in British Columbia. The popular, pragmatic Conservative significantly improved the province's once dismal credit rating and restored political stability. (Before he introduced party lines in 1903, the province had witnessed the selection of five different premiers during the five previous years; fourteen different men held the office between 1871 and 1903.)

The labor and socialist vote was for McBride a challenge to exercise his formidable political ingenuity and skill. While responsive to the appeals of Conservatives who warned that the party must try to win the labor vote or "the enemy will get it," he wasted little sympathy on the "Bourbon School" of Conservatives who, in the words of one supporter, seemed to believe that "one of their votes is equal to *five* of the common people."[21]

As life in British Columbia became more peaceful following the rash of strikes in 1903, McBride began to refer "with pride" to the Socialist support of his ministry in the legislative assembly. Critics, however, feared that the province had entered an unsettling era of "McBride-Hawthornthwaite Rule."

James Hawthornthwaite, one of the two Socialist legislators upon whom the McBride government depended for a majority after the election of 1903, was a master at reconciling revolutionary rhetoric and practical politics. Born in Ireland, educated in England, and variously employed as a real estate agent and night watchman, the canny Hawthornthwaite represented a Nanaimo riding in the legislative assembly from 1901 to 1908 and from 1909 to 1912. Elected to the seat vacated by Ralph Smith when he chose to run for the Dominion Parliament, Hawthornthwaite broke with the Liberal-Labor machine in Nanaimo a year later and embraced revolutionary socialism. British socialist J. Keir Hardie once said of Hawthornthwaite that his outspoken platform appearances revealed more honesty than diplomacy, but those who followed Hawthornthwaite closely were convinced that he had a "feline faculty for always landing on his feet." He could work constructively with McBride, yet, to the delight of those who liked their socialism served "boiling hot," he could also deliver an occasional revolutionary outburst replete with sarcasm and biting wit.

In September 1907, Hawthornthwaite upset a number of Conservatives by refusing to rise when Lieutenant Governor James Dunsmuir, the King's representative, entered the assembly chamber. A year later Hawthornthwaite moved to impeach Dunsmuir because the lieutenant governor refused to give assent to a literacy-test measure designed to exclude all Orientals from British Columbia. The impeachment motion lost, although future Liberal premier John Oliver voted with the Socialists. The Socialist party itself deplored the use of the "yellow peril" bogey, but Hawthornthwaite knew what good working-class socialist politics demanded. On another occasion, Hawthornthwaite denounced the Union Jack as an "old rag" and claimed that the people had the "constitutional right to tear it down and make a mock of it—to wash some of the blood stains out of it."[22]

Joining Hawthornthwaite in the legislative assembly in 1903 was Parker Williams, a thirty-year-old Welsh-born coal miner from the Ladysmith area. The Labor member of the legislative assembly (MLA) William Davidson, a Scottish-born metal miner from the Kootenays, worked closely with the two pioneer Socialist legislators to help force the McBride government into passing a number of measures sought by the working class. By late 1905 legislation had been enacted to provide special help for dependents of deceased workingmen, to exclude Asiatics from "positions of trust" in mining operations, and to penalize mine owners who kept employees underground for more than eight hours a day. Hawthornthwaite hoped to pressure the government, in addition, to enact measures providing for weekly payment of wages, female suffrage, old-age pensions, and a universal eight-hour workday.[23]

Although Hawthornthwaite and Williams gave a creditable performance in the legislative assembly, many of British Columbia's labor leaders remained wary of the Socialist party itself. They were determined to supplant it with a party less given to revolutionary theorizing and more concerned about the day to day needs of the working class. Sentiment favoring the creation of a Canadian labor party began surfacing several months before the 1906 Victoria convention of Canada's Trades and Labor Congress (TLC).

Many trade unionists, Samuel Gompers in particular, feared that British Columbia was hardly the proper place in which to launch a true labor party. They worried that the first Labor Congress gathering in Canada's Far West might fall under the domination of the socialists, ever so vigilant in British Columbia, and that delegates would adopt some kind of "radical socialist" declaration. Gompers consequently warned the heads of twenty-three international unions to send only trustworthy members to the Victoria gathering, and he ordered C. O. Young to travel to British Columbia to help the ex-president of the TLC, John Flett, keep the socialists at bay.[24]

When the TLC met in September 1906, the example of labor's recent political success in Great Britain filled the delegates with enthusiasm for a labor party. Debate on political action began when the Victoria Trades and Labor Council moved that a Canadian labor party be formed. R. Parm Pettipiece, a delegate from the Vancouver Trades and Labor Council, then proposed that the platform of the Socialist Party of Canada be endorsed by the congress, thus making the formation of a new party unnecessary. An attempt to compromise the issue by allowing workers in each locality to choose between either the Socialist party or a new labor party failed because the overwhelming desire of the delegates was to proceed with the formation of a national labor party. Secretary P. M. Draper put the socialists on the defensive by suggesting that the proposed party adopt the platform and principles of the Trades and Labor Congress. Although the socialists denounced the trade unionists for dividing the working class by promoting the formation of a separate labor party, they were outvoted in the Victoria convention.

If the congress had wanted to shut out the socialists, it erred in deciding to hold founding conventions for the Canadian Labor party in each of the provinces. In British Columbia, where they still had considerable influence in the labor movement, the socialists, rather than boycott the charter convention of the Labor party in Victoria, attended in force, unseated the convention's labor chairman, and persuaded delegates to adopt a form of proportional representation based on the numerical strength of each union represented, thus giving the radical miners' unions of the interior 81 of 142 votes. After this coup, the majority socialists wasted little time burying "dual partyism" by voting 99 to 41 to dissolve the Labor party.

Supporters of a labor party thereupon abandoned the convention to the socialists, moved across the hall, and formed a party based on the TLC platform and the delegates' perception of the "labor paradise" in New Zealand. The socialists' feat was not duplicated in other provinces, but as a result of the debacle in Canada's westernmost province, the Canadian Labor party became little more than a paper organization. In the 1907 provincial election the Labor party nominated only five candidates in British Columbia compared to the Socialist party's twenty-two. The Liberal party in the province used the socialists' coup in Victoria to woo labor reformers by arguing that socialism meant "subversion of individual liberty."[25]

As long as revolutionary theoreticians continued to guide the destiny of Pacific Northwest socialism, they would denounce any nonsocialist political effort by organized labor as an attempt to divide the working class. But not until the region's socialists resolved their internal differences to accommodate labor reforms would they be able to appeal realistically to the mass of workers. Events during the years from 1902 to 1909 offer insight into the failure of the early socialist movement to develop into a broad-based labor-socialist-reform organization.

CHAPTER 11

Revolutionaries Suffering from an Excess of Logic

The major difference between the socialist movements in Washington and British Columbia during the years 1902 to 1909 was that the British Columbia comrades enjoyed the sweet taste of political power and influence while the Washington socialists only seemed to argue bitterly with one another. Try as they might, the revolutionaries never seemed able to completely rout the reform socialists. And every time a reform-minded comrade attained political success, the party erupted in a convulsive ideological battle.

Beginning with the 1902 state Socialist convention, Washington's revolutionary socialists launched an all-out assault on "opportunism" within the party and particularly on the "Spokane influence toward Fusion." Dr. Titus and the revolutionaries were angry because the Spokane local refused to force the resignation of two of its members recently elected to public office on a broad-based reform ticket. At the center of the controversy was Judge William E. Richardson, one of the early socialists in the Inland Empire.[1]

Richardson demonstrated that socialism and political success were not incompatible, but his was the kind of eclectic socialism so despised by Titus and his followers. Richardson's career, nonetheless, illustrates the potential opportunities awaiting practical socialists. After graduating from the Christian College of Monmouth, Oregon, Richardson moved to Spokane for his health. He entered the legal profession there and was elected to the bench in

1896 on a fusionist ticket. A Populist and a member of the Knights of Labor, Richardson joined the Social Democracy of America and was also actively involved in the cooperative colony movement. Local 1 of the Cooperative Brotherhood, a branch of Burley Colony, met in his chambers in 1899. Richardson remained presiding judge of the Superior Court of Spokane County until succeeded in 1905 by Miles Poindexter, future United States senator and Progressive party activist.

When the Spokane socialists refused to expel Judge Richardson for participating in bourgeois politics, the revolutionaries used a statewide referendum to revoke the charter of the Spokane local. The Puget Sound theoreticians also attempted to reorganize locals at Northport and other Inland Empire communities.[2]

The socialists had cast 5.6 percent of the total vote in Washington in the 1902 state election, a figure exceeded that year only by socialists in Montana and Massachusetts; but as a result of the ideological strife in the socialist movement, the party was soon moribund in much of the area east of the Cascades. At the party's 1903 state convention, which the revolutionaries described as a straight workingmen's gathering, "class consciousness was very much the shibboleth of the party." To avoid future strife, the revolutionaries successfully promoted the idea that all new party members should be placed on probationary status.[3]

Titus and his revolutionary colleagues must have felt pleased when the party's national leadership recognized the apparent strength of socialism in Washington by allotting the state eleven delegates to the 1904 national convention of the Socialist party, a number surpassed only by the far more populous states of New York, Pennsylvania, Illinois, and California. At the 1904 gathering, Titus added his stridently revolutionary opinions to the more moderate ideas espoused by Victor Berger, Eugene Debs, and the other members of the platform committee. Seeking a wider audience for his ideas, Titus, in 1905, moved the *Socialist* from Seattle to Toledo, Ohio, where William Mailly, ex-national secretary of the Socialist party, became his business manager. Titus selected Toledo because he thought it to be the industrial center of the United States.[4]

While Titus was in Toledo expounding the distinction between revolutionary and reform socialism, Harry Orchard, a self-confessed bigamist, incendiary, and mass murderer, assassinated

Frank Steunenberg at his home in Caldwell, Idaho. Steunenberg had been elected governor of Idaho on a fusionist ticket in 1896. Although a former member of a printing trades union, he had alienated his labor supporters by the manner in which he reacted to violence in the Coeur d'Alenes in 1899. Just why Harry Orchard killed the ex-governor on 30 December 1905 is unclear, but when captured, he implicated the leadership of the Western Federation of Miners. The kidnapping of William D. Haywood, Charles Moyer, and George Pettibone in Colorado and their speedy removal to Idaho to stand trial for the Steunenberg murder became a *cause celebre* in the labor movement.

Following this high-handed abduction, the *Appeal to Reason* published a call from Eugene Debs encouraging workers to take revolutionary action. Entitled "Arouse Ye Slaves," the Debs piece so infuriated President Theodore Roosevelt that he asked the attorney general whether it was possible to take legal action against Debs. Although the president failed to secure Debs's arrest or to halt the publication of the *Appeal*, the postmaster general of Canada succeeded in temporarily barring the publication from Dominion mails.[5]

The assumption that Haywood, Moyer, and Pettibone were innocent caused trade unionists and socialists in North America to form a united front to protest a trial that rested solely on the dubious evidence contained in Orchard's "Confession." Titus used the trial to abandon his disappointing publishing effort in Toledo and move the *Socialist* to Caldwell, where he hoped to convert Idaho into "the First Socialist State."[6]

Titus remained in Caldwell barely three months. In the late fall of 1906, almost nine months before Haywood, Moyer, and Pettibone were acquitted of complicity in the Steunenberg murder, Titus returned to Seattle, ostensibly because of mounting financial troubles and ill health. He was not unmindful, however, of the amazing resurgence of reform socialism in Washington. The reform socialists of eastern Washington had not been eliminated after all but had operated as virtually autonomous organizations. Whitman County socialists, mostly farmers who had participated in the Populist movement, held a convention in 1904, wrote a reform platform, and entered a ticket in the fall election. C. B. Kegley served as county organizer. A similar socialist organization existed in Spokane County. During Titus' sojourn in Toledo reform socialists had even acquired a voice in the councils of the state organization and had formulated plans to launch a new party newspaper. Coinciding with the resurgence of the reform socialists, party membership in Washington climbed to 1,519 in 1906, a total exceeded only in Pennsylvania and California.[7]

"WHAT'S THE MATTER WITH SEATTLE?"

Titus heralded his return to Seattle by organizing "free-speech" fights to challenge a municipal ordinance forbidding certain types of street-corner speaking. During the next several months Titus was himself arrested six times. The free-speech fights were no doubt designed to embarrass Seattle's "labor mayor" and to cause workers to examine the socialist appeal more seriously, but many observers believed that Titus' antics were also designed to boost the flagging circulation of the *Socialist*.

Shortly after returning to Seattle, Titus became embroiled in an incredibly bitter fight with an old antagonist, Walter Thomas Mills, a Populist who had become a reform socialist. Like Titus, Mills had the credentials of an intellectual, a master's degree from Oberlin and Wooster and experience as a professor at the Kansas State Agricultural College, where he had been appointed by the Populists and later removed by the Republicans. He had established the People's University in Chicago and an affiliated Berrien College in Michigan. Because he operated the latter venture on the principle of work and study, Mills attracted the attention of cooperators in the Pacific Northwest. Mills, who was also a journalist, published his own paper in Michigan, and his articles publicizing reform socialism appeared in numerous socialist journals.

A minister, evangelist, and temperance lecturer, Mills and his muttonchop whiskers and wire-rim glasses were already well recognized on the Chautauqua circuit before he became an advocate of reform socialism. In his study *The American Socialist Movement*, Ira Kipnis has claimed that Mills was involved in a series of cooperative ventures of "doubtful legality" and that his trail from Chicago to Australia was strewn with charges of immorality, dishonesty, and fraud. Many of those charges could probably be traced to Hermon F. Titus, for whom Mills symbolized everything that was wrong with the socialist movement.[8]

Mills came to Washington to give a series of eight lectures shortly after Titus returned from Caldwell. Mills stayed on in Seattle to found the *Saturday Evening Tribune* and to rally the forces of reform socialism as represented by members recently expelled from the party for supporting the Municipal Ownership party. He used the Propaganda Club, an organization composed of the Seattle dissidents, to promote his ideas and to battle with Titus about the relative merits of reform and revolutionary socialism.[9]

Michael Harrington, a contemporary spokesman for socialism in America, has noted that the great and abiding problem of American socialists was their sectarianism. That tendency was nowhere better illustrated than in Washington between 1906 and 1909. Even the local socialists had to admit that the history of the party had become one of incessant internal quarreling, but neither Titus nor Mills seemed to realize or care that their ideological conflict was crippling the party. Each believed that, with the opposing faction eliminated, the party would grow in strength and harmony. Also, as cynics observed, the conflict seemed to encourage subscriptions to Seattle's rival socialist journals.[10]

The membership of the Propaganda Club rejoined the Socialist party in early 1907, but Mills, who became city organizer, had mistakenly allowed himself to be drawn into the quicksand of British Columbia's labor and socialist politics. As a result of some vague statements contained in a speech he had delivered in Victoria the previous December, revolutionary socialists in British Columbia angrily charged that Mills was advocating fusion between socialist and labor groups in the province, and Titus thereupon insisted that Mills be expelled from the party. A comic opera of sorts followed.

Mills retorted that Canadian socialists had no jurisdiction over Washington and charged that radicals simply had no patience with "rational, conservative, constructive work." Under the inflammatory banner "Pinkerton Socialists," Mills published a series of articles in the *Saturday Evening Tribune* accusing Titus and his "Bogus Organization" of being motivated solely by personal politics.[11]

Mills viewed the charge that he had endorsed fusion in his Victoria speech as part of a "malicious conspiracy" to disrupt the Socialist party in Washington. Mills, in his speech, had actually denounced the folly of fusion with bourgeois political groups by claiming that there were only two parties, the socialists and the non-socialists. He had also noted the trouble caused in the ranks of socialism by faction and compromise. In Mills's opinion, however, faction was more fatal than compromise, and so he had urged the socialists in Victoria to unite.

Mills apparently did not realize until later that to urge the socialists of Victoria to unite was tantamount to advocating fusion because that city's socialists had split into groups, the larger of which was composed of members associated with the new Canadian Labor party. In the eyes of British Columbia's revolutionary socialists, Mills's plea that the socialists of Victoria unite was thus a call for fusion. When the Seattle local refused to remove Mills, the State Central Committee expelled it. Supporters of "Titusism" in Seattle now formed a new local—one they hoped was purged of the taint of Walter Thomas Mills and fusion. The new Seattle local was headed by one of Titus' supposedly loyal colleagues in the recent free-speech fights, dentist and lawyer Dr. E. J. ("Doc") Brown.[12]

Mills, according to his enemies, had met his "Waterloo" in Washington, but ideological disputes between Titus and Mills partisans continued to plague the local socialist movement, and as long as socialists were battling one another they had little time to spend on making the party more appealing to the working-class voter. The party's national leadership decided something had to be done about the mess in Washington.

The Socialist Party of America adopted an amendment in November 1907 providing that the National Executive Committee should hold a referendum in any state where two factions requested official recognition. The Socialist party hoped to use this device to untangle the comrades in Washington, but Mills and Titus partisans were determined to take their fight to the floor of the party's 1908 national convention. Each side was given twenty minutes to place its case before the delegates. The Titus faction presented its usual diatribe against "opportunism," but the Mills faction contended, with some truth, that the revolutionaries were keeping trade unionists out of the party in Washington. The basic issue, said one Titusite, was that in Washington "you are either for fusion

or against fusion, and the two factions line up on that principle. . . ." After listening to the bizarre claims and counterclaims of
the Titus and Mills supporters, a majority of the delegates voted to
declare the party in Washington unorganized, a novel step designed
to give the confused and long-suffering rank-and-file members a
voice in determining the party's future. The wrangling continued,
however, and many a socialist no doubt wondered, "What's the
matter with Seattle?" [13]

In the months that followed the 1908 convention the national
leadership of the Socialist party made little effort to harmonize
party affairs in Washington. The party's national executive did
indicate its sympathies by refusing to commission a Titus lieutenant, Alfred Wagenknecht, as party organizer. That was the first
time such a decision had been based on explicit ideological grounds.

Since the badly factionalized Socialist party in Washington had
one of the highest memberships in the country in proportion to
population, the disappointingly small socialist vote in Washington
in the 1908 election led to a new round of recriminations. This time
the Titusites found their scapegoat in "Doc" Brown. Brown was
expelled from the party because he allegedly made a derogatory
statement about the party in one of Seattle's non-socialist daily
newspapers. Titus now lashed out against his latest bugaboo:
"Mills, Brown & Co."

The Socialist party's National Executive Committee (NEC) refused to send an organizer or lecturer to Washington because of the
continuation of the bizarre factionalism in the state. Titus charged
the NEC with supporting his opponents. Secure in the knowledge
that revolutionary socialists since the turn of the century had never
lost a fight to reformers at the annual state convention, he prepared
for a final showdown to eliminate his opposition in 1909. When the
smoke of combat cleared, however, Titus learned just how badly he
had ignored signs of change within the Socialist party in
Washington. [14]

During the first half of 1909 Titus had become obsessed with his
campaign for greater "proletarianization" of the party. Affairs of
the party, argued the middle-class physician and erstwhile Baptist
theologian, should be placed in the hands of proletarians or those in
sympathy with the proletarian policy. If the party were to reach out
to laborers, the state executive committee must itself be composed

of wage workers, Titus asserted, and he urged delegates to the forthcoming Everett convention to commit the party unequivocally to the fundamental principle of proletarian supremacy.

The Everett convention, which included delegates who were Titusites, reform socialists or "opportunists," and utopian, foreign-language socialists or "impossibilists," was not the sort of gathering that could have been expected to draft a statement of proletarian supremacy. With apparent encouragement from the NEC, the "opportunists" and the "impossibilists" clasped hands to run the proceedings, and the Titusites thereupon boycotted the meetings to protest what they described as a "Gag Convention." In an interesting about-face, the Titusites sought to regain control of the state organization by appealing to the party's national leadership.[15]

As the Titusites saw it, what had happened at the Everett convention was a victory of a business faction, led by followers of Walter Thomas Mills and E. J. Brown, over a worker faction, led by Titus and his associate, Emil Herman. Titus claimed that the middle-class reformers had triumphed because the NEC had decided to "invade" Washington to support Mills and because those socialists who spoke little English were confused by the complicated convention proceedings. According to Emil Herman, the Titusites had been routed by a disparate coalition of their old political enemies. Because six of the locals represented at the Everett convention had voted to support Mills in 1907 and another thirty-three locals had not been represented at all, Herman called for a referendum to declare the proceedings unconstitutional.[16]

The NEC at first refused the request but then reversed itself. The purpose of the referendum, explained National Secretary J. Mahlon Barnes, was to determine whom the individual socialists in Washington wished to have as their state secretary. Titus, who saw the referendum as an opportunity to regain his influence in the party, warned Washington socialists about the problems he imagined would result from middle-class domination of the party. But W. H. Waynick, a sawmill worker and temporary state chairman, in a smarting reference to the non-proletarian background of the intellectual leader of the old guard, suggested that members pay no attention to Titus' "college-bred adjectives."

The referendum dashed Titus' hopes of regaining power in the

Socialist party since a majority of the members voted to uphold the actions of the Everett convention, to move party headquarters to Everett, and to have Frans Bostrom, proprietor of a Marxist bookstore, serve as the new state secretary. Some of the dissidents earned the title of "injunction socialists" when they sought to contest the referendum results by legal action, but Titus and some of his followers in Seattle abandoned the Socialist party to the reformers and the "impossibilists" and created a new body, the United Wage Workers' party, to continue the battle for true "scientific socialism."[17]

For Titus, the events of 1909 marked the culmination of a nine-year struggle in Washington between revolutionary and reform socialists. He was convinced that the party's national leadership had become "hopelessly" middle class and had "shamelessly" sacrificed principle to secure the votes of the landowning class. The local Socialist party, according to Titus, had turned "Populist" when the Mills-Brown faction voted to support an amendment pledging the party not to collectivize the land belonging to small farmers. Titus regarded the socialists of British Columbia as still "fairly proletarian," but he had become convinced of the need to form a new "party of the proletarians" to replace the discredited Socialist Party of America. He also attempted to define more precisely than before just who were the "Slaves of Capital," a phrase that had long appeared on the masthead of the *Socialist*, by adding the prefacing word "Wage." For Titus, the vote by itself had become an "ineffectual" way for "Wage Slaves" to destroy capitalism; and so although he had previously urged class-conscious workers to "vote" their emancipation, he now admonished that they "win" their emancipation by all possible means. The Wage Workers' party, a hybrid organization that stressed both politics and collective industrial action by workers, was the embodiment of Titus' new convictions.[18]

Although Titus and his associates held as many as five meetings a night to build the Seattle membership of the Wage Workers' party, this vestige of rebellion against the new leadership of the Socialist party soon collapsed in the face of competition from the Socialist Labor party, the resurgent Socialist party, and the new Washington State Labor party. A few members of the defunct Wage Workers' party later became influential in the Industrial

Workers of the World (IWW). One of Titus' associates in the Wage Workers' party was William Z. Foster, a twenty-nine-year-old native of Portland, Oregon, who had worked as an itinerant railroader in the Pacific Northwest until the Panic of 1907 gave him the leisure time to think about the economic system. As a reporter for the *Workingman's Paper*, the successor to the *Socialist*, Foster covered the free-speech fight that the IWW conducted in Spokane. His demonstration of sympathy for the downtrodden of the Inland Empire earned him two months in jail. Foster joined the IWW to continue a commitment to radicalism that culminated in his becoming head of the American Communist party.[19]

Titus did not accompany members of the Wage Workers' party into other organizations, although he briefly agitated for the IWW. The man whom Foster once described as a "brilliant speaker, a forceful writer, and an energetic agitator" but possessed of an "incurable 'leftism'" and a strong tendency to "bureaucratic arbitrariness," staked his hopes on the four-hour workday, an idea first advanced by a Seattle carpenter. A publication issued by Titus and his youthful friend, E. B. Ault, set 1 May 1920 as the target date for the introduction of the four-hour day.[20]

Titus left Seattle in 1912 to promote his short-hours scheme. According to Ault, Titus fell in love with a massage girl during this period and left Mrs. Titus, who remained in Seattle, where she ran a small hotel that was a rendezvous for radicals. Titus himself disappeared into myth and speculation. Hulet Wells, a close associate, claimed that Titus later became an official in an elevator operators' union in Chicago, but according to other accounts he ended his career in the late 1920s or early 1930s working as a doorman in a swanky New York apartment house. Ironically, his wife later became a revered figure in the Seattle labor movement. Trade unionists gave her a house in appreciation for her loyalty to the labor movement, and in the late 1920s and early 1930s they staged an annual "Mother" Titus Ball.[21]

The Mills-Titus-Brown fight almost destroyed the Socialist party in Seattle, but elsewhere in the state the party appeared to be in good health. In Spokane, more than a thousand people attended a May Day demonstration in 1910 to hear the Reverend Henry Victor Morgan of Portland speak on "The Impending Revolution and the Dawn of the Age of Cooperation and Comradeship." Orations with such titles no doubt caused revolutionary theoreticians to cringe, but reform socialists in Washington were convinced that the state party was at last ready to emulate the example of the comrades in Milwaukee, where trade unionists and socialists had worked together to elect the cautious and evolutionary Victor Berger as the first Socialist congressman. It is probable that the "slick dentist," as Foster described E. J. Brown, expected to use reform socialism to acquire similar power in Seattle. What Brown and other reform socialists soon learned, however, was that the revolutionaries, although weakened, were still capable of disrupting the socialist movement in Washington.[22]

SCHISMATIC SOCIALISTS IN BRITISH COLUMBIA

The Socialist Party of Canada (SPC), which had been formed out of the Socialist Party of British Columbia in late 1904,[23] expected to do well in the 1907 provincial election. A tour of the province a few months earlier had convinced Socialist representative James Hawthornthwaite that "things look good in British Columbia from the Revolutionary standpoint" because workers in the major industries were becoming class conscious. Overflowing with optimism, the SPC nominated twenty-two candidates, five of whom were in the Vancouver riding, where the party had never before put up a full slate.

The election campaign revealed a marked eroding of the Liberal middle ground between Conservatives and Socialists. Both parties regarded provincial Liberals as objects of scorn. The *Colonist*, which had once editorialized that "because a man is a socialist he is not necessarily less a good man or a good citizen," no doubt spoke for many Conservatives when it announced that it preferred a good Socialist to a poor Liberal. The Socialists believed that their party must sweep the deck clean of the "middle-class reform rubbish" represented by Liberalism in order to radicalize the working class. As Hawthornthwaite and Williams explained to their followers, Socialist legislators cooperated with Conservatives to eliminate the Liberal party and hasten the final showdown between the Socialists and the Conservatives who stood for "untrammeled capitalist development."

As election day approached, Liberals denounced ever more vigorously the unholy parliamentary alliance beteween the Socialists and Conservatives. Several prominent Liberal candidates proclaimed that if their party became dependent upon "Revolutionary Socialists," it would return to the voters and seek reelection.

The Liberals need not have worried, for in the 1907 election Conservatives captured twenty-six of the forty-two seats in the legislative assembly. Although the Socialists ran far behind Conservatives and Liberals in Vancouver and Laborite William Davidson was defeated in his Slocan riding, the SPC won a third seat in the legislative assembly when workers in the Grand Forks riding elected John McInnis, president of the Phoenix Miners' Union. In some ways the gain of an additional representative represented an empty victory, however, for the Socialist legislators suffered a measurable loss of influence when the election freed the Richard McBride government from dependence on them.[24]

The outcome of the provincial election of 1907 bitterly disappointed those millenarian socialists who had been predicting a Socialist majority in the legislative assembly by 1907 or 1908, and contributed to the mounting criticism of the revolutionary theoreticians who led the party in British Columbia. Before the election, Ramsay MacDonald, the future Labour party prime minister of Great Britain, had chided the British Columbia socialists who led the movement in Canada for "grinding away" at their "cold, aggressive, academic formulae" and denouncing every person who does not agree with them as a "fakir or a scoundrel of some degree or other."

The *Winnipeg Voice* attributed the Socialists' 1907 electoral defeat in British Columbia to the "excess of logic" and the lack of understanding of human nature that had been so prominent in "much of the so-called propaganda work of the past few years." Keir Hardie, the virtual embodiment of the Labour party for many Canadians, also commented on the inability of socialists and trade unionists in North America to reach a mutual understanding. At the 1908 convention of the Dominion's Labor Congress, Hardie told delegates that the term "socialism" did not have the restricted meaning in Great Britain that it had in Canada, where the socialists and labor leaders were behaving in a "pure and simple" way that kept them apart. Dominated by the revolutionary theoreticians of British Columbia, the SPC, as Canadian Communist leader Tim

Buck later observed, degenerated into a kind of "dogmatic passivity" and "anti-working-class snobbery."[25]

The slow progress of the socialist movement in Canada was especially upsetting to some members of the Vancouver local of the SPC. The electorate, they noted, had more than doubled during the past several years, but the SPC was declining in popularity because its propaganda had been of "too purely a negative character" and because of the party's often sweeping condemnation of trade unions.[26]

As in Washington, the ideological split between revolutionary and reform socialists in British Columbia was worsened by the controversy surrounding Walter Thomas Mills's speech in Victoria in late 1906. When the SPC subsequently canceled its sponsorship of Mills's speaking engagements in Vancouver because of his alleged fusionist tendencies, Ernest Burns personally arranged for Mills to speak in the city. When the SPC suspended Burns and his wife for this action, they were joined by more than sixty seceders. Burns and his group, which avidly studied the reformist ideas of Victor Berger, considered joining forces with the Socialist Party of America but decided instead to form the Social Democratic Party of Vancouver. Social Democratic party locals also appeared in several other British Columbia communities.[27]

When Daniel DeLeon visited the Pacific Northwest later in 1907, he must have been pleased by the discomfiture of his old enemies. He noted that "vagabond journalists" like E. T. Kingsley were claiming that DeLeon had sent Mills to break up the socialist movement. "The innocents are sincere about it too," DeLeon remarked with no small hint of delight. Like most other observers, DeLeon was correctly convinced that Titus and Kingsley had invited schism by their own obtuse actions.[28]

Outside of British Columbia, several other groups split away from the SPC. Foreign-language locals in Winnipeg had long been dissatisfied with the SPC and the scorn it heaped on immediate demands and palliative measures; a number of locals in Winnipeg left the SPC in 1910 because of its "impossibilism" and formed a local Social Democratic party to promote a "constructive, practical policy." In 1910 the various groups calling themselves the Social Democratic party claimed to have thirty-five hundred members in 133 locals as compared with the SPC's two thousand members in 100 locals. A year later the seceders from the SPC united to form the

Social Democratic Party of Canada, which, according to Tim Buck, was the forerunner of the Communist party in Canada. Although it was at times heavily dominated by foreign-language groups, particularly the Finns, the protean nature of the Canadian Social Democratic party also made it a forerunner of the Cooperative Commonwealth Federation and the New Democratic party.[29]

Unlike members of the SPC, Social Democrats promoted reform socialism, contested municipal elections, and strongly supported trade unions. They also maintained official ties to socialists in other countries. Because members of the Social Democratic party in Vancouver believed that "Socialists should be sociable" in order to convert "the stranger," their gatherings were likely to be devoted more to entertainment than to abstruse theorizing.[30]

In the 1909 provincial election in British Columbia, the SPC nominated nineteen candidates for the Legislative Assembly and received more than eleven thousand votes, compared to the five thousand votes it had received two years before. In the constituencies it contested, the party received approximately 22 percent of the total vote, and party members took some comfort that Hawthornthwaite and Williams had been reelected by "good class-conscious" votes. The SPC, however, had already lost much of its influence outside British Columbia, and the election, in effect, signaled little more than the start of a new round of schisms in the provincial socialist movement.[31]

THE LEGACY OF THE REVOLUTIONARY SOCIALISTS

In both Washington and British Columbia, the revolutionary factions that dominated the local socialist parties in the early twentieth century had shunned cooperation with middle-class reformers even on such issues as municipal ownership. The ideological rigidity of the party's leadership in Washington had not only discouraged trade unionists from joining the movement but also invited ridicule from more pragmatic comrades in other parts of the United States. The *Social Democratic Herald* of Milwaukee averred in 1908 that the Titus wing of the party in Washington was "so orthodox that its spokesmen have decided that a union man, being a skilled worker, is not a proletarian because he has a skill to sell, whereas a proletarian is one who possesses only his (unskilled) labor power."

The party's failure at the polls was sometimes blamed on the revolutionary theorists who allegedly kept ten socialists outside the party for every one in it; ironically, however, socialists in the Pacific Northwest enjoyed their greatest successes in those British Columbia ridings where the most rabid expressions of socialist ideology were common. This seems to confirm the observation that socialists were successful only in those locales where their ideology corresponded to reality.[32]

Socialist victories in pre-World War I British Columbia were totally confined to three ridings: Nanaimo, Newcastle, and Grand Forks. The first two of these electoral districts contained a large number of coal miners, who in the provincial elections of 1903, 1907, 1909, and 1912 comprised between 40 and 50 percent of the eligible voters. In the provincial election of 1907, in which the Socialist candidate carried the Grand Forks riding, hardrock miners, smeltermen, and laborers comprised almost 60 percent of the electorate in the district.

Despite the alleged radicalism of British Columbia's coal and metal miners, socialist electoral success in the province was as much a product of special circumstances, such as the intransigence of the Dunsmuirs, as it was of occupation. The Fernie riding, for example, contained an electorate composed of from 25 to 35 percent coal miners, but in the four provincial elections held during the decade from 1903 to 1912 the Socialist candidates were unable to carry the riding even when the non-socialist vote was split between two candidates.

Although the socialists frequently occupied positions of leadership in the metal mining unions of southeastern British Columbia, rank-and-file metal miners did not support Socialist candidates with any great regularity. The number of metal miners in the elctorate of the Kaslo riding ranged from 49 percent in 1903 to 33 percent in 1912, but local socialists never once contested a provincial election during that time. The Rossland City riding was almost totally urbanized, and metal miners comprised between 40 and 50 percent of the electorate from 1903 to 1912, but the Socialist vote in those years only once climbed as high as 26 percent of the total. To the radicalized coal miners of Vancouver Island revolutionary solutions seemed both desirable and feasible, but most workers in the rest of British Columbia were simply not desperate enough to embrace

revolutionary socialism instead of the more practical solutions proposed by labor and labor-leaning candidates.[33]

The political strength of revolutionary socialism in the Nanaimo
and Newcastle ridings not only helped sustain the power of the
revolutionary theoreticians in the Socialist party in British Columbia but also tended to blind many socialist leaders to the abject
condition of the party in other areas of the province. The limited
nature of socialist support was illustrated in the 1909 provincial
election when twelve of the nineteen Socialist candidates failed to
gain at least one-half as many votes as their weakest opponent.
Vancouver, the seat of party leadership, typically had a low
Socialist vote despite the large number of wage workers in the
community. This is probably explained, in part, by the degree of
upward social mobility in the city, which seemingly lessened the
appeal of revolutionary socialism.[34]

Left-wing unionism, far more than political power, was the real
legacy of the revolutionary socialists in Washington and British
Columbia. These revolutionaries had been remarkably successful in
combating the twin threats of reform socialism and "dual partyism"
as represented by the various labor parties, but they nearly destroyed the socialist parties in the process. Ironically, however, by
weakening the socialist parties the revolutionary theoreticians
opened the way to a rapprochement between the socialist and trade
union movements in the Pacific Northwest on the eve of World
War I.

CHAPTER 12

Wobblies and Progressives:

Class Consciousness
versus Reform Consciousness

During the decade that preceded the outbreak of world war in 1914, the Industrial Workers of the World (iww) emerged as ubiquitous, determined, and outrageously colorful fighters on the front lines of class war. Until the free-speech fights began in 1909, the activities of the Wobblies continued in the tradition of the Western Federation of Miners (wfm) and the regional labor unions, the Western Labor Union (wlu) and the American Labor Union (alu).

With few exceptions, early iww locals in British Columbia were established in communities long noted for radicalism. The locals formed in 1906 were thus all located in the Kootenay region. In Nelson, the iww simply took over the membership in the American Federation of Labor (afl) and alu federal unions.

In Spokane, the iww built on the foundation provided by the alu, but in western Washington, the iww was forced to build anew. Beginning with a nucleus of support among the intellectuals of Home Colony, located near Tacoma, the iww established locals in Tacoma, Bellingham, and possibly other Puget Sound communities by the summer of 1906. In western Washington, the "Industrious Wreckers of the Workers," as the *Union Record* dubbed the iww, encountered the same stiff resistance from the trade unions as the wlu and alu once had.

The iww acknowledged that it had little power in Seattle but claimed four thousand members in Spokane, where it had a meet-

ing hall seating eight hundred. The powerful Spokane local of the
IWW also published the *Industrial Worker*, beginning in 1909.[1]

The IWW at first had no prominent organizer in the Pacific
Northwest. After his acquittal in the Steunenberg murder trial,
William D. Haywood toured the Pacific Northwest several times to
work for the socialists, but his interest in the IWW had temporarily
waned. On one such tour he discovered Ed Boyce, former president of the WFM, working as the "petty manager" of a hotel in
Portland. On another occasion Haywood was arrested in North
Yakima for violating the state law forbidding the smoking of
cigarettes. "Of all the indictments I have been subject to,"
Haywood later remarked, "this was my first conviction." Perhaps it
was his encounter with Hermon Titus and his strange brand of
socialism that caused Haywood to renew his interest in the IWW. In
any case, Haywood and several other socialists became indefatigable organizers for the IWW. In their efforts they were helped by the
peculiar structure of the Pacific Northwest labor market and by the
free-speech fights that erupted in Missoula in 1909 and spread to
Spokane, Vancouver, and other communities before culminating in
the Everett Massacre in 1916.[2]

Complaints about employment agencies or "sharks" triggered the
free-speech fight in Spokane. Of the thirty-one such agencies in the
city in 1909, most were poorly managed, and some were simply
dishonest. Both the Spokane Labor Council and the IWW launched a
crusade against these agencies in September 1908; a year later the
IWW deliberately violated a city ordinance forbidding street-corner
speaking, which led to the free-speech fight. During the next five
months Wobblies were jailed, beaten, and tortured by city police.
Elizabeth Gurley Flynn, "the Rebel Girl," particularly embarrassed the city fathers by publishing a description of her experiences
in the Spokane jail. The resulting outcry of moral indignation caused
the city to provide better treatment for women prisoners. The
police halted the printing of the *Industrial Worker*, but the paper
reappeared on the streets after arrangements had been made to have
it printed in Seattle.[3]

The *Pasco Express* declared that Spokane was "getting about what
she is entitled to," because city officials had long harbored the
employment sharks. On the other hand, Governor Marion Hay
characterized the free-speech movement as crazy" and spoke of the

protestors as "poor, misguided fellows." The AFL criticized reformers for supporting the movement, and Secretary Frank Morrison
dispatched AFL organizer C. O. Young to prevent an IWW victory in
Spokane. Under increasing pressure, the Spokane City Council
revoked the licenses of nineteen employment agencies, and the
Washington state legislature later passed a law forbidding the establishment of private employment agencies in the state.[4]

IWW organizers usually toured the Kootenay region after visiting
Spokane, and the *Industrial Worker* circulated freely on both sides of
the border. Fred Heslewood, once a member of the Greenwood,
British Columbia, Miners' Union, became a national organizer for
the IWW and made his headquarters in Spokane, where he was for a
time editor of the *Industrial Worker*. Other former members of the
WFM organized an IWW local in Prince Rupert. By 1911 Wobblies
claimed to have established nine locals in Canada, all in British
Columbia, and boasted of a Canadian membership of almost four
thousand out of the IWW total of twenty-eight thousand. Most
Canadians, however, were probably unaware of the IWW's existence
in the Dominion until Wobblies led British Columbia's numerous
railway construction workers in a series of strikes beginning in
1911.[5]

Although the IWW has often been identified with the timber industry of the Pacific Northwest, Wobblies in British Columbia
concentrated most of their organizational activity along the lines of
the Canadian Northern and Grand Trunk Pacific railways. Conditions in the primitive and isolated construction camps of these two
railways provided workers with a great incentive to join the IWW.
Several thousand workers walked off their jobs in the Grand Trunk
Pacific in January 1912. Subsequent work stoppages kept the construction camps in a turmoil. Pressured for funds, the IWW appealed
to the Vancouver Trades and Labor Council for financial help, and
the council voted to send a contribution to the railway workers and
issued a financial appeal to its affiliates. C. O. Young, however, was
furious when he learned that labor leaders in Vancouver were aid-
ing the IWW.[6]

Trouble erupted in Vancouver a few months later when Parm
Pettipiece attempted to address a mixed crowd of Wobblies,
socialists, and unemployed trade unionists. The open-air gathering
was attacked and dispersed by police, and Pettipiece was arrested

for "unlawful assembly." The Trades and Labor Council then established a defense fund to support free speech in Vancouver and to raise legal fees for Pettipiece, who was later acquitted of his participation in Vancouver's "Bloody Sunday."[7]

William Z. Foster was engaged about this same time in a "hobo agitation tour" to promote his new Syndicalist League of North America among the province's railway construction workers. The tour ended in Kamloops, when two policemen stopped Foster and escorted him to the local police station, a veritable arsenal. The officers were angry because American Wobblies had recently taken a Canadian nonunion cook to the edge of the river and threatened to throw him in if he did not join the IWW. "Think of it," one officer stormed, "those bastards were actually going to throw a Canadian citizen into our Fraser River."[8]

Popular feelings of anti-Americanism no doubt aided railway officials and law officers to break all the IWW-led strikes in 1912. A year later, however, the unscrupulous entrepreneurs William Mackenzie and Donald Mann complained to British Columbia's attorney general that Wobblies were secretly organizing among the laborers on their Canadian Northern line and that construction was being delayed because workers were becoming restless and prone to strike. The attorney general apparently could do nothing, but the Ottawa government ordered prominent Wobbly Joseph Ettor deported from British Columbia in March 1913, and prohibited Bill Haywood and other Wobblies from entering Canada.[9]

Violence erupted in Seattle on a spring afternoon in 1912 when Wobblies marched through the city carrying a red flag alongside the Stars and Stripes. Colonel Alden J. Blethen, editor and publisher of the *Seattle Times* and a bitter foe of the IWW, excoriated the city's labor-leaning mayor, George Cotterill, for having permitted the IWW to endanger the safety of the community. Blethen's continuing fulminations against the Wobblies were perhaps partly responsible for further violence a year later when drunken sailors brawled with Wobblies and then ransacked Socialist party headquarters. Fear and hatred of the IWW were so strong on Puget Sound that in 1917 a deputy sheriff in Seattle was convinced he had captured some dangerous Wobblies when he arrested two girls who "dared convention" by cutting their hair short and wearing overalls.[10]

The Wobblies so captured the public imagination by their free-speech fights that more conventional developments in the Pacific Northwest labor movement were often overlooked. British Columbians, for example, acquired a new voice in Canada's Trades and Labor Congress (TLC) when delegates elected J. C. Watters of Victoria in 1911. One of the province's young but experienced socialist trade unionists, Watters remained the leader of the congress until 1918.[11]

At about the same time as Watters became president of the TLC a majority of the trade unions in British Columbia voted to form the first provincial federation of labor in Canada, the British Columbia Federation of Labor. Although the WFM objected to the creation of the new federation because the miners already had a strong district organization in the province, the WFM joined the federation in 1912. Parm Pettipiece, as secretary of the new organization, attempted to give it a moderately radical orientation.[12]

There were approximately twenty-two thousand union members in British Columbia in 1911 as compared with an estimated twenty thousand in much more populous Washington. The British Columbia unions accounted for almost 22 percent of the total membership of organized labor in Canada. Approximately 32 percent of the members of organized labor in British Columbia were concentrated in the Vancouver area, where the local Trades and Labor Council was the only central body in the province affiliated with both the AFL and the TLC; the other five centrals in the province were affiliated only with the TLC. There was a strong feeling in the Vancouver labor movement that although Samuel Gompers had once done yeoman work for the labor movement, the era of the hand-tool and craft union was about over. In Washington, likewise, there was a growing conviction among AFL members that the organization lacked aggressiveness in confronting the new problems faced by workingmen.[13]

William Blackman, the long-time leader of the Washington State Federation of Labor, resigned in 1907, and the organization languished as the result of frequent leadership changes until Ernest Marsh was elected president in 1913. Marsh, an executive in the Shingle Weavers' Union, had begun working in the Everett mills as a young man. Rising rapidly in the trade union movement, he was selected to head the local labor council, and he edited the *Everett Labor Journal*. Originally a firm supporter of the AFL leadership,

Marsh became an admirer of Eugene Debs in 1909. Although he never became a socialist and was uncomfortable with the socialists' rejection of craft unionism, Marsh came to believe that the industrial pattern of organization was appropriate in some industries, and he hoped to persuade the AFL to accommodate industrial unions. Marsh also hoped to keep the State Federation of Labor at the forefront of the Progressive movement in Washington.[14]

A RISING REFORM CONSCIOUSNESS

British Columbians were aware of the rising reform consciousness in the United States after the turn of the century. Muckraking articles circulated on both sides of the 49th parallel, and accounts of the activities of "Fighting Bob" LaFollette and Theodore Roosevelt appeared regularly in Canadian newspapers. International trade unions served as sources of information about the new reform crusades south of the border. A concerned British Columbian could join one of the local counterparts to the conservation groups, uplift organizations, and consumers' leagues that spearheaded the middle-class fight in the United States for better public health and industrial safety, workmen's compensation, and the eradication of child labor, exploitation of women, and poverty.[15]

Because common problems often plagued the societies on both sides of the 49th parallel, legislators in Victoria and Olympia enacted a number of strikingly similar measures during the thirty years after 1890. Periodic concern about habit-forming drugs, food adulteration, impure milk, and diseased meat prodded legislators to pass a series of often poorly enforced remedial measures. When women got the vote in Washington in 1910, women's groups, organized labor, and prominent Liberals in British Columbia were encouraged in their campaign for female suffrage, which was finally secured in the province in early 1917. Likewise, the prohibitionists' victory in Washington in 1914 aroused general interest in Victoria and Vancouver. After following Washington's "noble experiment" with keen interest, British Columbia also went "dry" in 1917.[16]

The Washington state legislature passed the nation's first compulsory workmen's compensation act in 1911. Designed to fix insurance costs and reduce disturbing and often costly litigation, the act elicited praise from both labor and businessmen. Theodore

Roosevelt and the governors of several states requested a copy of the law, and the leadership of the AFL recommended the Washington plan as a model to be followed by other states. The British Columbia legislative assembly, which had previously enacted several unsatisfactory compensation laws, carefully studied Washington's new system of workmen's compensation and finally, in 1916, after investigation by a royal commission, enacted a compensation measure for the province.[17]

The efforts by Canadians to duplicate American reform legislation appeared mindless in some instances. After Washington's voters approved direct legislation amendments to the state constitution in 1912, interest in the subject increased in British Columbia. Although direct legislation had long attracted some reformers in the Dominion, many Canadians were convinced that direct legislation was "wholly un-British" and better suited to correcting the abuses in the American legislative system than in the British-style parliamentary system. The three Prairie provinces enacted direct legislation measures between 1913 and 1916, but the Privy Council declared Manitoba's initiative and referendum statute unconstitutional because it interfered with the office of the lieutenant governor and the principle of executive control over the legislature. Despite this precedent as well as opposition from the Conservatives and Socialists, John Oliver, a rough-and-ready debater and British Columbia's Liberal premier between 1918 and 1927, successfully pushed a direct legislation measure through the legislative assembly in 1919. For Socialist representative James Hawthornthwaite, the direct legislation measure was an example of "freak legislation," but Liberals saw the statute as an integral part of their party's traditional reform package.[18]

To be a Liberal in certain parts of British Columbia during the years of McBride prosperity was to court political and social ostracism. Tied to Prime Minister Sir Wilfrid Laurier and his opposition to anti-Oriental legislation, the Liberals in British Columbia sought to regain popularity in 1911 by supporting reciprocity with the United States, but Premier McBride and a majority of British Columbians opposed the idea. The fortunes of the Liberals continued to sag.[19]

Despite attempts to rebuild the party, the Liberals fared no better in the provincial election of 1912 than they had in 1909. The

Vancouver Sun, which the Liberals had founded to aid in the rebuilding of the party, claimed that McBride's Conservation platform was planked with "second-hand railroad ties," but the "Colossus of Roads," as one cartoonist pictured McBride, was reelected by voters who supported his "Progressive Policy" of building railroads and developing natural resources. The Liberal platform contained sixty-four planks designed to build a coalition of moral and labor reformers. Many planks were subsequently incorporated into an enduring Liberal creed, but middle-class discontent in 1912 was a poor weapon to use against a party that stood for prosperity. The Liberals and Socialists each had only two seats in the legislative assembly after the 1912 election, and Sir Richard McBride, knighted in recognition of his growing stature as an imperial statesman, could accurately be described as the most popular first minister in the British Empire.[20]

McBride's power began to decline not long after the election of 1912. He underestimated the growing popular interest in reform and allowed his party to grow complacent. As a partisan warned him in 1913, the Conservative party in Victoria had deteriorated to such an extent that "it is only your own personality which keeps it together." Economic collapse on the eve of World War I further contributed to the declining popularity of British Columbia's Conservative government. In 1914 McBride begged Donald Mann to continue railway construction work on Vancouver Island because it would be "very disastrous to me" if work stopped. A few months later the Ministerial Union of the Lower Mainland published a pamphlet, "The Crisis in British Columbia," denouncing the government for all sorts of corruption, and its charges were soon reiterated in a score of different ways. As an optimist, McBride had difficulty coping with the mounting personal criticism and economic depression.[21]

McBride professed to believe in late 1915 that the economic situation in British Columbia had "greatly improved" over that of the previous year, and he optimistically predicted an "excellent" year in 1916. By the time his observations appeared in print in early 1916, however, McBride had resigned to become head of the oldest provincial agency in London, and the once admired Conservative government had become a popular scapegoat for the depression and growing industrial unrest.[22]

William Bowser, provincial attorney general and boss of the Vancouver Conservative machine, succeeded McBride as premier. A paternalistic man devoid of much personal charm, Bowser inherited the whirlwind. He became a convenient target for local muckrakers and the object of labor hatred after his actions during a coal strike on Vancouver Island. So thoroughly disliked was Bowser that in 1916 he came to be characterized as the "Kaiser" of provincial politics.[23]

Conservative by-election defeats helped convince Bowser that it was necessary to outflank the reformers. The government had passed several reform measures in 1915, and Bowser cautiously pushed for additional reforms. His action, however, failed to satisfy the popular demand for change. Liberals described the 1916 provincial election as a fight between the "forces of Bowserism" and those striving for a constitutional government. By successfully equating the Conservative party with graft, despotism, and extravagance, the Liberals won thirty-seven seats to the Conservatives' eight in the legislative assembly.

Harlan C. Brewster, wealthy cannery owner and prominent Baptist layman, became the new premier, and Ralph Smith, the erstwhile "Gompers of Canada," became minister of finance. Responding to middle-class discontent, the Liberals sought to provide British Columbia with a government characterized by honesty and efficiency. The Liberals also secured the enactment of a number of measures of interest to the working class, including legislation guaranteeing workers in major industries the fortnightly payment of wages, establishing a system of workmen's compensation, creating a department of labor, and providing the eight-hour workday for miners. Legislation to secure greater rights for women was pushed by Mary Ellen Smith, who, after the death of her husband, Ralph, became the first woman elected to a provincial legislature in Canada.[24]

Although provincial legislators had copied freely from American reformers, most British Columbians probably did not regard the passage of reform legislation in the province between 1915 and 1919 as analogous to Progressivism in the United States. Earlier, muckraking articles like Lincoln Steffens' "The Shame of Minneapolis" and David Graham Phillips' "The Treason of the Senate" had tended to confirm Canadians' beliefs about the shortcomings of the

American political system. Although Upton Sinclair's *The Jungle* probably stirred more interest in the Dominion than any other American muckraking piece did, some Canadians saw the rising concern about Chicago sausages as an opportunity for Canada and Australia to capture the world's market for meat. Progressivism, as Miles Poindexter, Washington's future Progressive senator, explained to British Columbians in 1910, sought to curb the trusts and interests, to conserve natural resources, and to protect the weak against the strong. Because Canadians typically regarded such reforms as products of America's need to impose order on the confusion resulting from adherence to a laissez-faire philosophy, the *Colonist* could declare in 1912, "We have what the Progressive Party seeks to obtain for the people of the United States."[25]

PROGRESSIVISM IN WASHINGTON

The Progressive party, which for some Canadians was apparently the apotheosis of Progressivism, actually had very little to offer the people of Washington. In fact, its formation in 1912 helped to end a remarkable era of reform in the state that had begun seven years earlier. After the demise of the Populist party, popular interest in reform had languished in Washington until the railroad lobby allegedly captured the Tacoma convention of the Republican party and dictated its 1904 platform. The main issue of the 1904 campaign became that of railroad regulation. Although the Republicans won the election, the new governor, Albert E. Mead, recommended that the legislature establish a railway commission and enact labor legislation similar to that proposed by the Washington State Federation of Labor. Concern about the power of the railroad lobby led to the creation of a railroad commission in 1905 and the adoption of the direct primary in 1907.[26]

The direct primary, a device that allowed voters to bypass the discredited convention system in choosing public officials, laid the foundation for Washington's anti-party, issue-oriented political system. The Direct Primary League, which was organized in 1906 to secure this reform, contributed importantly to the interest in reform developing in the state. The state's voters elected in 1906 a number of legislators pledged to support the direct primary, and these "insurgents" became the first significant reform element in the legislature since the demise of the Populists. Pressured by farmer and labor groups as well as by the Direct Primary League, dissident Republicans and the liberal Democrats led by the reformer George Cotterill enacted the direct primary. As passage of the direct primary law illustrates, Progressivism in Washington was not a mass crusade born of frustration or desperation but rather the product of popular education and pressure politics by highly organized groups and committed individuals.[27]

Although reformers such as Cotterill and C. B. Kegley remained outside the Republican party, the liberal wing of the party was growing stronger, particularly during the administration of Governor Marion Hay, a small-town merchant from eastern Washington. Elected lieutenant governor in 1908 primarily as a result of the new direct primary law, Hay succeeded to the office of governor a few months later. Although a large amount of reform legislation was enacted during his tenure as governor, Hay's commitment to reform was questioned because he supported development of the state's natural resources in addition to their conservation. Hay also suffered from a drab personality; he lacked the flair that characterized many of the nation's leading Progressives. His preference for moral reform, moreover, drew criticism from leaders of the farmer-labor alliance. Like President William Howard Taft, Hay became concerned about insurgency in the Republican party, and, like Taft, this led him to cooperate with conservative factions, which later resulted in his undoing at the polls. Hay's continued support for Taft was, in fact, another reason he found it difficult to convince voters that he was a Progressive reformer.[28]

Insurgents in Washington scored an important electoral victory in 1910, and the legislature that convened the next year distinguished itself as one of the most reform-minded in the state's history. A united front of labor, agrarians, and urban, middle-class reformers encouraged legislators to pass a pure food and drug law and an eight-hour workday for women, ratify the federal income tax amendment, and set up the system of workmen's compensation alluded to earlier. Legislators also approved direct legislation amendments to the state constitution that were submitted to the voters in 1912.[29]

Progressivism in Washington had no leader comparable to Robert M. LaFollette in Wisconsin, but the movement gradually became identified with Miles Poindexter, United States senator from 1911 to 1923. Moving to Washington from Virginia, Poindexter remained a Democrat until he became alienated by the triumph of fusion in 1896. After 1904, a growing awareness of the problems that unfair railway rates were causing for Spokane convinced Poindexter that the people were being exploited by "the interests." Working closely with Spokane businessmen and others who supported reform, Poindexter was elected to Congress in 1908. He first distinguished himself as an insurgent Republican by opposing the autocratic Speaker of the House, Joseph G. Cannon, and then he broke with President Taft as a result of the Ballinger-Pinchot controversy over government conservation policy. Taft opposed Poindexter's election to the Senate in 1910, describing him as a "blatant demagogue," but Poindexter was supported by a broad coalition of reform interests that included Samuel Gompers, C. B. Kegley, and the Spokane Chamber of Commerce.[30]

A number of Progressive organizations formed in eastern Washington beginning in late 1909 to work for reform within the Republican party. This movement was closely tied to support for Miles Poindexter. Poindexter himself became a member of the Progressive Republican League that was organized in January 1911.[31]

In what was perhaps a symbolic gesture to get as far away as possible from the influence of Miles Poindexter and the reform interests in eastern Washington, the conservative leaders of the Republican party chose Aberdeen as the site for the party's 1912 state convention. Even before the Aberdeen convention met, however, county Republican organizations had begun to split on the issue of whether to select Taft or Roosevelt as the party's presidential standard-bearer. As a result of the clash between the two forces at Aberdeen, Washington's Republican party sent rival delegations to the national convention in Chicago. There the Taft forces triumphed over Roosevelt's vociferous and determined supporters.[32]

Roosevelt apparently did not consult with Poindexter before deciding to form a third party, but like most Progressives in Washington, Poindexter probably saw little need for a separate Progressive party since the state's Progressives had already achieved most of the reforms advocated by the new "Bull Moose" party in its 1912 platform. Roosevelt's supporters had considerable difficulty in organizing their party in Washington, and they were unable to form local organizations in many of the state's counties. In November, however, Roosevelt carried the state with 113,000 votes, approximately 36 percent of the total; Woodrow Wilson ran second to Roosevelt with 86,000 votes; Taft received 70,000 votes; and Eugene Debs polled a remarkable 40,000 votes or 12 percent of the total.

Governor Hay, who chose to remain with the regular Republicans, was defeated by approximately six hundred votes by the Democratic candidate, Ernest Lister, a moderate reformer. Lister, the first Democrat elected to statewide office since John R. Rogers in 1900, benefited from a last-minute switch by Progressives who had come to learn that their gubernatorial candidate had a past record of personal follies. Every Progressive candidate for major state office was defeated, and although a total of thirty-five Progressives were elected to the state legislature, Republicans retained a working majority in both houses.[33]

The Progressive candidates generally fared best in the state's urban areas. Half of the total Progressive vote came from the state's three most urbanized counties, King (Seattle), Pierce (Tacoma), and Spokane, and most of the Progressive members of the new legislature were elected from these three counties. Both Roosevelt and Wilson did well in eastern Washington, where many people still regarded large business combinations as dangerous. Wilson, however, generally ran better than Roosevelt in the poorer, more rural counties that had once been Populist strongholds. Most of the counties carried by Taft were located in the conservative, far western part of the state centering about Aberdeen. The Debs vote was heaviest in the urban counties of western Washington.[34]

As in several other states, organized labor in Washington played a major role in generating interest in reform but played almost no part in the Progressive party. Although Progressivism, like Populism, represented an attack on laissez faire, the overwhelming majority of the members of the Progressive party were former Republicans who idolized Roosevelt and had very little in common with Populists. Membership in the Progressive party was heavily based in the Protestant middle class, with lawyers and businessmen providing the leadership. Although some Progressives attempted to appeal to workingmen, others could scarcely disguise their animosity toward organized labor.[35]

Organized labor in Washington was not disappointed by the results of the 1912 election. Although Governor Lister had been a businessman at the time of his election, he had also once been a leader in the labor movement. Born in Halifax, England, forty-two years before, Lister had migrated to the United States at the age of fourteen and later settled in Tacoma. An ardent prohibitionist and an active Populist, Lister had been prominent in Tacoma municipal politics, and he held a statewide post in the administration of John R. Rogers. As a member of the Iron Molders' Union, Lister also became secretary-treasurer of the Tacoma Trades Council.[36]

In the 1913 session of the Washington state legislature, the Progressives supported the program of the Joint Legislative Committee. Represented in Olympia by Kegley, H. L. Hughes, and other reformers, the Joint Legislative Committee was particularly interested in securing legislation to prohibit employment agencies from charging job seekers a fee, sanction the operation of cooperative businesses, and permit voters to amend the constitution by initiative. The legislature, however, enacted few measures of interest to organized labor. The *Union Record* was willing to "forgive" the lawmakers for their "many major sins" because they enacted a mothers' pension and a minimum wage measure, but a disappointed Ernest Marsh came away from the 1913 session with his belief in direct legislation "more firmly entrenched than ever."[37]

Marsh and other observers had no way of knowing that few additional pieces of progressive legislation would be enacted in the pre-World War I era. Reformers had been remarkably successful working within the structure of the Republican party, but the schism in 1912 allowed the conservatives to regain full control of the state's major party. Even the eventual reconciliation of the Republicans and the Progressives signified little more than a continuation of the political swing to the right that had begun when voters reacted to economic decline and an apparent increase in labor radicalism.[38]

After the 1913 legislative session the farmer-labor reform coalition decided to rely on direct legislation as a substitute for political parties in securing measures of interest to the coalition. Rather than seeking to commit legislative candidates to the program of the Joint Legislative Committee, the reformers proposed to place that program directly before the voters in 1914. The several initiative measures, described as the farmers' and workers' response to the fish combine, the lumber trust, and other special interests, included labor's long-sought demand for a general eight-hour workday. The Republicans had introduced such a bill in the preceding legislature in the hope of splitting the farmer-labor coalition, but when the farmers' representatives had raised no objection to the controversial measure, the chagrined Republicans were forced to kill their own proposal. To defeat the initiatives at the polls, the standpatters formed the Stop-Look-Listen League, which was considered by opponents to be "worse than the old railroad lobby."[39]

Marsh, who by pledging to achieve the eight-hour day without a strike had tacitly linked the future of the State Federation of Labor to the success of direct legislation as a tactic, suffered a crushing defeat in the November election when the eight-hour initiative received the approval of less than 36 percent of the state's voters. In Whitman County, where the Stop-Look-Listen League had apparently convinced many farmers to oppose the measure, the eight-hour initiative was rejected by 86 percent of the voters. The voters not only humiliated Marsh and thus helped to encourage the emergence of a radical leadership in several trade unions, but they also elected an "economy" legislature that appeared determined to snatch from organized labor many of the hard-won reforms of the preceding seven years.

Members of the 1915 legislature sought to render the initiative inoperative by attempting deliberately to complicate the process of gathering signatures and to subdue the trade unionists by an anti-picketing bill. Organized labor was able to delay implementation of the anti-picketing measure by invoking a referendum, but the legislators, perhaps encouraged by the recent defeat of the eight-hour initiative and the slumping economy, voted to repeal the law providing an eight-hour day on public works. Governor Lister vetoed the bill, however, and his veto was sustained. The rampaging conservatives even attacked Professor J. Allen Smith, a middle-class reformer whose book *The Spirit of American Government* enraged prominent businessmen in Seattle, by introducing an amendment to a University of Washington appropriations bill that proposed to abolish the Political Science department, in which Smith taught. It is no wonder that Marsh, speaking for organized labor, described the 1915 legislature as the "most reactionary" in the state's history.[40]

In the 1916 election the leaders of organized labor in Washington found themselves in the rather anomalous position of having to urge members to vote "no" on all seven referendum measures. Three of the objectionable items, including an anti-picketing law, had been signed by Governor Lister. Although Lister was the only Democrat other than Woodrow Wilson to carry a statewide race in 1916, the governor had been forced to announce the "error of his ways" and oppose the referendum measures. The voters rejected the referenda and elected a legislature less reactionary than the previous one. Ernest Marsh unhappily now felt obliged to warn that the people could be "fooled and confused" on matters of direct legislation.[41]

The epoch often described as the Progressive Era in the United States was preeminently a time of transition for Washington's reformers. Long-sought measures such as women's suffrage, prohibition, and direct legislation were enacted into law, but as Ernest Marsh and others discovered, the results were sometimes disappointing. Likewise, the growing impotence of the reform coalition inclined the state's labor movement toward the kind of class-conscious action that increasingly typified organized labor in British Columbia.

CHAPTER 13

The Limits of Dissent:

The North Pacific Industrial
Frontier in Transition

British Columbians had been riding a wave of prosperity and growth since the turn of the century. The population of the province more than doubled between 1901 and 1911. The boom became especially noticeable after 1910. The *Vancouver World* could truthfully claim to be Canada's "biggest" newspaper because of the number of pages it contained devoted to real estate advertisements. Observers found it a "dull day" when someone failed to start a sixteen-story building in Vancouver, and Kamloops advertised itself in 1911 as the "Los Angeles" of Canada. Recession, however, began creeping over the Pacific Northwest in 1912, and the next several years were anything but prosperous.

Business failures increased markedly in Vancouver after 1912, and the amount of new construction fell precipitously, eliminating many unions in the building trades. Unskilled and semi-skilled workers suffered even more than the skilled. As mills, mines, and logging camps shut down, unemployment became a major problem in most of the region's larger cities. In Seattle a citizens' committee secured abandoned buildings to provide shelter for five thousand, and farmers living near the city hunted rabbits and sent them to feed the growing number of indigents. The beginning of World War I brought little relief to unemployed Canadians, and soon even British Columbians fortunate enough to have jobs began to receive notices reading, "Your King and Country need you—we can spare you." When Vancouver dropped two thousand persons from the city's relief rolls in early 1915, the unemployed rioted.[1]

Among the casualties of the economic collapse in British Columbia was the single tax. Although the single tax had never amounted to anything more than a precipitant of reform in Washington, Henry George's scheme had come to fruition in pre-World War I Vancouver. For the single taxers, Vancouver had become a "city upon a hill." The single tax was most closely associated in Vancouver with L. D. ("Single Tax") Taylor, a friend of labor and the oft-times mayor of the city.[2]

The *Union Record* claimed that as a result of the single tax more building permits had been issued in 1912 in one suburb of Vancouver than in all of Seattle. Many single-tax advocates were convinced that Vancouver had seized the opportunity Washington had rejected, but the socialists wondered, "If the Single-Taxers claim credit for the building boom, how will they dodge the responsibility for the resultant slump?"[3]

The economic slump that wiped out confidence in the single tax was accompanied by an increase in labor unrest. In Washington, the years between 1912 and 1915 were characterized by a growing number of strikes, lockouts, and Wobbly-led demonstrations. No industrial development, however, was quite as upsetting to trade unionists as the increasing intervention in labor disputes by employers' associations and others supporting the open shop. Beginning in 1915 employers aggressively attacked the recently formed International Timber Workers' Union, and the union's membership fell rapidly as a result. As of 1 February the union was engaged in fifteen different strikes and lockouts in as many towns in Washington; by the end of 1915 the Timber Workers had experienced fifty-five lockouts and had almost been destroyed.

In Everett, lumbermen declared war on the shingle weavers, the backbone of the Timber Workers' Union, by proclaiming an open shop and cutting wages 20 percent. The increasing social tension in the community resulted in the Everett Massacre, in which a mob of armed "citizen deputies" led by the county sheriff clashed with a boatload of Wobblies arriving to participate in the Everett free-speech fight. When the two-minute battle was over, the *Verona* retreated out into the bay; four Wobblies lay dead on its decks, one man was dying, and thirty-one others were wounded. "An unknown number of passengers," Melvyn Dubofsky notes, "had also fallen into the water, their bodies washed away, unknown, unidentified, and unmourned." On shore, two deputies were killed, and another twenty were wounded in the melee.[4]

VIOLENCE ON VANCOUVER ISLAND

Major labor violence in the Vancouver Island coal fields accompanied the growing stature of the United Mine Workers of America (UMW) in the Pacific Northwest. The UMW had been steadily organizing coal miners in Washington since the formation of a small local in Wilkeson in 1901. Although the coal miners lost several of their early strikes, the formation of an employers' association to deal collectively with the UMW paradoxically encouraged some of the state's more recalcitrant operators to recognize the union. The UMW also benefited from operators' fears of the more radical Western Federation of Miners (WFM), which had likewise begun to organize miners in the Cascade coal fields shortly after the turn of the century. The WFM's local at Roslyn was claiming more than four hundred members in 1903. The WFM withdrew from the Washington coal fields two years later, but a radical residue remained in the camps on the eastern slope of the Cascades.

UMW District 10 was thrown into turmoil in 1910 when radicals at Roslyn and Cle Elum supported a young Marxian socialist for district president while the locals on the western side of the mountains supported a more conservative candidate. Although the UMW's efforts to create a joint conference and a common scale for coal miners in Washington, Wyoming, Colorado, and British Columbia foundered on the ideological conflict in the Cascades, District 10 continued to grow until it had more than five thousand members in thirteen locals. In 1913 the *Union Record* began providing an entire page for news of interest to the state's coal miners, who were prospering as a result of a strike by four thousand miners on Vancouver Island.[5]

A gas explosion that killed thirty-two miners at Extension in October 1909 prompted a revival of interest in union organization in the Vancouver Island coal fields. The UMW leadership at first seemed reluctant to become involved in an organizational drive on the island because of the miners' discouraging history of defeat, but when determined miners at Ladysmith formed the first local in the Canadian Federation of Miners they helped force the UMW to act. District 28 was built on the foundation of the Canadian Federation of Miners and the struggling UMW locals on Vancouver Island. In 1912 the two UMW districts in British Columbia affiliated with the provincial Federation of Labor, which now represented virtually all labor organizations except the IWW and the railway brotherhoods.[6]

The Vancouver Island coal strike which began in September 1912 lasted for two years, was Canada's most expensive strike up to that time, and was the first major labor dispute in British Columbia in almost nine years. Workers at the Ladysmith, Extension, and Cumberland mines, recently sold by the Dunsmuir interests to railway promoters Mackenzie and Mann, charged that they were being forced to purchase blasting powder from the company at a high price, that their wages were too low, and that union members suffered discrimination. The company retaliated against the strikers with a lockout and then reopened the mines, using Chinese and imported strikebreakers from as far away as Britain. Violence directed against the scabs led the government to send a contingent of special provincial police to Cumberland to protect the strikebreakers. Despite attempts by the British Columbia Federation of Labor to encourage the provincial government to settle the dispute, Premier McBride refused to intervene.[7]

Rather than surrender, the UMW expanded the strike to include all of District 28. In mid-August 1913, after provocation from the strikebreakers and the company, strikers rioted and burned mine buildings at Extension. The increasing violence, accompanied by management's claim that the strike was a plot inspired by the Industrial Workers of the World (IWW), led Attorney General William Bowser to send several hundred militiamen to the island coal fields. In the words of Paul Phillips, "The government, loath to act as long as only the miners' livelihood was threatened, moved quickly as soon as the company's property was endangered." Earlier the special police had irritated the strikers; now the militia solidified the ranks of the workers by arresting 256 men, including the president of the Ladysmith UMW local, the vice-president of District 28, and John Place, a Socialist recently elected to the legislative assembly. Most of the defendants were given harsh prison sentences, but twenty-two of them were pardoned, and none ever served his full term. The formation of a Miners' Liberation League to defend the miners on trial and to urge the release of those jailed brought together representatives from the British Columbia Federation of Labor, the Trades and Labor councils in Victoria and Vancouver, the UMW, the IWW, the Socialist Party of Canada, and the Social Democratic party and further increased the possibility of real class conflict in the province.[8]

Interest in a general strike began growing in the British Columbia labor movement in late 1912, but when delegates from the Cumberland UMW local proposed this at the annual convention of the provincial Federation of Labor, the gathering rejected the idea largely because of the depressed state of the economy. After this first serious consideration of the general strike, the Miners' Liberation League advocated using such a weapon to force the release of the imprisoned miners; and in 1914, when the British Columbia Federation of Labor referred a proposal for a general strike to its members, they approved it by a five-to-two margin. Nothing, however, was done to implement the resolution because only a few unions responded and because the influential Trades and Labor Council in Vancouver tabled the proposal as impractical.[9]

Mother Jones, a prominent and popular figure among the coal miners of the United States, arrived in British Columbia in June 1914 to agitate for the strikers, but the depression and the ongoing expenses of the strike so drained the UMW treasury that the union soon agreed to settle the strike in accordance with terms proposed by Premier McBride. The demand for union recognition was abandoned, but miners won the right to belong to a union. Employers, however, soon reneged on the agreement, and blacklisting and discrimination were the net result of the two-year struggle for many workers. In the minds of many workers, however, the idea of a general strike had only been tabled for the duration of the war, not abandoned.[10]

Premier McBride had been inclined to see the miners' strike as the work of a disorderly proleteriat, and he had in his possession a copy of a Nanaimo paper which argued that Canadian coal miners were suffering so that miners in Washington might prosper. Certainly, miners south of the 49th parallel benefited from the strike, but Washington miners had threatened to stage a sympathy strike to support their Canadian brothers. Anti-Americanism once again served as a potent weapon in a Canadian labor dispute. Ironically, however, a royal commission later reported that the large corporations, which refused to bargain collectively with international labor unions, were themselves controlled by aliens.[11]

The coal strike led to an increase of unemployment on Vancouver Island. In a confidential memo to Premier McBride, the provincial secretary estimated that there were almost five hundred unemployed men at Ladysmith, two hundred at South Wellington, and a thousand at Nanaimo. In the fall of 1914 a number of families were living in tents near Nanaimo. When the rains came, leaks soaked the bedding, and children went without shoes during the winter months. McBride received scores of letters from the estimated 12,500 unemployed workers in the province. Some writers included pictures of their families and, as Christmas approached, begged the premier to help them support their wives and children. A small piece of meat, a few beans, a loaf of bread, and a piece of cheese were sometimes provided from the soldiers' barracks on Vancouver Island to help sustain starving families. There was even some talk of sending British Columbia's unemployed workers to help with the harvest in Saskatchewan, but officials there advised that miners and lumberjacks without farm experience were not needed.[12]

Workers in the Pacific Northwest fortunate enough to have jobs found wages rising much more slowly than the spiraling cost of living. The cost of living in Canada had risen steadily between 1900 and 1914, but prices leaped upward more rapidly than ever before in 1915 and 1916. Prices far outdistanced wages in Washington also, although the war improved economic conditions for American workers after 1917 by stimulating the economy and decreasing immigration.[13]

"ROTTEN RIPE FOR CONSTRUCTIVE SOCIALISM"

When popular reform cleric Mark Matthews urged the unemployed in Seattle to join the army in 1915, the *Union Record* wondered how a Christian could reconcile advice to join the army, "a machine for killing men," with the teachings of the "gentle Galilean." Organized labor's vociferous opposition to war and conscription, the alarming cycle of depression and inflation, and anti-labor brutality in Colorado and the Michigan copper country as well as the Vancouver Island coal strike and Everett Massacre heightened the class consciousness of workers in the Pacific Northwest.

Within the local movement, class consciousness was also being encouraged by three significant developments: growing interest in industrial unionism, the socialists' acquisition of power in the councils of organized labor and in its publications, and the increasing isolation of trade unionists in Washington from the middle class as a result of the collapse of the reform coalition in the state. Possibly only the involvement in a European war and the resulting upsurge in patriotism helped reduce class consciousness enough to prevent class war in certain parts of the Pacific Northwest.[14]

Differing in background from most eastern trade unionists and confronting a uniquely structured labor market, a number of labor leaders in the Pacific Northwest had distinguished themselves as staunch advocates of industrial unionism. At the American Federation of Labor's (AFL) annual conventions, trade unionists from the Pacific Northwest could usually be counted on to support the industrial-union resolutions that were regularly introduced between 1901 and World War I.[15]

Some trade unionists in the Pacific Northwest had been proclaiming for years that industrial unionism was the "logical and next evolutionary stage" to be attained by organized labor, and beginning in 1910 they won more support for their idea than ever before. The British Columbia Federation of Labor endorsed industrial unionism at its first convention in 1910, and the Dominion Trades and Labor Congress (TLC) convention in Calgary the following year described craft unions as "inadequate" and endorsed industrial unionism by a vote of 70 to 52. The TLC soon retreated from its strong condemnation of craft unions, but sentiment favoring industrial unionism remained strong in the congress. The Vancouver Trades and Labor Council by a unanimous vote in August 1912 became the first city central in Canada to endorse industrial unionism. It then sent its views on the subject to over five hundred labor organizations in the United States and Canada. As a result of this action, the IWW regarded the Vancouver Council as the "most revolutionary body" in the entire AFL. By the summer of 1913 industrial unionism had been endorsed by central bodies in Victoria, Seattle, Spokane, and Aberdeen, and by the Washington State Federation of Labor at its annual convention.[16]

Support for industrial unionism was only one of several points of contention between the conservative leadership of the AFL and the trade unionists in the Pacific Northwest. Shortly after Premier McBride, in 1912, admonished the provincial Federation of Labor to "never forget there is such a thing as moderation," the federation defiantly endorsed socialism by a referendum vote of 1,488 to 289. Central labor councils in Victoria and Vancouver also declared in favor of socialism. At the 1914 annual convention of the Washington State Federation of Labor, delegates voted to support "the collective ownership and democratic management of all the means of production and distribution." The *B. C. Federationist*, with Pettipiece as managing editor, began running a page for socialists in 1911 and soon gave its official support to the movement.[17]

In Washington, several former associates of Dr. Hermon Titus acquired power in the local labor movement. E. B. Ault, who as editor of the *Young Socialist* in 1902 had endorsed the American Labor Union (ALU) because it had "no ties of tradition and fealty to leaders to bind it to the past," became secretary of the Seattle Central Labor Council in 1912 and editor of the *Union Record* a short time later. Having modified his youthful radicalism into an advocacy of labor solidarity within the AFL, Ault converted the *Union Record* into a daily and pushed subscriptions to twenty-five thousand. Hulet Wells, who had once crusaded for "free speech" in Seattle with Titus, was elected president of the Central Labor Council in 1915. Serving for one year, Wells noted that he was the "radical" president of a body that during his term in office "always had a conservative majority."[18]

Gompers had been at odds with the socialist minority within the AFL for many years. Several delegates from the Pacific Northwest and two unions with strong regional ties, the WFM[19] and the Shingle Weavers, joined with other dissidents at the 1912 AFL convention to support the socialist Max Hayes, who was contesting the AFL presidency with Gompers.

In 1915, E. B. Ault characterized the insults traded by Gompers and the socialists as "simply silly." Praising both Gompers and the socialists for their good work in behalf of labor, Ault noted that it was time for organized workers to refuse to allow political antagonisms to divide them on industrial matters. Such solidarity was at that time being fostered within the Pacific Northwest labor movement by the self-destructive tendencies of the local socialist parties.[20]

The Socialist Party of America had benefited from the popular interest in Progressivism. Voters in a number of cities elected Socialist governments, and Victor Berger, as we have seen, became the first Socialist congressman. By 1912 voters who had once considered socialism a form of heresy were apparently embracing it at the polls. Eugene Debs received a record 6 percent of the popular vote in the 1912 presidential election, and hundreds of Socialists were elected to state and local offices. Debs, however, had warned in 1911 that "voting for socialism is not socialism any more than a menu is a meal." The impressive Socialist vote, as a matter of fact, was a poor indicator of the health of the Socialist party.[21]

In 1912, the voters of Mason County, Washington, situated in the heart of the region controlled by the large timber interests, elected the first Socialist ever sent to the Washington state legislature. Representative William H. Kingery, who attended Stanford in the early 1900s but quit when a professor was dismissed for advocating government ownership of railroads, distinguished himself in the 1913 session by supporting labor legislation. The Socialist party leadership in Washington, however, had nothing to do with him because he was a farmer. Revolutionary theoreticians, who loathed the Progressive party because it attempted to reform the existing system, severely criticized Kingery for supporting a Progressive for speaker of the house. "They contended that I should have nominated and voted for myself, I being the only socialist," Kingery remarked.

Kingery, whose socialist enemies identified him with the party's "yellow" or reform faction, generally worked with the Progressives because they supported every reform measure "that had developed public sentiment enough to give it any semblance of a chance to pass." In contrast to his counterparts in the British Columbia legislative assembly, Kingery also sought to make the Socialist party's first appearance in the state legislature "respectable." Washington, said Kingery, was "rotten ripe for constructive socialism." As he realized only too well, factionalism was continuing to debilitate the local socialist movement.[22]

After Titus quit the party in 1909, the Socialists had for a time appeared determined to accommodate themselves to reality. The party had not only chastised comrades in the rest of the country for failing to regard Chinese labor as a threat to the proletarians in the Pacific Northwest but also had contested local elections on reform platforms. Judge Richard Winsor, a fusionist officeholder once described as the "Father of Populism" in Seattle, was elected in 1911 to be the first Socialist director of that city's public schools. A Mills partisan in the 1907 battle with Titus, Winsor had been appointed by John R. Rogers to be a regent of the University of Washington. Believing that public schools existed solely to perpetuate capitalism and that teachers were victims of the system, socialists began a statewide campaign in 1912 to "capture" the schools for socialism by electing school boards that would appoint socialist teachers. The Socialist candidates for the school board in Tacoma in 1913 demanded the establishment of kindergartens, the landscaping of school grounds, ample playgrounds, baths and a gymnasium, the teaching of sex hygiene, and teacher organizations.[23]

Socialists elected a mayor and treasurer in Edmonds in late 1910 and the following year captured three seats on the Tacoma city council. In the Seattle municipal election of 1911, the Socialist message supposedly reached more voters than ever before, although the *Union Record* wondered why the Socialists received only 9 percent of the vote when over 90 percent of the population was composed of workers. Hulet Wells ran for mayor of Seattle in 1912 but lost to labor reformer George Cotterill, whom Wells characterized as close enough to the Socialists to "steal their thunder." Although the Socialists captured the entire Pasco municipal ticket in 1913 and began publishing their own paper, they soon realized the validity of Debs's observation regarding the growing Socialist vote. When Pasco's Socialist mayor resigned a year later and moved to Rossland to enter the cigar business, Pasco's fling with municipal socialism came to an inglorious end.[24]

The reform socialists were particularly strong in Spokane, where H. L. Hughes and David C. Coates continued to lead the local movement. Coates's tenure as commissioner of public works elicited praise from Samuel Gompers, but his participation in Spokane's first nonpartisan election engendered the first major party split since the 1909 schism. Coates's election on an alleged "fusion" ticket caused party leaders to demand his resignation. When he refused to do so, the Spokane local sustained him, but Coates and his local were read out of the party in 1912 by a convention vote of 128 to 58. After that, he lost interest in the party but not in reform socialism itself.[25]

The socialist movement in Seattle as of 1912 was badly split between the "yellows" and the "reds." The "reds" demanded immediate revolution, but, as Harvey O'Connor has noted, it would be a mistake to conclude that they were actually ready for revolution. Most of them were solid burghers, with rose gardens around their homes and a stake in the community. Indeed, the issue of middle-class morality caused a major split in the Seattle movement when two prominent comrades were discovered living together unmarried. The factionalism that continued after the departure of Titus culminated in Tacoma in the spring of 1913 when the "yellows" or reputable socialists, led by Joseph Gilbert, organized a new Socialist party to appeal to the Progressives and other reformers. Denouncing the "iww faction" supposedly led by George Boomer, the seceders claimed to have more than one-third of the six thousand Socialist members in Washington.[26]

The Socialist party's National Executive Committee was once again called in to investigate the charges and countercharges being hurled by the comrades in Washington. The seceders claimed that the local party leadership had degenerated into a "powerful machine" composed of "anarchists, direct actionists, impossibilists, inebriates, down-and-outers, free lovers and worse." They had allegedly ridiculed preachers, religion, and morality, and driven doctors, lawyers, and businessmen out of the party. The party leadership, on the other hand, charged that the seceders were a remnant of Populism. Both sides agreed, however, that the schism resulted from the continuing influence of the philosophy once espoused by Titus. The regular Socialists claimed to have triumphed over the seceders by mid-1914, but the internecine struggle actually continued until the government began to suppress radicals during World War I.[27]

Perhaps the only beneficiaries of the interminable squabbling that the *Union Record* described as the party's "second childhood" were the local socialist journalists. So many factional papers appeared that one Seattle entrepreneur maintained a "Red News Wagon" stocked with the latest radical publications. The *Red Feather* described itself as a "corrective iconoclast, a sarcastic pragmatist," and the *Truth* of Tacoma claimed to be "so red that it sizzles." After the demise of Titus' *Socialist*, the Everett-based party began publishing the *Commonwealth*. Maynard Shipley, a student at Stanford during the furor over government ownership of railroads and the editor of the *Commonwealth* beginning in 1913, took the bold step of refusing to print any items concerning party squabbles. Unlike most other socialist editors in the state, Shipley did not believe that people were converted to socialism by the continual airing of party difficulties. Shipley's action, however, failed to prevent party disaster in the election of 1916. After polling more than forty thousand votes in Washington in 1912, the party received less than twenty-three thousand votes four years later. The number of Socialists elected to public office also declined markedly.[28]

Socialist developments in British Columbia closely paralleled those in Washington. No one could deny that the Socialist Party of Canada had made hundreds of committed rebels; neither could one ignore the fact that the party, isolated in British Columbia, was dying. Growing ideological friction caused militants in the Nanaimo local to expel James Hawthornthwaite in 1911 as an "enemy to the revolutionary working class." Although the party's provincial executive sustained Hawthornthwaite and revoked the charter of the Nanaimo local, Hawthornthwaite chose not to contest the 1912 provincial election. Only a few months before he resigned his seat in the legislative assembly, Hawthornthwaite had emerged briefly as the first Socialist in the British Empire to lead His Majesty's Loyal Opposition.[29]

By 1912 the Socialist Party of Canada was suffering not only as a result of internal ideological tension and its alienation from the bulk of organized labor but also from the scorn heaped on the party by a onetime ally, Premier McBride. During the provincial election campaign McBride characterized socialists as men with "strenuous voices, shouting about wage slavery and the labour market, and similar rubbish. This narrow-minded class should not exist in British Columbia, where the man with the pick and shovel to-day may own a saw-mill or mine to-morrow." McBride refused to debate with Socialists in Greenwood because he did not wish to hear himself denounced as a "slave of capital." Parker Williams was returned to the legislative assembly by miners in the Ladysmith area and "radical" John Place was elected as a Social Democrat in Hawthornthwaite's old Nanaimo constituency, but elsewhere the 1912 election results demonstrated to many Socialists that "unless lots of pick and shovel work is done from now on, we will not be a factor" in the next election.[30]

After McBride and the Conservatives swept the 1912 election, the *Saturday Sunset* noted that "Mr. Williams and his colleague, Mr. Place, are to be envied. In all British Columbia they are the only two who have an opportunity, even though it be rare, to stand up and tell the government what they think about it." They were also praised as the only members of the legislative assembly who did not "truckle to the whim of the autocratic rulers of British Columbia." As Parker Williams lamented, however, "no one realizes better than I do the farcical nature of this opposition. No two men, be they ever so able, could form an efficient opposition. It is a physical impossibility."

Convinced that the Socialists were keeping the Conservatives in power in British Columbia by dividing the opposition, Williams supported a Liberal candidate in a Vancouver by-election in February 1916. The Socialists subsequently expelled him, and the *B. C. Federationist* denounced Williams as a "wanderer in the wilderness of old party politics" who had "lost his bearings" the day that James Hawthornthwaite left the legislative assembly. Williams successfully contested the 1916 provincial election in his old constituency by running as a Liberal who remained a socialist at heart, but a few months later he resigned his seat and was appointed to the workmen's compensation board by the new Liberal government.[31]

NEW DIRECTIONS: 1917 AND AFTER

The North Pacific industrial frontier essentially lasted from 1885 to 1917. By 1917, such cities as Seattle and Vancouver could no longer be regarded primarily as regional entrepôts. The draft, enacted in both the United States and Canada in 1917, symbolized as perhaps nothing else the changes overtaking the region. Coal miners and loggers from the remotest parts of Vancouver Island and the Olympic Peninsula were sent to fight in the trenches alongside pipefitters and carpenters from New York City and Toronto. With the stroke of a pen, desk-bound bureaucrats in wartime Washington, D.C.; and Ottawa were dramatically changing the everyday lives of virtually every citizen of the Pacific Northwest.

Especially for the radicals of the Pacific Northwest, 1917 was the end of one era and the beginning of another. British Columbia's socialists, for example, finally began to realize their need to work constructively with labor leaders. The withering of the two socialist parties in the province, neither of which elected any members to the legislative assembly in 1916, and the class consciousness engendered by the great coal strike on Vancouver Island encouraged such a step.

After several false starts, British Columbians created the Federated Labor party in early 1918. Highly representative of the provincial labor movement, the new party was supported by a number of AFL craft unionists as well as by old-line socialists such as Pettipiece and Hawthornthwaite. E. T. Kingsley, who presided over the party's Vancouver branch, was determined to keep the new organization from straying too far down the path to bourgeois reformism. Trade unionists, to be sure, had triumphed in the formation of the Federated Labor party, but its platform was essentially socialistic. A list of labor planks in the platform was capped by a demand for the collective ownership and democratic operation of the means of production. The British Columbia labor movement thus approached the end of World War I more highly united than ever.[32]

The socialist movement in Washington, likewise, left the age of innocence behind in 1917. Soon, the most committed revolutionaries would be the Communists with their slavish adherence to a party line laid down in Moscow. Reform socialists generally abandoned what was left of the old Socialist party. In the mid-1920s, "Doc" Brown was twice elected mayor of Seattle on a nonpartisan ticket. The flamboyant Brown later became a perennial office seeker on the Democratic ticket. Hulet Wells became an aide to Democratic congressman Marion Zioncheck in the mid-1930s.

E. B. Ault, too, drifted into Democratic politics. A few of the members of Washington's Socialist party joined their old adversaries, the Socialist Laborites.[33]

Like the local socialists, organized labor in Washington entered a new and unpredictable era in 1917. The amazing resurgence of the IWW in the timber industry would so threaten the nation's war effort that the federal government was forced to step in and help the timber workers secure the basic amenities of life for which the IWW had so long fought. Radicalism was also growing in several of the state's central labor councils.[34]

For several years, organized labor in Washington had tied its political hopes to the continued viability of the bourgeois reform coalition, but that too began to change in 1917. A noticeable swing in public mood had become evident several years earlier. Direct legislation signatures were far more difficult to obtain in 1916 than they had been two years before. As the middle class at least temporarily lost interest in reform, it became easy to characterize the state's remaining reformers as "boat rockers." During the period of depression that preceded American entry into World War I business antagonism to organized labor increased, and the IWW bogey was used to discredit the entire labor movement. Criminal syndicalism laws were enacted in the Pacific Northwest in early 1917 that made it illegal to advocate crime, sabotage, and violent methods of terrorism as a means of accomplishing industrial or political reform.[35]

As a result of the strains that were placed upon it, Washington's influential farmer-labor coalition unraveled on the eve of World War I. The intrusion of the liquor issue in the election of 1914 had seriously weakened the coalition. Although he realized that prohibition appealed to farmers living in eastern Washington, Ernest P. Marsh agonizingly decided on economic grounds to commit the State Federation of Labor against the reform. C. B. Kegley appeared before the 1915 convention of the Washington State Federation of Labor to dispel rumors that the alliance of producers was falling apart, but statistics demonstrated that the farmers were losing interest in helping workers obtain reforms by direct legislation.[36]

When Kegley died in 1917, he was succeeded as leader of the

Grange by an enthusiastic supporter of the Non-Partisan League, a socialist-like movement that had originated among the farmers of North Dakota in 1915. The Grange joined with organized labor in Washington to oppose American entry into World War I, but a growing number of farmers drew away from their erstwhile trade-union allies as labor on Puget Sound became caught up in the revolutionary excitement that began with the overthrow of the Czar of Russia in early 1917. The Joint Legislative Committee maintained a nominal existence until 1919, and after the war a new Farmer-Labor party appeared, but events during the war destroyed the farmer-labor coalition as an effective pressure group by alienating the moderate and conservative farmers from the growing body of class-conscious workers.[37]

The war had a disastrous impact on the lives of many of Washington's radicals. Reform was equated with subversion, and opponents of war such as Hulet Wells and Emil Herman went to prison during the war years. Herman, the German-born secretary of the Socialist party in Washington, was arrested because some "disloyal" books were discovered in his office, and he was sentenced to ten years in federal prison for violating the Espionage Act.[38]

In early 1918 the federal government of Canada launched a similar crackdown on radicalism in the Dominion. A number of suspected radical organizations were banned, and a Dominion police officer threatened to arrest the editor of the *B. C. Federationist* because the journal's alleged policy of "glorifying" the Bolshevik objectives in Russia supposedly tended to "justify" a similar movement in Canada.[39]

Government suppression, employer hostility, and the rising cost of living brought a new mood of militancy to the Pacific Northwest labor movement. Products of different historical and political environments yet sharing a common radical heritage, organized labor in both Washington and British Columbia displayed a growing class consciousness that after World War I burst forth in the form of unprecedented strikes and bold new opposition to the conservative leadership of the AFL. But manifestations of radicalism, so long tolerated as a feature of life on the relatively isolated North Pacific industrial frontier, seemed unacceptably menacing in an unstable world frightened by the crumbling of ancient empires and creeds and convinced of the reality of an international Bolshevist conspiracy. Ironically, though the strikes were broken and the radical movement decimated, the radical heritage endured. Down through the years that heritage has been manifested time and time again in subtle and not so subtle ways.[40]

CHAPTER *14*

Radical Heritage in Perspective

Endless prairie plains and the backbone of a continent separated workers in the Pacific Northwest from their brothers in Cincinnati, Toronto, Hamilton, or Boston; by contrast, the international boundary separating Washington and British Columbia seemed almost invisible. Whether they were hardrock miners or lumberjacks, stevedores or stationary engineers, workers on both sides of the 49th parallel shared common job-related concerns that transcended local differences in matters of history, culture, and government.

The evolution of the labor movement in the Pacific Northwest did not differ notably from that in other parts of the United States until the 1890s. Artisans in Victoria and Seattle formed trade unions for the same reasons as artisans in Pittsburgh and Peoria—to raise wages, improve working conditions, and protect their jobs. The presence of the Knights of Labor in the Pacific Northwest in the 1880s was not exceptional, aside from the Knights' involvement in the race riots that shook Tacoma and Seattle. In the 1890s, however, the declining influence of the Knights, the isolation of the region from the main centers of America Federation of Labor (AFL) activity, and the unique problems posed by the structure of the local labor market, with its emphasis on unskilled and semi-skilled labor in large-scale extractive industries, caused workers in the Pacific Northwest to develop a variety of responses to industrialism that were different from those adopted by workers in other parts of the United States and Canada. Although craft unions represented a realistic response to local industrial conditions for workers in some parts of the Pacific Northwest, the reformist ideas espoused by the Knights of Labor continued to appeal to a significant portion of the labor movement in Spokane and its tributary areas for the same reason. The advent of the AFL in Washington and British Columbia after the turn of the century encouraged local trade union leaders to define the character and purpose of organized labor in a narrow fashion, but largely as a result of the lingering influence of the Knights in Spokane, the growing prominence of the Western Federation of Miners (WFM) in the Northern Rockies, and the radicalization of the Dunsmuir miners on Vancouver Island, industrial unionism, dual unionism, and political radicalism became the hallmarks of the Pacific Northwest labor movement prior to World War I.

Lacking direct guidance from the leadership of the AFL until the early twentieth century, trade unionists in the Pacific Northwest pragmatically forged the local patterns of labor's political involvement. As a comparison of developments in Washington and British Columbia indicates, labor was far more likely to reflect national differences in matters of history, governmental institutions, and popular ideology in its political role than in its structure. Participation in the Populist movement had convinced trade unionists in Washington that a community of interests existed between the state's farmers and workers. Aided by a lack of class consciousness and by the political circumstances that gave lobbies a powerful influence in the state legislature, Washington's labor leaders perfected the tools of pressure politics. Labor leaders in British Columbia, on the other hand, were inclined to independent political action by such factors as class consciousness, the parliamentary system of government, and the lack of recognized party lines in the legislative assembly. The growing presence of the AFL in the Pacific Northwest after the turn of the century did not materially alter the patterns of political involvement adopted by organized labor in Washington and British Columbia during the 1890s.

At a time when the ills of modern industrial society were becoming apparent in some parts of the Western world, the Pacific Northwest remained a region still largely unscarred by the industrial revolution. The tremendous natural abundance of the land and sea and the almost profligate beauty of scenery that first attracted a mass of settlers to Washington in the 1880s seemed especially to draw those people who dreamed of implementing the social reform schemes then gaining widespread attention. Living in a society characterized by impatience with the present and optimism about the future, and with only the most rudimentary strictures of tradition to inhibit them, reformers dotted the shores of Puget Sound with their cooperative colonies while others gained a respectful hearing for their ideas in the legislative chambers of Olympia. For many of the same reasons, reformers were also drawn to British Columbia in the late nineteenth century.

One of the many "isms" attracting a following in the Pacific Northwest was socialism. Aspects of the socialist dream of a more humane society appealed to farmers and workers alike, but when the local socialists formed political parties to institutionalize their proposals for social and economic change, ideological conflicts inevitably followed. These factional disputes helped vitiate the socialist movement in the Pacific Northwest during the years preceding World War I. By claiming to represent the political arm of organized labor, the political socialists also provoked numerous conflicts among trade unionists. It would be a mistake, however, to conclude that socialism was at best an endless tale of schism and at worst an instrument to divide the working-class vote. The general campaign of reform education conducted by the socialists helped to win for the working classes of the Pacific Northwest far more benefits than could have been obtained at that time through collective bargaining alone.

"If Socialism did no more than arouse public attention to the evils and excrescences of the present social system," the *Week* observed, "it would have justified its existence. . . ." Keir Hardie noted in 1912 that "the fear of Socialism is the beginning of social reform." Many a progressive legislative measure was no doubt enacted in Washington and British Columbia to lessen the socialist appeal. Socialists also served to goad their trade union allies into greater political involvement to secure social and economic reforms of benefit to the working class.[1]

Beatrice Webb once noted that in America a reform was proposed and accepted, yielded a crop of extravagant hopes and fears, and then was forgotten long before it had taken practical shape. In Washington, however, the ongoing combined efforts of farmers and workers in the quarter century before World War I resulted in a remarkable amount of practical reform legislation. Washington's lawmakers had often seemed willing enough to provide basic protection for women and children, just as for sea gulls and honeybees, but even minimal protection for adult male workers would not have been enacted in that era of laissez faire without a long, arduous educational campaign. Although the political methods used by organized labor and its reform allies differed in Washington and British Columbia, the net result was the beginning of a more secure and abundant life for the working class of the Pacific Northwest. That was probably the most significant and enduring aspect of the region's radical heritage.[2]

The study of the development of the labor movement in the Pacific Northwest prior to World War I provides a comparative framework that helps to explain the lack of a viable labor or socialist party in the United States. Why, it may be asked, should the socialist movement in Washington have died a lingering death after World War I while the socialists in British Columbia joined with trade unionists and other reformers to establish a successful labor-socialist-reform party?

It would be tempting to blame the failure of socialism in Washington on the theoretical eccentricities of Hermon Titus and his revolutionary socialist allies, but the revolutionary theoreticians were no less prominent in the early socialist movement in British Columbia, and there the movement survived after World War I. Similarly, the course of trade unionism in Washington and British Columbia does not account for the markedly different fates awaiting socialism in the two areas in the 1920s and 1930s.

Trade union developments in British Columbia following World War I did not differ appreciably from those in Washington. General strikes in Seattle and Winnipeg and sympathy strikes in British Columbia in 1919 not only heightened labor's sense of solidarity but also evoked an anti-labor reaction and strengthened the "open shop" movement in the United States and Canada. The economic slump that crippled the Pacific Northwest in the early 1920s was accompanied by widespread unemployment and a general atrophy of the labor movement. Labor's lean years culminated in the Great Depression, which, ironically, provided the circumstances leading to a renewal of organizational activity and a remarkable increase in the number of unionized workers in Washington and British Columbia.[3]

Politically, however, organized labor in Washington and British Columbia continued to diverge along the paths established during the formative decade of the 1890s. Continuing to favor pressure politics, the AFL, the CIO, and the railway brotherhoods in Washington formed a "joint labor lobby" in Olympia in the 1930s that John Gunther called "the only one of its kind in America." Labor has remained one of the most important pressure groups in the state and has obtained many of the reform measures advocated by the labor-socialist-reform party in British Columbia.[4]

The labor movement in British Columbia in the 1920s and 1930s pursued the partisan political activity that it had first used haltingly in the 1880s and 1890s. Organized labor's several forays into provincial politics in the 1920s proved disappointing, but the formation of the Cooperative Commonwealth Federation (CCF) in 1932, a confederation of labor and socialist organizations, helped encourage labor's continued interest in partisan politics. Even though an important segment of the labor movement in British Columbia did not at first endorse the CCF, the labor movement by the 1950s had become the primary supporter of the CCF in the province. When the CCF reorganized as the New Democratic party (NDP) in 1961, labor organizations affiliated directly with the party, and the NDP emerged as the political arm of the Canadian labor movement.[5]

The amazing growth of the CCF and NDP in British Columbia not only indicates that socialists in North America could modify their revolutionary ideology to accommodate reality but also raises a question about the alleged power of the early AFL leadership to check the growth of socialist and labor parties in areas of AFL influence. Gompers' opinion of socialism was well known by the turn of the century, but he could not prevent socialists from attaining positions of strength in certain of the affiliated national unions. Furthermore, despite socialist claims to the contrary, it is unlikely that a mere change of national leadership in the AFL would have convinced rank-and-file workers to support socialist candidates. As developments in the WFM-dominated hardrock mining districts of British Columbia demonstrated, socialist leadership in a trade union was no guarantee of socialist political success. On the other hand, the conservative national leadership of the AFL could not have prevented the growth of support for socialism among rank-and-file workers if conditions had been favorable. Local circumstances and not AFL leadership were the primary determinants of whether or not organized labor supported socialist candidates in Washington and British Columbia.[6]

Harold Winch, a pioneer member of the CCF in British Columbia and leader of the CCF opposition in the legislative assembly beginning in 1941, campaigned for socialism in both Washington and British Columbia in the 1930s, but when asked to account for the success of the movement in British Columbia and its failure in Washington, he observed, "I haven't the foggiest notion." Perhaps it frustrated a dedicated socialist like Winch to realize that intangibles such as class consciousness and the political culture of a locale were far more important determinants of the success or failure of the socialist movement than matters of leadership or trade union structure.[7]

Very simply, bourgeois American society in the late nineteenth century venerated individualism and took a dim view of collectivist schemes such as socialism. Many Canadians did too, but Canadian society in general was more open-minded on the subject. The *Colonist*, for example, declared in 1906 that the basic tenets of socialism were "very beautiful" because they abolished individualism. Lacking the ideology of individualism so pervasive in the United States, Canadians had little reason to regard socialism as "un-Canadian." It thus remained possible for Canadians to discuss socialism freely without arousing the "all-silencing cry of treason."

R. Parm Pettipiece noticed how the American attitude toward socialism permeated the AFL. Pettipiece, who was sent to represent the Dominion's Labor Congress at the 1910 convention of the AFL, reported back to the Canadian congress, "I found that my political affiliation had preceded me and it was difficult to start a thaw." In time, however, he remarked, the delegates came to realize "it was no crime to the trade unions of America to belong to the International Socialist Party."

Furthermore, socialists entering the political arena were confronted by the fact that governmental structures in Washington and British Columbia were fundamentally different. To have attained real political power, socialists in Washington would have had to capture the governorship. But a statewide race unquestionably entailed doctrinal compromise if not outright fusion.

Realizing that to be politically successful the party had to develop a popular appeal, Washington's reform socialists had struggled to fashion a program of social and economic amelioration that also accepted many of the tenets of individualism. The resulting ideological battles sapped the movement of its political vitality at the same time as the two major parties co-opted many of the Socialist party's more moderate reform demands.

Even if Washington socialists had been able to capture the legislative and executive branches and enact a radical program into law, they still faced a probable judicial challenge. Thus lacking the access to power and the ideological legitimacy of its British Columbia counterpart, and with its political program in a shambles, the Socialist party in Washington had by World War I lost its *raison d'être*.

By contrast, the NDP eventually emerged as one of the two major parties in British Columbia. The NDP and its free enterprise counterpart, the Social Credit party, virtually eliminated all other parties in the 1975 provincial election.[8]

Reflecting on an outburst of radicalism in Washington in the mid-1930s, Postmaster General James Farley is supposed to have offered a toast to the forty-seven states and the "Soviet of Washington." More recently, in December 1977, *Time* portrayed Washington as a kind of unspoiled utopia lacking much of the urban blight, street crime, racial trouble, and chronic unemployment that so worries citizens in other parts of America. Contemporaneously, the *Atlantic Monthly* referred to British Columbia as a province of "bizarre social and political contrasts. A bastion of British colonial tradition, it is also a haven for various counter culture groups." Washington and British Columbia are still portrayed as the last utopia because an earlier generation of settlers, variously described as visionaries and eccentrics, reformers and rebels, realized that utopia was less a geographic location than a result of an ongoing quest for a loving, concerned human society.[9]

Notes

Notes have generally been collected at the end of a paragraph or passage. Volume numbers are included in citations only in the case of professional journals and multivolume books and reports. In some instances, the reader seeking more extensive bibliographical information should consult Carlos A. Schwantes, "Left-Wing Unionism in the Pacific Northwest: A Comparative History of Organized Labor and Socialist Politics in Washington and British Columbia, 1885–1917" (Ph.D. dissertation, University of Michigan, 1976).

PREFACE

1. Irving Bernstein, "Trade Union Characteristics, Membership, and Influence [in California, Oregon, and Washington], 1849–1959," *Monthly Labor Review*, May 1959, pp. 530–35; James Robert Shields, "The Significance of the Relationships between the International Unions and their Canadian Affiliates" (M.A. thesis, University of Washington, 1954), pp. 12, 28.

2. Allan Fotheringham, "A Socialist in the Land of Plenty," *Maclean's*, June 1973, p. 32.

3. Ibid., p. 70. Barrett was defeated along with the New Democratic party in the December 1975 provincial election, but he described the loss as "a temporary setback." As Barrett noted, "The war for a more mature, loving, human society goes on." *Vancouver Sun*, 12 December 1975, p. 1; *Victoria Times*, 12 December 1975, p. 1.

4. David Potter, *People of Plenty: Economic Abundance and the American Character* (Chicago: University of Chicago Press, Phoenix Books, 1964); David Potter, "A Commentary," in S. F. Wise and Robert Craig Brown, *Canada Views the United States: Nineteenth-Century Political Attitudes* (Seattle: University of Washington Press, 1967), pp. 126, 127.

Notes

CHAPTER 1

1. Robert R. Martin, "The Inland Empire of the Pacific Northwest: A Regional Study" (Ph.D. dissertation, University of Washington, 1935); Ruth K. Wood, *The Tourist's Northwest* (New York: Dodd, Mead & Company, 1916), p. 255.

2. Robert F. Harrington, "The Kootenay Area of British Columbia," *Canadian Geographical Journal* 63 (December 1961): 200. See also, John Fahey, *Inland Empire: D. C. Corbin and Spokane* (Seattle: University of Washington Press, 1965); Donald W. Meinig, *The Great Columbia Plain: A Historical Geography* (Seattle: University of Washington Press, 1968).

3. Stephen Jones, "The Cordilleran Section of the Canada-United States Borderland," *Geographical Journal* 89 (June 1937): 439; Griffith Taylor, "British Columbia, a Study in Topographic Control," *Geographical Review* 32 (July 1942): 372-402; Margaret Ormsby, "Agricultural Development in British Columbia," *Agricultural History* 19 (January 1945): 11-30.

4. Richard L. Rapson, *Britons View America: Travel Commentary, 1860–1935* (Seattle: University of Washington Press, 1971); Robert G. Athearn, *Westward the Briton* (New York: Charles Scribner's Sons, 1953).

5. Stewart H. Holbrook, *Far Corner: A Personal View of the Pacific Northwest* (New York: Ballantine Books, 1952), p. 4.

6. Charles Reginald Enock, *Farthest West: Life and Travel in the United States* (London: John Long, 1910), pp. 91–92.

7. Dorothy O. Johansen, "A Working Hypothesis for the Study of Migrations," *Pacific Historical Review* 36 (February 1967): 11–12. The method is not without its perils unless a fairly representative sampling is taken. Deliberate misrepresentation is a common problem. The following study of the images projected for Washington and British Columbia hardly pretends to be exhaustive; care was taken, nonetheless, to include a representative sampling of opinion from Canadians, British, and Americans. One must also be aware of possible change in an image over time. A more complete sample of the literature of travel and promotion is contained in Carlos A. Schwantes, "Left-Wing Unionism in the Pacific Northwest: A Comparative History of Organized Labor and Socialist Politics in Washington and British Columbia, 1885–1917 (Ph.D. dissertation, University of Michigan, 1976), pp. 17–22.

8. Elia Peattie, *A Journey Through Wonderland* . . . (St. Paul: Northern Pacific Railroad, 1890), p. 66; "Settler's Guide to Oregon and Washington Territory . . ." (St. Paul: Northern Pacific Land Department, [ca. 1880]), p. 13; William G. Blaikie, *Summer Suns in the Far West; A Holiday Trip to the Pacific Slope* (London: Thomas Nelson and Sons, 1890), p. 115; Harry F. Giles, *Homeseekers' Guide to the State of Washington* (Olympia: State of Washington, Department of State, 1914), p. 8; L. P. Brockett, *Our Western Empire* (Philadelphia: Bradley, Garretson & Company, 1882), p. 1213.

9. Kinahan Cornwallis, *The New Eldorado; or British Columbia* (London: Thomas Cautley Newby, 1858), p. 27; "Land and Agriculture in British Columbia," *Bulletin 10* (Victoria: Bureau of Provincial Information, 1906), p. 14; A. J. Langley, *A Glance at British Columbia and Vancouver's Island in 1861* (London: Robert Hardwicke, 1862), p. 6; Walter Woehlke, "Unlocking British Columbia," *Sunset*, September 1912, p. 236; Henry Tanner, *British Columbia: Its Agricultural and Commercial Capabilities and the Advantages it Offers for Emigration Purposes* (Montreal: Dawson Brothers, 1887), p. 31; *Information for Emigrants* (Victoria: British Colum-

bia, Minister for Agriculture, 1884), p. 23. See also, Craig Donald Andrews, "British Columbia: A Study of the Influence of the Themes of Hardship and a Sterile Land upon its Literature both Descriptive and Historical, 1628–1914" (M.A. thesis, Washington State University, 1968).

10. Thomas Shaw, *A Farmer's Paradise: The Columbia River Valley as a Land of Grain and Fruit* (Portland, Oregon: Oregon Railroad and Navigation Company, 1898); E. V. Smalley, "The New Northwest," *Century*, October 1882, p. 869; Helen H. Jackson, *Glimpses of Three Coasts* (Boston: Roberts Brothers, 1886), p. 143; *Washington Territory: Information for Immigrants* (Seattle: Washington Territory Immigrant Aid Society, 1879), p. 8.

11. *West Shore*, February 1887, p. 10; Charles T. Conover, "Should Young Men Go West?" *Washington Magazine*, April 1890, p. 44; *Guide Map of Tacoma, Washington Territory* (n.p.: Northern Pacific Railroad, [1889]); *Okanogan Record*, 18 January 1907, p. 1.

12. J. Despard Pemberton, *Facts and Figures Relating to Vancouver Island and British Columbia, Showing What to Expect and How to Get There* (London: Longman, Green, Longman and Roberts, 1860), p. 135; C. J. Lee Warner, "The Evolution of Farming in British Columbia," *Westward Ho! Magazine*, September 1907, p. 44; *Land of the Okanagan, British Columbia* (n.p.: Okanagan Land and Development Company, [1891?]), p. 27; Edward Roper, *By Track and Trail; a Journey through Canada* (London: W. H. Allen & Company, 1891), p. 449; *Hand Book of British Columbia, Canada* ([Victoria]: Bureau of Provincial Information, [ca. 1907]), p. 61; Thomas Rawlings, *The Confederation of the British North American Provinces; Their Past History and Future Prospects . . .* (London: Sampson Low, Son, and Marston, 1865), p. 120; *British Columbia as a Field for Emigration and Investment* (Victoria: Richard Wolfenden, 1891), p. 9.

13. William H. Barneby, *Life and Labour in the Far, Far West . . .* (London: Cassell & Company, 1884), p. 141; Marcus Lee Hansen and John Bartlet Brebner, *The Mingling of the Canadian and American Peoples* (New Haven: Yale University Press, 1940), p. 228.

14. Earl S. Pomeroy, *The Territories and the United States, 1861–1890* (Philadelphia: University of Pennsylvania Press, 1947); Dorothy O. Johansen, "Washington Territory," *American Heritage* 4 (Summer 1953): 54, 55; Charles Miles and O. B. Sperlin, eds., *Building a State: Washington, 1889–1939* (Tacoma: Washington State Historical Society, 1940).

15. Margaret Ormsby, *British Columbia, a History* ([Toronto]: Macmillan, 1958), pp. 111–132 *passim*; John S. Helmcken, "Reminiscences," Helmcken manuscripts, 5: 76–77, Public Archives of British Columbia, Victoria; British Columbia Legislative Council, *Debate on the Subject of Confederation with Canada* (Victoria: Government Printing Office, 1870); George W. Shelton, ed., *British Columbia and Confederation* (Victoria: University of Victoria, 1967).

16. Cornwallis, *The New Eldorado*, pp. 138, 139; Barneby, *Life and Labour in the Far, Far West*, pp. 126, 150; *Industrial Canada*, August 1910, pp. 20, 21.

17. Rudyard Kipling, *Letters of Travel: 1892–1913* (Garden City, N. Y.: Doubleday, Page & Company, 1920), p. 203.

18. Stella Higgins, "British Columbia and the Confederation Era," and Susan D. Scott, "The Attitude of the Colonial Governors and Officials Towards Confederation," both in Shelton, *British Columbia and Confederation*, pp. 18, 150; Wood, *The Tourist's Northwest*, p. 389.

19. K. A. Mackirdy, "Conflict of Loyalties: The Problem of Assimilating the Far Wests into the Canadian and Australian Federations," *Canadian Historical Review* 32 (December 1951): 346; K. A. MacKirdy, "Regionalism: Canada and Australia" (Ph.D. dissertation, University of Toronto, 1959); Sir Charles P. Piers, *Sport and Life in British Columbia* (London: Heath Cranton, [1923]), pp. 112–13.

20. Lloyd G. Reynolds, *The British Immigrant: His Social and Economic Adjustment in Canada* (Toronto: Oxford University Press, 1935); Cliftoɹ K. Yearly, *Britons in American Labor: A History of the Influence of the United Kingdom Immigrants on American Labor, 1820–1914* (Baltimore: Johns Hopkins University Press, 1957); Rowland Berthoff, *British Immigrants in Industrial America* (Cambridge: Harvard University Press, 1953); S. D. Clark *The Developing Canadian Community*, 2nd ed. (Toronto: University of Toronto Press, 1968), p. 196.

21. Unless otherwise noted, all population statistics are drawn from the official decennial census reports issued by the respective governments of Canada and the United States.

22. Commander R. C. Mayne, *Four Years in British Columbia and Vancouver Island* (London: John Murray, 1862), p. 26; Alexander A. Boddy, *By Ocean, Prairie and Peak; Some Gleanings from an Emigrant Chaplain's Log, on Journeys to British Columbia, Manitoba and Eastern Canada* (London: Society for the Promotion of Christian Knowledge, 1896), p. 170; E. Catherine Bates, *A Year in the Great Republic* (London, Ward & Downey, 1887), 1:149.

23. Douglas Sladen, *On the Cars and Off* . . . (London: Ward, Lock & Bowden, 1895), p. 368; J. A. Hobson, *Canada To-day* (London: T. Fisher Unwin, 1906), p. 28.

24. Norbert MacDonald, "Seattle, Vancouver and the Klondike," *Canadian Historical Review* 49 (September 1968): 234–38; Boddy, *By Ocean, Prairie and Peak*, p. 178; C. B. Yandell, "The Seattle Spirit," *Pacific Monthly*, February 1907, pp. 237–40 *passim*; Rudyard Kipling, *From Sea to Sea* (Leipzig: Bernhard Tauchnitz, 1900), pp. 184–87.

25. Samuel Bowles, *Across the Continent* (Springfield, Mass.: Samuel Bowles & Company, 1866), p. 183; Lady Mary Rhodes Carbutt, *Five Months' Fine Weather in Canada, Western United States, and Mexico* (London: Sampson Low, Marston, Searle, & Rivington, 1889), p. 76; J. M. Murphy, *Rambles in North-Western America, From the Pacific Ocean to the Rocky Mountains* (London: Chapman and Hall, 1879), p. 47.

26. [A. T. Hawley], *Portland, Oregon, The Metropolis of the Pacific Northwest* (Portland, Oregon: The Oregon Immigration Board, [ca. 1888]).

27. *Canadian Annual Review, 1908*, pp. 534–35.

28. James N. Tattersall, "The Economic Development of the Pacific Northwest to 1920" (Ph.D. dissertation, University of Washington, 1960); "Fourth Biennial Report of the Bureau of Labor of the State of Washington, 1903–1904," in *Washington Public Documents, 1903–1904*, 2: 166; William Z. Foster, *Pages From a Worker's Life* (New York: International Publishers, 1939), pp. 36–37; William O. Douglas, *Go East, Young Man: The Early Years; The Autobiography of William O. Douglas* (New York: Random House, 1974), pp. 76–78.

29. "First Annual Report of the Inspector of Factories, 1910," in *British Columbia Sessional Papers, 1911*, pp. 1–9.

30. Hobson, *Canada To-day*, p. 32; "Report of the Royal Commission on Labour," in *British Columbia Sessional Papers, 1914*, 2: m-1, m-2.

Notes

CHAPTER 2

1. Harry W. Stone, "Beginning of Labor Movement in the Pacific Northwest," *Oregon Historical Quarterly* 47 (June 1946): 155–64; Paul Phillips, *No Power Greater: A Century of Labour in British Columbia* (Vancouver: Boag Foundation, 1967), pp. 1–18 *passim*.

2. Robert V. Bruce, *1877: Year of Violence* (Indianapolis: Bobbs-Merrill, 1959).

3. Ray Stannard Baker, "The Great Northwest," *Century*, March 1903, p. 653.

4. H. M. Hyndman, "Lights and Shades of American Politics," *Fortnightly Review*, 1 March 1881, p. 349.

5. *Seattle Daily Call*, 19 November 19 1885, p. 2.

6. Robert E. Wynne, "Reaction to the Chinese in the Pacific Northwest and British Columbia" (Ph.D. dissertation, University of Washington, 1969); Jules A. Karlin, "Anti-Chinese Outbreaks in Seattle, 1885–1886," *Pacific Northwest Quarterly 39 (April 1948): 103–30*; Phillips, *No Power Greater*, pp. 9–15.

7. Gerald N. Grob, *Workers and Utopia: A Study of Ideological Conflict in the American Labor Movement, 1865–1900* (Evanston, Ill.: Northwestern University Press, 1961); Norman J. Ware, *The Labor Movement in the United States, 1860–1895* (New York: D. Appleton and Company, 1929).

8. Knights of Labor, *General Assembly Proceedings, 1978*, p. 26; *1879*, p. 64; *1884*, pp. 217, 219; *Journal of United Labor*, August 1882, p. 291; February 1884, pp. 651, 693, 813; Ira Cross, *A History of the Labor Movement in California* (Berkeley: University of California Press, 1935), pp. 152, 153; Phillips, *No Power Greater*, pp. 12–15.

9. *Victoria Daily Colonist* (hereinafter cited as the *Colonist*), 8 September 1885, p. 3; 11 October 1885, pp. 1, 2; *Industrial News* (Victoria), 26 December 1885, p. 1.

10. Chester McArthur Destler, *American Radicalism, 1865–1901: Essays and Documents* (New London, Conn.: Connecticut College, 1946), pp. 78–104 passim; *Truth in Small Doses* (San Francisco), 23 May 1886, p. 4.

11. *Truth* (San Francisco), 11 February 1882, p. 1; 18 February 1882, p. 1; 7 June 1882, pp. 1, 3; *Haskell Journal*, May 1898, p. 46; International Workingmen's Association material in the Burnette Haskell papers, Bancroft Library, University of California, Berkeley.

12. Morris Hillquit, *History of Socialism in the United States* (1910; reprint ed., New York: Dover Publications, 1971), p. 231; Henry David, *The History of the Haymarket Affair: A Study in the American Social-Revolutionary and Labor Movement*, 2nd ed. (New York: Russell & Russell, 1958); "What the I. W. A. Is," (n.p.), pamphlet in the Haskell papers; Robert Saltvig, "The Progressive Movement in Washington' (Ph.D. dissertation, University of Washington, 1966), pp. 4–13 *passim*.

13. Knights of Labor, *General Assembly Proceedings, 1886*, p. 1848; idem, *General Assembly Proceedings, 1887*, 2: 1056, 1057; idem, *General Assembly Proceedings, 1888*, pp. 2–5; Ware, *The Labor Movement in the United States*, pp. 66, 114; *Model Commonwealth* (Port Angeles, Wa.), 10 June 1887, p. 10. In July 1887, the Knights of Labor reported district assemblies in Seattle with 1,210 members, in Butte with 772, in Portland with 310, and in Vancouver with 300 in six local assemblies.

14. Meryl E. Rogers, "The Labor Movement in Seattle, 1885–1905" (M.A. thesis, Pacific Lutheran University, 1970), p. 29; Woodrow R. Clevinger, "The Western Washington Cascades: A Study of Migration and Mountain Settlement" (Ph.D. dissertation, University of Washington, 1955), p. 96.

15. The Irish and Welsh dominated the Roslyn field on the east side of the Cascades, and British and Scottish miners had difficulty obtaining employment; on the western slope, a large English and Scottish element lived at Newcastle while the Welsh predominated at Black Diamond. In the Carbon Valley, which included the camps of Wilkeson, Carbonado, and Fairfax, the European-born represented 60 percent of the population before 1914. Frederick E. Melder, "A Study of the Washington Coal Industry with Special Reference to the Industrial Relations Problem" (M.A. thesis, University of Washington, 1931), p. 57; Clevinger, "The Western Washington Cascades," p. 58.

16. Alan A. Hynding, "The Public Life of Eugene Semple: A Study of the Promoter-Politician on the Pacific Northwest Frontier" (Ph.D. dissertation, University of Washington, 1966), pp. 167–86 *passim*; John Howard to Elijah Smith, 30 May 1888, Oregon Improvement Company papers, box 58, folder 25, Archives and Manuscripts Division, University of Washington Library, Seattle; petition dated 29 August 1888, and signed by A. H. Harris and others, in the Eugene Semple papers, box 11, folder 16, Archives and Manuscripts Division, University of Washington Library.

17. Alan A. Hynding, "The Coal Miners of Washington Territory: Labor Troubles in 1888–1889," *Arizona and the West* 12 (Autumn 1970): 221–36; Eugene Semple to William Galvani, 6 September 1888, Semple papers, box 1, folder 15. For additional information on Semple and his handling of the labor disturbances in the coal fields, see Alan A. Hynding, *The Public Life of Eugene Semple: Promoter and Politician of the Pacific Northwest* (Seattle: University of Washington Press, 1973).

18. John Howard to Elijah Smith, 30 May 1888, Oregon Improvement Company papers, box 58, folder 25; Hynding, "The Coal Miners of Washington Territory," pp. 222–23.

19. Mark J. Stern, "To Bring Forth the Hidden Wealth: The Knights of Labor in the Coalfields of King County, Washington, 1885–1891" (B.A. thesis, Reed College 1973); C. William Thorndale, "Washington's Green River Coal Company [Country]: 1880–1930" (M.A. thesis, University of Washington, 1965).

20. Beverly Paulik Rosenow, ed., *The Journal of the Washington State Constitutional Convention, 1889* (Seattle: Book Publishing Company, 1962). Newton refused to sign the completed document because the convention voted down proposals for better mine safety. The delegates were not anti-labor, however; they merely wanted to avoid turning the proposed constitution into a code of laws.

21. John S. Hittell, *The Commerce and Industries of the Pacific Coast of North America* (San Francisco: A. L. Bancroft & Company, 1882), p. 309; Harold Griffin, *British Columbia: The People's Early Story* (Vancouver: Tribune Publishing, 1958), pp. 43–47 *passim*. The Washington mines were not notably safer than those on Vancouver Island (see the statistics in the *Seattle Union Record*, 23 September 1916, p. 2).

22. *Guide to the Province of British Columbia for 1877–8* (Victoria: T. N. Hibben & Company, 1877), p. 56; Brian R. D. Smith, "A Social History of Early Nanaimo" (B.A. thesis, University of British Columbia, 1956); Allan Donald Orr, "The Western Federation of Miners and the Royal Commission on Industrial Disputes in 1903 with Special Reference to the Vancouver Island Coal Miners' Strike" (M.A. thesis, University of British Columbia, 1968).

23. Knights of Labor, *General Assembly Proceedings, 1891*, pp. 2, 75.

24. *Northern Light* (Tacoma, Seattle, and Spokane), 11 October 1890, p. 4.

25. For further details, see Allan D. Orr, "The Western Federation of Miners and the Royal Commission on Industrial Disputes in 1903."

Notes

26. Federation of Organized Trades and Labor Unions in the United States and Canada, *Convention Proceedings, 1881*, p. 8; Cross, *The Labor Movement in California*, pp. 204, 206; Minutes of the Western Central Labor Union, 26 August 1891, 31 May 1893, Archives and Manuscripts Division, University of Washington Library; *Coast Seamen's Journal*, 17 June 1891, p. 4.

27. *Coast Seamen's Journal*, 17 June 1891, p. 4; 30 September 1891, p. 5; 31 May 1893, p. 8; American Federation of Labor, *Convention Proceedings, 1891*, p. 17; idem, *Convention Proceedings, 1892*, p. 16.

28. Robert L. Friedheim, *The Seattle General Strike* (Seattle: University of Washington Press, 1964), p. 29; Minutes of the Western Central Labor Union, 31 May 1893, 1 July 1898, 4 January 1899.

29. *Union Record*, 31 January 1914, p. 4.

30. American Federation of Labor, *Convention Proceedings, 1892*, pp. 8, 17; idem. *Convention Proceedings, 1896*, p. 90; idem, *Convention Proceedings, 1898*, pp. 36, 92; Stone, "Beginning of Labor Movement," pp. 155–64.

31. The best account of the AFL struggle for hegemony in Canada is Robert H. Babcock, *Gompers in Canada: A Study in American Continentalism before the First World War* (Toronto: University of Toronto Press, 1974). See also, Eugene Forsey, "Insights into Labour History in Canada," *Relations Industrielles* 20 (July 1965): 445–77; Harold A. Logan, *Trade Unions in Canada: Their Development and Functioning* (Toronto: Macmillan, 1948).

CHAPTER 3

1. *West Shore*, June 1879, p. 73; *Colonist*, 19 August 1913, p. 4; Eric F. Goldman, *Rendezvous with Destiny: A History of Modern American Reform* (New York: Alfred A. Knopf, 1952); S. D. Clark, "Economic Expansion and the Moral Order," *Canadian Journal of Economics and Political Science* 6 (May 1940): 206.

2. Norman E. Clark, *The Dry Years: Prohibition and Social Change in Washington* (Seattle: University of Washington Press, 1965); Albert J. Hiebert, "Prohibition in British Columbia" (M.A. thesis, Simon Fraser University, 1969).

3. *Sandon Paystreak*, 16 September 1899, p. 4; *Western Clarion* (Vancouver), 30 April 1910, p. 1; *Vancouver Daily Province*, 23 December 1901, p. 6.

4. *B. C. Saturday Sunset* (Vancouver), 5 March 1910, p. 2; *Week* (Vancouver), 18 January 1913, p. 1; *B. C. Federationist* (Vancouver), 22 June 1912, p. 1; 23 April 1919, p. 4; *Western Clarion*, 9 December 1905, p. 1; 19 June 1909, p. 2; 31 July 1909, p. 2; 26 November 1910, p. 1.

5. E. V. Smalley, "Discontent of the Laboring Class," *Northwest Magazine*, February 1886, p. 25.

6. *Palladium of Labor* (Hamilton, Ont.), 19 April 1884, p. 1; *Labor Advocate* (Toronto), 3 July 1891, p. 244.

7. Frederick Lewis Allen, *The Lords of Creation* (New York: Harper & Brothers, 1935), p. 158; Richard T. Ely, *The Labor Movement in America* (New York: Thomas Y. Crowell, 1886), p. 284; *Colfax Commoner*, 21 November 1890, p. 4.

8. Henry George, *Progress and Poverty; An Inquiry into the cause of Industrial Depressions and of Increase of Want with the Increase of Wealth . . . The Remedy* (1879; reprint ed., New York: Robert Schalkenbach Foundation, 1962); Goldman, *Rendezvous with Destiny*, pp. 85–104 *passim*. Hayes is quoted in Daniel Aaron, *Men of Good Hope: A Story of American Progressives* (New York: Oxford University Press, 1951), p. 88.

9. F. W. Watt, "The National Policy, the Workingman, and Proleterian Ideas

in Victorian Canada," *Canadian Historical Review* 40 (March 1959): 10, 17; *Palladium of Labor*, 2 August 1884, p. 4; 9 August 1884, p. 1.

10. *Industrial News* (Victoria), 17 July 1886, p. 2; *Light* (Vancouver), 2 June 1894, p. 1; *Single Tax Review*, 25 July 1901, p. 50. See also, Arthur N. Young, *The Single Tax Movement in the United States* (Princeton: Princeton University Press, 1916).

11. *Spokane Spokesman-Review*, 2 February 1914, p. 6; *Single Tax Review*, September-October 1908, pp. 56, 57; *Standard*, 29 October 1887, p. 3; *Western Clarion*, 29 April 1911, p. 2.

12. P. E. Maher, "Laurence Gronlund: Contributions to American Socialism," *Western Political Quarterly* 15 (December 1962): 618–24; Laurence Gronlund, *The Co-Operative Commonwealth*, ed. Stow Persons (1884; reprint ed., Cambridge: Harvard University Press, 1965).

13. Laurence Gronlund to Henry Demarest Lloyd, 28 June 1897, Henry Demarest Lloyd papers, box 8, State Historical Society of Wisconsin, Madison; Elizabeth Sadler, "One Book's Influence: Edward Bellamy's *Looking Backward*," *New England Quarterly* 11 (December 1938): 739–72; Edward Bellamy, *Looking Backward, 2000–1887* (1888; reprint ed., Chicago: Packard and Company, 1946), p. 174.

14. Michael Harrington, *Socialism* (New York: Saturday Review Press, 1970), p. 109; Theodore Roosevelt, "Socialism: Where We Cannot Work With Socialists," *Outlook*, 20 March 1909, pp. 619–23; Theodore Roosevelt, "Socialism II: Where We Can Work With Socialists," *Outlook*, 27 March 1909, p. 662.

15. *Colonist*, 21 January 1911, p. 4; J. W. Longley, "Socialism—Its Truths and Errors," *Canadian Magazine*, February 1896, p. 297; Chehalis *People's Advocate*, 14 July 1893, p. 4. See also, John H. M. Laslett and Seymour Martin Lipset, *Failure of a Dream? Essays in the History of American Socialism* (Garden City, N. Y.: Doubleday, Anchor Press, 1974).

16. *Western Clarion*, 9 July 1904, p. 4.

17. *Slocan Drill*, 18 May 1900, p. 4; *Seattle Union Record*, 8 July 1911, p. 6; *Co-Operator* (Burley, Wa.), 22 September 1900, p. 2; Eugene V. Debs, "Socialist Ideals," *Arena*, November 1908, p. 432; Eugene V. Debs, "The Social Democratic Party," *Independent* (New York), 23 August 1900, p. 2019.

18. *Firebrand* (Portland), 24 February 1895, p. 1; 22 November 1896, p. 1; *The People* (New York), 1 May 1899, p. 2; Silver City, Idaho, Western Federation of Miners Local 66 papers, Bancroft Library.

CHAPTER 4

1. Donald D. Saltvig, "The Progressive Movement in Washington" (Ph.D. dissertation, University of Washington, 1966), pp. 9–17 *passim*. See also, Meryl E. Rogers, "The Labor Movement in Seattle, 1885–1905" (M.A. thesis, Pacific Lutheran University, 1970), pp. 10, 55–61 *passim*.

2. Melvin G. De Shazo, "Radical Tendencies in the Seattle Labor Movement as Reflected in the Proceedings of its Central Body" (M.A. thesis, University of Washington, 1925), pp. 4, 6; Minutes of the Western Central Labor Union, 11 July 1894, Archives and Manuscripts Division, University of Washington Library.

3. James A. Halseth, "Social Disorganization and Discontent in Late Nineteenth Century Washington" (Ph.D. dissertation, Texas Tech University,

1974), pp. 133–39 *passim*; Minutes of the Tacoma Trades Council, 3 April 1890 to 30 June 1892, Archives and Manuscripts Division, University of Washington Library.

4. Margaret J. Thompson, "Development and Comparison of Industrial Relationships in Seattle" (M.B.A. thesis, University of Washington, 1929), p. 20. On the eve of the depression of 1893, the Tacoma Trades Council claimed 796 members and the WCLU 1,648. *Coast Seamen's Journal*, 14 June 1893, p. 9.

5. *Spokane Review*, 7 June 1893, p. 4; *Colfax Commoner*, June 9 1893, p. 1; Charles Hoffmann, "The Depression of the Nineties," *Journal of Economic History* 16 (June, 1956): 137–64; *Oregon Populist* (Albany), 4 January 1893, p. 1; Alan Morley, *Vancouver: From Milltown to Metropolis*, 2nd ed. (Vancouver: Mitchell Press, 1969), pp. 111,117.

6. *Tacoma Weekly Ledger*, 7 July 1893, p. 4; *New Whatcom Blade*, 15 September 1894, p. 2; *Northwest Magazine*, March 1894, p. 32. See also, David P. Thelen, *The New Citizenship: Origins of Progressivism in Wisconsin, 1885–1900* (Columbia, Mo.: University of Missouri Press, 1972); Donald L. Kinzer, *An Episode in Anti-Catholicism: The American Protective Association* (Seattle: University of Washington Press, 1964).

7. *Journal of the Knights of Labor*, 20 August 1891, p. 4. The best overall account of the Populist movement in Washington is Thomas W. Riddle, "The Old Radicalism in America: John R. Rogers and the Populist Movement in Washington, 1891–1900" (Ph.D. dissertation, Washington State University, 1976).

8. Saltvig, "The Progressive Movement," p. 18; Minutes of the Western Central Labor Union, 16 December 1891; Halseth, "Social Disorganization and Discontent in Late Nineteenth Century Washington," p. 165.

9. David Burke Griffiths, "Populism in the Far West, 1890–1900" (Ph.D. dissertation, University of Washington, 1967), p. 195.

10. The 1893 legislation, after voting for forty-one different persons on 101 consecutive ballots, gave up trying to pick a United States senator; the position remained vacant for the next two years. *Legislative Manual, State of Washington, 1893–1894*, pp. 206–56 *passim*, 374–79.

11. Ezra Carr, *Patrons of Husbandry on the Pacific Coast* (San Francisco: A. L. Bancroft & Company, 1875); Harriet Ann Crawford, *The Washington State Grange, 1889–1924* (Portland, Ore.: Bindfords & Mort, 1940); Fred R. Yoder, "The Farmers' Alliances in Washington—Prelude to Populism," *Research Studies of the State College of Washington* 16 (September-December 1948).

12. Thomas Wayne Riddle, "Whitman County Populism and Washington State Politics: 1889–1902" (M.A. thesis, Washington State University, 1971).

13. *Colfax Commoner*, November 21 1890, p. 3; Frances Fuller Victor, *Atlantis Arisen; or, Talks of a Tourist About Oregon and Washington* (Philadelphia: J. B. Lippincott, 1891), pp. 379, 380; Gordon B. Ridgeway, "Populism in Washington," *Pacific Northwest Quarterly* 39 (October 1948): 289; Stephen Henry Peters, "The Populists and the Washington Legislature, 1893–1900" (M.A. thesis, University of Washington, 1967), p. 15; Robert Allen Henderson, "The *Spokesman-Review*, 1883–1900: A Mirror to the History of Spokane" (Ph.D. dissertation, Washington State University, 1967), pp. 50, 52.

14. Riddle, "Whitman County Populism and Washington State Politics," pp. 7–10 *passim*; Ridgeway, "Populism in Washington," p. 285; Peters, "The Populists and the Washington Legislature," p. 4; Yoder, "The Farmers' Alliances in

Washington," p. 144; *Report of the Secretary of Agriculture, 1893* (Washington, D.C.: Government Printing Office, 1894), p. 472.

15. Herman C. Voeltz, "Coxey's Army in Oregon, 1894," *Oregon Historical Quarterly* 65 (September 1964): 263–95; *Industrial Army News*, 20 April 1894, pp. 1, 4; Rogers, "The Labor Movement in Seattle," pp. 106, 107; Riddle, "The Old Radicalism in America," pp. 166–74. See also Donald L. McMurry, *Coxey's Army: A Study of the Industrial Army Movement of 1894* (Seattle: University of Washington Press, 1929).

16. Philip S. Foner, *History of the Labor Movement in the United States* (New York: International Publishers, 1955), 2: 254–259; *Railway Times*, 1 January 1894, p. 4; 1 June 1894, p. 4; 2 July 1894, p. 4; Minutes of the Western Central Labor Union, 27 June 1894, 11 July 1894; Henry Demarest Lloyd to Clarence Darrow, 23 November 1894, Lloyd papers, Microfilm Reel 5, State Historical Society of Wisconsin, Madison.

17. *Tacoma Weekly Ledger*, 25 August 1893, p. 1; *Weekly Olympian*, 24 May 1894, p. 2; 14 June 1894, p. 1.

18. Robert F. Durden, *The Climax of Populism* (Lexington, Ky.: University of Kentucky Press, 1965); Henry D. Lloyd, "The Populists at St. Louis," *Review of Reviews*, September 1896, 298–303.

19. Boone, "The Washington State Legislature of 1897," p. 18; Carroll H. Wooddy, "Populism in Washington: A Study of the Legislature of 1897," *Washington Historical Quarterly* 21 (April 1930): 103–19.

20. Robert Bridges, "Scrapbook III," University of Washington Library; Norman F. Tjaden, "Populists and Progressives of Washington: A Comparative Study" (M.A. thesis, University of Washington, 1960), pp. 2, 78.

21. *Tacoma Weekly Ledger*, 20 October 1896, p. 1; "Abstract of Votes Polled in the State of Washington, 1896," available from the secretary of state's office, Olympia. See also, Tjaden, "Populists and Progressives of Washington" for an analysis of the election returns.

22. *New Whatcom Blade*, 24 September 1896, p. 2; *Northwest Magazine*, March 1897, p. 25.

23. A character sketch of Rogers is contained in Riddle, "The Old Radicalism in America," pp. 44–67.

24. Margaret H. Thompson, "The Writings of John Rankin Rogers" (M.A. thesis, University of Washington, 1947), p. 29; John Rankin Rogers, *Free Land, the Remedy for Involuntary Poverty, Social Unrest and the Woes of Labor . . .* (Tacoma: Morning Union, 1897), p. 10.

25. John Rankin Rogers, "Reformers I Have Known," *Tacoma Morning Sun*, March 1894, p. 12; Rogers, *Free Land*, pp. 15, 17; David B. Griffiths, "Far-Western Populist Thought: A Comparative Study of John R. Rogers and Davis H. Waite," *Pacific Northwest Quarterly* 60 (October 1969): 183–92; Boone, "The Washington State Legislature of 1897," p. 30.

26. Boone, "The Washington State Legislature of 1897," p. 68; Peters, "The Populists and the Washington Legislature," pp. 86, 92, 126–27 *passim*.

27. *New Whatcom Blade*, 12 November 1898, p. 2; *Weekly Olympian*, 13 September 1900, p. 2; *Yakima Herald*, 3 August 1900, p. 4; 8 November 1900, p. 1.

28. Griffiths, "Populism in the Far West," p. 232; Boone, "The Washington State Legislature of 1897," p. 27. Tjaden's "Populists and Progressives of Washington" is the best study of the composition of Populist leadership as compared with that of the Democrats, Republicans, and Progressives of 1912. The

Populist vote in King, Spokane, and Pierce counties, which together contained 43 percent of the state's population in 1900 and also served in each case as a focal point for the labor movement, generally accounted for between 36 and 41 percent of the total Populist vote cast in statewide elections between 1892 and 1898. Except in 1896, when the Populist vote in Spokane rose markedly because of the silver issue, the percentage of the Populist vote cast in the elections of 1892, 1896, and 1898 in each of the state's three most populous counties remained remarkably stable. Election figures are drawn from official voting abstracts available from the secretary of state's office, Olympia, or *Legislative Manuals* for the State of Washington.

29. *New Whatcom Champion*, May 1894, pp. 1, 2; R. H. Norton to John R. Rogers, 13 November 1896, John R. Rogers public papers, Washington State Archives, Olympia; Thompson, "The Writings of John Rankin Rogers," p. 42.

CHAPTER 5

1. John D. Hicks, *The Populist Revolt; A History of the Farmers' Alliance and the People's Party* (Minneapolis: University of Minnesota Press, 1931); Richard Hofstadter, *The Age of Reform; From Bryan to F. D. R.* (New York: Alfred A. Knopf, 1955); Norman Pollack, *The Populist Response to Industrial America; Midwestern Populist Thought* (Cambridge: Harvard University Press, 1962); Lawrence Goodwyn, *Democratic Promise: The Populist Movement in America* (New York: Oxford University Press, 1976).

2. J. M. S. Careless, *Canada: A Story of Challenge* (Toronto: Macmillan of Canada, 1953), pp. 5, 10; Arthur R. M. Lower, *Canadians in the Making: A Social History of Canada* (Toronto: Longmans, Green and Company, 1958), p. 273.

3. *Oregonian's Handbook of the Pacific Northwest* (Portland, Ore.: The Oregonian Publishing Company, 1894), p. 576; Joseph Nimmo, Jr., *Canadian Aggression upon American Commerce . . .* (Washington, D.C.: Gibson Brothers, 1888), pp. 7–10 *passim*; *Industrial Canada*, October 1903, p. 134.

4. *Colonist*, 10 June 1894, p. 4; Edward J. Chambers, "Late Nineteenth Century Business Cycles in Canada," *Canadian Journal of Economics and Political Science* 30 (August 1964): 391–412; *British Columbia Commercial Journal*, 29 August 1893, p. 8; *Canadian Manufacturer*, 2 March 1894, p. 179.

5. Neil Roy Knight, "History of Banking in Washington" (Ph.D. dissertation, University of Washington, 1935); *Colonist*, 5 October 1893, p. 4.

6. H. M. P. Eckardt, "Canadian Banking," *Annals of the American Academy of Political and Social Sciences* 45 (January 1913): 158–70. For all its strength when compared to the American banking system, the Canadian banking system was unable to prevent the failure of the Home Bank of Canada in 1923.

7. Irwin Unger, *The Greenback Era: A Social and Political History of American Finance, 1865–1879* (Princeton: Princeton University Press, 1964); John Reid Watt, "Introduction to the Economic and Labor History of Western Washington" (M.A. thesis, University of Washington, 1942), pp. 67, 171; Joseph Ellison, "The Currency Question on the Pacific Coast during the Civil War," *Mississippi Valley Historical Review* 16 (June 1929): 50–66.

8. "Statistics on Silver Production," in Cominco papers, box 2, folder 10, Public Archives of British Columbia, Victoria; John S. Church, "Mining Companies in the West Kootenay and Boundary Regions of British Columbia, 1890–1900, Capital Formation and Financial Operations" (M.A. thesis, University of British Columbia, 1961), pp. 16, 17; John Davidson, "Canada and the Silver Question,"

Quarterly Journal of Economics 12 (January 1898): 139–52; James H. Baker, "International Bimetallism, Speech in the Legislative Assembly of B.C." ([Victoria?]: n. p., [ca. 1894]), pp. 1, 11; *Colonist*, 5 October 1895, p. 4; 6 June 1896, p. 4; 30 July 1896, p. 4.

9. *Colonist*, 17 January 1894, p. 5.

10. *Colonist*, 5 November 1896, p. 4; 10 July 1897, p. 4; *Sandon Paystreak*, 2 September 1896, p. 2.

11. Michael Bliss, "Another Anti-Trust Tradition: Canadian Anti-Combines Policy, 1889–1910," *Business History Review* 47 (Summer 1973), 177–88.

12. Erwin C. Hargrove, "On Canadian and American Political Culture," *Canadian Journal of Economics and Political Science* 33 (February 1967): 107–11; W. L. Morton, *The Canadian Identity*, 2nd edition (Madison, Wis.: University of Wisconsin Press, 1972), pp. 58–87 *passim*.

13. Margaret A. Ormsby, *British Columbia: a History* ([Toronto]: Macmillan of Canada, 1958), p. 306; Paul Phillips, *No Power Greater: A Century of Labour in British Columbia* (Vancouver: Boag Foundation, 1967), pp. 21–22; Minutes of the Regular Meetings of the Vancouver Trades and Labor Council, 6 November 1890; 17 July 1891, in the Vancouver Trades and Labor Council papers, Special Collections Division, University of British Columbia Library, Vancouver, The Vancouver Trades and Labor Council was organized in late 1889 by craft unionists and members of the Knights of Labor. Minutes of the Regular Meetings of the Vancouver Trades and Labor Council, 21 November 1889.

14. *Nanaimo Free Press*, 27 May 1890, p. 1; 3 June 1890, p. 1; 4 November 1890, p. 1.

15. Trades and Labor Congress, *Convention Proceedings, 1892*, pp. 23, 33; Thomas Robert Loosmore, "The British Columbia Labor Movement and Political Action, 1879–1906" (M.A. thesis, University of British Columbia, 1954), pp. 70, 76; Phillips, *No Power Greater*, pp. 23, 24; *People's Journal* (Vancouver), 18 February 1893, p. 3; 3 June 1893, p. 2.

16. *Kaslo Kootenaian* as quoted in the *Colonist*, 25 December 1899, p. 8; *Colonist*, 25 August 1899, p. 4.

17. T. L. Grahame, "British Columbia Politics," *Canadian Magazine*, August 1900, pp. 330–36.

18. *Colonist*, 17 January 1897, p. 4; 8 October 1897, p. 4; 16 April 1898, p. 4; 19 May 1898, p. 6; *New Westminster Daily Columbian*, 28 January 1897, p. 1; Margaret A. Ormsby, "The United Farmers of British Columbia—An Abortive Third-Party Movement," *British Columbia Historical Quarterly* 17 (January-April 1953): 53, 54; Margaret A. Ormsby, "The History of Agriculture in British Columbia," *Scientific Agriculture* 20 (September 1939): 61–73.

19. An excellent summary of the reasons usually given to explain the peculiarities of labor politics in the United States is Charles Rehmus, "Labor in American Politics," in William Haber, ed., *The Vista of American Labor*, Voice of America Forum Lectures (Washington, D.C., U.S. Information Agency, ca. 1966), pp. 281–96 *passim*.

20. Hubert Howe Bancroft, *History of Washington, Idaho, and Montana; 1845–1889* (San Francisco: The History Company, 1890), p. 71.

21. Eleanor Brown Mercer, "Political Groups in British Columbia, 1883–1898" (M.A. thesis, University of British Columbia, 1937), p. 100. See also, R. MacGregor Dawson, *The Government of Canada*, 5th ed., revised by Norman Ward (Toronto: University of Toronto Press, 1970).

22. Henry Steele Commager, *The American Mind: An Interpretation of American Thought and Character since the 1880's* (New Haven, Conn.: Yale University Press, 1950), p. 361; *Cotton's Weekly* (Cowansville, Que.), 5 January 1911, p. 1; *Colonist*, 27 May 1895, p. 4; 9 July 1908, p. 4.

23. Sidney Fine, *Laissez Faire and the General-Welfare State: A Study of Conflict in American Thought, 1865–1901* (Ann Arbor: University of Michigan Press, 1956), pp. 136, 140, 141; Almont Lindsey, *The Pullman Strike* (Chicago: University of Chicago Press, Phoenix Books, 1964), p. 242.

24. *Colonist*, 17 August 1897, p. 4; A. W. R. Carrothers, *A Study of the Operation of the Injunction in Labour-Management Disputes in British Columbia, 1946–1955* (Toronto: CCH Canadian Limited, [1956]), pp. xxiii, xxiv.

25. Joseph F. Tripp, "Progressive Labor Laws in Washington State (1900–1925)" (Ph.D. dissertation, University of Washington, 1973).

CHAPTER 6

1. Melvyn Dubofsky, *Industrialism and the American Worker, 1865–1920* (New York: Thomas Y. Crowell, 1975), pp. 63, 64.

2. Howard Quint, *The Forging of American Socialism: Origins of the Modern Movement* (Columbia, S.C.: University of South Carolina Press, 1953), pp. 142–74 *passim*; Socialistic Labor party, *Platform, Constitution and Resolutions, 1877* (Cincinnati: n.p., 1878), in Socialist Labor party papers, Microfilm Reel 35, State Historical Society of Wisconsin.

3. *Workingmen's Advocate* (New York), 26 July 1890, p. 3; Henry Addis to the National Executive Committee, 12 November 1891, Socialist Labor party papers, Microfilm Reel 4; *The People* (New York), 5 April 1891, p. 5; 22 May 1892, p. 3; 5 November 1894, p. 4.

4. *The People*, 17 April 1898, p. 4; 21 August 1898, p. 1. Socialists in Seattle did not completely vanish during the depression years. In late 1895 a small group of them published the *Socialist* for a short period. There was even some interest among various socialists on the West Coast in holding a regional convention. *Socialist* (San Francisco), 16 November 1895, p. 3.

5. *The People*, 6 March 1898, p. 1; 17 July 1898, p. 1; 15 October 1899, p. 1; *Spirit of '76* (Tacoma), 3 December 1899, p. 4; *Freemen's Labor Journal* (Spokane), 13 October 1899, p. 4.

6. *The People*, 1 January 1899, p. 3; *Class Struggle* (San Francisco), 26 July 1899, p. 3; Ross Alfred Johnson, "'No Compromise—No Political Trading': The Marxian Socialist Tradition in British Columbia" (Ph.D. dissertation, University of British Columbia, 1975), pp. 55–56. The *Pathfinder* was edited by Thomas Robinson and Charles Dinsmore. *The People*, 25 October 1899, p. 2.

7. *Class Struggle*, 26 July 1899, p. 3; Minutes of the British Columbia Socialist Trades and Labor Alliance, Socialist Labor party papers, Microfilm Reel 41; *Weekly People* (New York), 3 January 1903, p. 3.

8. Samuel Gompers, *Seventy Years of Life and Labor: An Autobiography* (New York: E. P. Dutton, 1925), 1: 383; Samuel Gompers, "Socialist Methods versus Trade Union Methods, *American Federationist*, February 1912, p. 39; *American Federationist*, January 1904, p. 45; *Seattle Union Record*, 13 October 1900, p. 4.

9. Edward and Eleanor Marx Aveling, *The Working-Class Movement in America*, 2nd ed., enlarged (London: Swan, Sonnenschein and Company, 1891).

10. Howard H. Quint, "Julius A. Wayland, Pioneer Socilist Propagandist,"

Notes

Mississippi Valley Historical Review 35 (March 1949): 585–606; David A. Shannon, *The Socialist Party of America* (New York: Macmillan, 1955), pp. 29, 30.

11. Ray Ginger, *Eugene V. Debs: A Biography* (New York: Macmillan, Collier Books, 1959); Eugene V. Debs, "How I Became a Socialist," reprinted in Jean Y. Tussey, ed., *Eugene V. Debs Speaks* (New York: Pathfinder Press, 1970), p. 48; *Railway Times*, 15 October 1894, p. 1; 15 November 1895, p. 4; *Coming Nation*, 16 March 1895, p. 1.

12. *Railway Times*, 13 January 1896, p. 1; 1 August 1896, p. 2.

13. *Spokane Spokesman-Review*, 14 March 1895, p. 5; 15 March 1895, p. 5; *Railway Times*, 1 April 1895, p. 3; 15 November 1895, p. 5.

14. *Social Democrat* (Chicago), 1 July 1897, p. 4.

15. *Model Commonwealth* (Port Angeles, WA.), 10 June 1887, pp. 3, 8; 17 June 1887, p. 6; 22 July 1887, p. 1; 7 October 1887, p. 3. The best study of the communitarian settlements in western Washington is Charles P. LeWarne, *Utopias on Puget Sound, 1885–1915* (Seattle: University of Washington Press, 1975).

16. Alexander Kent, "Cooperative Communities in the United States," Department of Labor, *Bulletin 35* (July 1901), p. 617; Quint, *The Forging of American Socialism*, p. 288.

17. G. E. Pelton to Henry Demarest Lloyd, 14 December 1897, Lloyd papers, box 8, State Historical Society of Wisconsin; *New York Herald* as quoted in Margaret H. Thompson, "The Writings of John Rankin Rogers" (M.A. thesis, University of Washington, 1947), p. 41; *Chehalis People's Advocate*, 2 July 1897, p. 4; *Co-Operator* (Burley, Wa.), 21 August 1899, p. 4. Communitarian experiments were less prominent in British Columbia than in Washington, but a short-lived Ruskin Colony was established in 1896 near Hastings, and a group of Finnish socialists founded a colony on Harmony Island. John I. Kolehmainen, "Harmony Island: A Finnish Utopian Venture in British Columbia, 1901–1905," *British Columbia Historical Quarterly* 5 (April 1941): 111–23.

18. Charles P. LeWarne, "Equality Colony: The Plan to Socialize Washington," *Pacific Northwest Quarterly* 58 (July, 1968): 137–46; E. B. Ault papers, box 5, folder 7, Archives and Manuscripts Division, University of Washington Library.

19. *Coming Nation*, 11 September 1897, p. 4; *Social Democrat*, 16 September 1897, p. 4; 2 December 1897, p. 4; *Social Democratic Herald* (Chicago), 28 July 1898, p. 3; *Co-Operator*, 18 September 1899, p. 1.

20. George Knoles, "Populism and Socialism, with Special Reference to the Election of 1892," *Pacific Historical Review* 12 (September, 1943): 295–304; *Appeal to Reason*, 9 October 1897, p. 3; Frank B. Tracy, "Menacing Socialism in the Western States," *Forum*, May 1893, 332–42 *passim*; *Okanogan Record*, 5 May 1905, p. 4.

21. Henry Demarest Lloyd to Bayard Holmes, 13 July 1896, Lloyd papers, Microfilm Reel 8.

22. *Tacoma Weekly Ledger*, 26 June 1896, p. 6; *Spokesman-Review*, 26 April 1896, p. 3; 4 June 1897, p. 2; *Colfax Commoner*, 10 December 1897, p. 2; *Freemen's Labor Journal*, 11 March 1898, p. 4; copy of the *Socialist* (Seattle), 16 November 1895, p. 2, in Robert Bridges, "Scrapbook II," University of Washington Library.

23. David B. Griffiths, "Populism in the Far West: 1890–1900" (Ph.D. dissertation, University of Washington, 1966), p. 165; *Chehalis People's Advocate*, 28 February 1898, p. 2; 16 September 1898, p. 1; *New Whatcom Blade*, 27 August 1898, p. 1; 8 September 1898, p. 1; 12 November 1898, p. 2.

24. *New Nation* (Boston), 7 February 1891, p. 34; *Nationalist* (Boston), Sep-

tember 1889, p. 174; January 1890, p. 78; *Labor Advocate* (Toronto), 13 March 1891, p. 114.

25. *Co-Operator*, 30 January 1899, p. 6; Robert D. Saltvig, "The Progressive Movement in Washington" (Ph.D. dissertation, University of Washington, 1966), pp. 145, 406, 407.

26. *Sandon Paystreak*, 23 September 1897, p. 2; 27 October 1897, p. 4; *New Westminster Daily Columbian*, 21 June 1897, p. 2; 20 October 1897, p. 2; *Winnipeg Voice*, 6 January 1911, p. 6; *Seattle Socialist*, 2 November 1907, p. 4; *Union Record*, 11 November 1905, p. 1; 25 November 1905, p. 1; 16 December 1905, p. 1; 8 September 1906, p. 2; 22 February 1908, p. 1.

27. *Vancouver Daily Province*, 11 January 1901, p. 1; *New Westminster Daily Columbian*, 14 December 1898, p. 2; Robert A. Henderson, "The *Spokesman-Review*, 1883–1900; A Mirror to the History of Spokane" (Ph.D. dissertation Washington State University, 1967), pp. 93–95 *passim*; David A. Shannon, ed., *Beatrice Webb's American Diary, 1898* (Madison, Wis.: University of Wisconsin Press, 1963), p. xi.

28. *Union Record*, 11 May 1907, p. 2; *Direct Legislation Record*, July 1898, p. 17; *Independent* (Vancouver), 23 November 1901, p. 4; Jonathan Bourne, Jr., "Initiative, Referendum and Recall," *Atlantic Monthly*, January 1912, pp. 122–30. Samuel Gompers, "Initiative, Referendum and Recall," *American Federationist*, August 1912, pp. 618, 619. In late 1912 Gompers advocated direct legislation in a series of articles that appeared in the *American Federationist*.

29. *Social Democratic Herald*, 29 October 1898, p. 3; 12 August 1899, p. 3; 11 November 1899, p. 1; 23 November 1899, p. 1; *Seattle Socialist*, 25 November 1900, p. 1; 6 January 1901, p. 7.

30. *Social Democratic Herald*, 7 April 1900, pp. 2, 4; 19 May 1900, p. 3; 23 June 1900, p. 3; 1 September 1900, p. 4; *Co-Operator*, 14 July 1900, p. 2; *Freemen's Labor Journal*, 6 July 1900, p. 1.

31. *Seattle Socialist*, 12 August 1900, p. 3; 2 December 1900, p. 1; 20 July 1902, p. 2; *Social Democratic Herald*, 24 February 1900, p. 3.

32. *Seattle Socialist*, 5 January 1902, p. 1; *Everett Commonwealth*, 24 July 1913, p. 4; *Appeal to Reason*, 26 March 1898, p. 2; 2 April 1898, p. 3; Harvey O'Connor, *Revolution in Seattle: A Memoir* (New York: Monthly Review Press, 1964), p. 18.

33. *Seattle Socialist*, 12 August 1900, p. 3; 4 August 1901, p. 8; Hermon F. Titus, "Revolutionary Socialism and Reform Socialism," *Socialist* (Toledo), 7 January 1906, p. 1; Hermon Titus to George Cotterill, 24 February 1906, in George Cotterill papers, box 8, folder 5, Archives and Manuscripts Division, University of Washington Library. The best biographical study of Hermon Titus is Paul B. Bushue, "Dr. Hermon Titus and Socialism in Washington State; 1900–1909" (M.A. thesis, University of Washington, 1967).

34. Melvin G. De Shazo, "Radical Tendencies in the Seattle Labor Movement as Reflected in the Proceedings of its Central Body" (M.A. thesis, University of Washington, 1925), p. 12; *Seattle Socialist*, 12 August 1900, pp. 1, 2.

35. *Union Record*, 19 September 1908, p. 2.

36. *Seattle Socialist*; 11 November 1900, p. 4; 25 November 1900, p. 1; Hulet M. Wells, "I Wanted to Work," manuscript in the Hulet M. Wells papers, box 2, Archives and Manuscripts Division, University of Washington Library; *Appeal to Reason*, 16 November 1901, p. 3.

37. *Nelson Miner*, 7 January 1893, p. 6; *Co-Operator*, 7 August 1899, p. 3; 6 November 1901, p. 2; *Freemen's Labor Journal*, 11 March 1898, p. 4. Saywell is incorrect when he states: "Socialism appeared first in 1895, when the Kootenay

miners affiliated with the Western Federation of Miners." John Tupper Saywell, "Labour and Socialism in British Columbia: A Survey of Historical Development Before 1903," *British Columbia Historical Review* 15 (July-October 1951): 129–50. The WFM and the related Western Labor Union did encourage miners to participate in politics. See the *Pueblo Courier* for the years 1898–1900.

38. *Citizen and Country* (Toronto), 11 March 1899, pp. 1–4 *passim*; *Canadian Socialist* (Toronto), 6 June 1902, p. 1; *Social Democratic Herald*, 30 December 1899, p. 4; *The People*, 9 April 1899, p. 1; *Social Democrat*, 30 December 1897, *Freemen's Labor Journal*, 18 November 1898, p. 4.

39. Johnson, "'No Compromise—No Political Trading,'" pp. 65, 66.

40. *Citizen and Country*, 9 September 1899, p. 1.

41. Harry Keith Ralston, "The 1900 Strike of Fraser River Sockeye Salmon Fishermen" (M.A. thesis, University of British Columbia, 1965); Peter Guy Silverman, "Military Aid to Civil Power in British Columbia: The Labor Strikes at Wellington and Steveston, 1890, 1900," *Pacific Northwest Quarterly* 61 (July 1970): 156–61.

42. *Citizen and Country*, 15 June 1900, p. 1; *Class Struggle*, 28 June 1899, p. 3; *The People*, 9 April 1899, p. 1.

43. *Slocan Drill*, 1 June 1900, p. 4; *Colonist*, 10 May 1900, p. 4; *Independent*, 19 May 1900, p. 1; 2 June 1900, p. 4; 7 July 1900, p. 1; Thomas Robert Loosmore, "The British Columbia Labor Movement and Political Action, 1879–1906" (M.A. thesis, University of British Columbia, 1954), p. 99.

44. *Sandon Paystreak*, 10 April 1900, p. 1; *Colonist*, 19 April 1900, p. 2; *Independent*, 28 April 1900, pp. 1, 2; *Rossland Industrial World*, 26 May 1900, p. 4.

45. *Independent*, 28 July 1900, p. 1; *Slocan Drill*, 9 November 1900, p. 4; *Rossland Industrial World*, 6 October 1900, p. 1; *Lardeau Eagle* (Ferguson, B.C.), 21 October 1900, p. 1; Ronald Grantham, "Some Aspects of the Socialist Movement in British Columbia (M.A. thesis, University of British Columbia, 1942), p. 12.

CHAPTER 7

1. Harvey O'Connor, *Revolution in Seattle: A Memoir* (New York: *Monthly Review Press*, 1964), p. 13; *Colonist*, 29 August 1893, p. 4; *Seattle Socialist*, 7 September 1907, p. 4.

2. F. J. Dean to H. Kuhn, 3 January 1898, Socialist Labor party papers, box 19, State Historical Society of Wisconsin, Madison.

3. David A. Shannon, *The Socialist Party of America* (New York: Macmillan, 1955).

4. *Western Clarion* (Vancouver), 11 September 1909, p. 2; 27 May 1911, p. 2; Socialist Labor party, *Convention Proceedings, 1900*, in Socialist Labor party papers, Microfilm Reel 35; *International Socialist Review*, May 1912, p. 777; Daniel DeLeon, "Reform or Revolution," reprinted in Albert Fried, ed., *Socialism in America: From the Shakers to the Third International* (Garden City, N.Y.: Doubleday & Company, Anchor Books, 1970), pp. 244–55.

5. *Seattle Socialist*, 26 August 1900, p. 2; 7 July 1901, p. 1; 27 April 1902, p. 2; 1 May 1909, p. 4.

6. *Mason County Socialist Campaign Book* (n. p., [ca. 1912]); *Inland Empire News* (Hillyard, Wa.), 19 February 1914, pp. 2, 3.

7. *Social Democratic Herald* (Chicago), 9 September 1899, p. 3; *Weekly People* (New York), 19 October 1901, p. 5.

Notes

8. *Workingman's Paper* (Seattle), 30 October 1909, p. 1; *Seattle Socialist*, 6 January 1901, p. 1; 13 January 1901, p. 1; 26 October 1902, p. 2; *Spokane Spokesman-Review*, 7 January 1901, p. 3; *Social Democratic Herald*, 18 February 1899, p. 6.

9. *Colfax Commoner*, 18 July 1902, p. 1; *Yakima Herald*, 20 June 1901, p. 8; 17 October 1902, p. 7; *Appeal to Reason*, 16 November 1901, p. 3.

10. *Citizen and Country* (Toronto), 23 February 1900, p. 3; *Lardeau Eagle* (Ferguson, B.C.), 12 December 1901, p. 4; 28 December 1901, p. 3; *Seattle Socialist*, 30 June 1901, p. 2.

11. *Western Clarion*, 12 January 1907, p. 1; *Seattle Socialist*, 1 March 1901, p. 2; 29 December 1901, p. 4; 12 January 1902, p. 4; *Western Socialist* (Vancouver), 14 February 1903, p. 2; *Canadian Socialist* (Toronto), 20 June 1902, p. 3.

12. *Ferguson Eagle*, 14 February 1900, p. 1; 25 April 1900, p. 1; *Lardeau Eagle*, 28 December 1901, p. 3; *Citizen and Country*, 30 December 1899, p. 4; 13 January 1900, p. 3; 10 August 1900, p. 4.

13. *Independent* (Vancouver), 28 June 1902, p. 1; *Western Clarion*, 9 July 1904, p. 3; *Weekly People*, 7 November 1903, p. 1.

14. *Seattle Socialist*, 23 June 1901, p. 2; 29 December 1901, p. 1; 18 May 1902, p. 4; *Canadian Socialist*, 20 June 1902, p. 3.

15. *Seattle Socialist*, 24 March 1901, p. 2; 28 April 1901, p. 3; *New Charter* (San Francisco), 10 February 1897, p. 4; *Colonist*, 8 February 1903, p. 12; *Western Clarion*, 16 June 1904, p. 4; 16 July 1904, p. 2; 6 August 1904, p. 2; Dorothy G. Steeves, *The Compassionate Rebel: Ernest E. Winch and His Times* (Vancouver: Boag Foundation, 1960), p. 14.

16. *Canadian Socialist*, 2 August 1902, p. 4; *Western Clarion*, 13 October 1906, p. 1; 12 January 1907, p. 2; G. Weston Wrigley, "Another Red Spot on the Socialist Map," *International Socialist Review*, January 1904, pp. 398–403.

17. Robert W. Smith, *The Coeur d'Alene Mining War of 1892: A Case Study of an Industrial Dispute* (Corvallis, Ore.: Oregon State University Press, 1961); Vernon Jensen, *Heritage of Conflict: Labor Relations in the Nonferrous Metals Industry up to 1930* (Ithaca: Cornell University Press, 1950), pp. 26–30 *passim*; Richard E. Lingenfelter, *The Hardrock Miners* (Berkeley: University of California Press, 1974), pp. 196–212 *passim*.

18. *Miners' Magazine*, 2 July 1914, p. 7; *Freemen's Labor Journal*, 1 September 1899, p. 7; Philip Taft, *The A. F. of L. in the Time of Gompers* (New York: Harper & Brothers, 1957), p. 153.

19. *Freemen's Labor Journal*, 1 September 1899, p. 7; Smith, *The Coeur d'Alene Mining War of 1892*, p. 112; John H. M. Laslett, *Labor and the Left: A Study of Socialist and Radical Influences in the American Labor Movement, 1881–1924* (New York: Basic Books, 1970), p. 243; *Constitution and By-Laws of the Western Federation of Miners*, rev. ed. (Butte: Bystander Printers, 1895).

20. Philip S. Foner, *History of the Labor Movement in the United States* (New York: International Publishers, 1964), 3: 413–38 *passim*; Melvyn Dubofsky, "The Origins of Western Working Class Radicalism: 1890–1905," *Labor History* 7 (Spring 1966): 131–54.

CHAPTER 8

1. John Fahey, *Inland Empire: D. C. Corbin and Spokane* (Seattle: University of Washington Press, 1965). For a history of the economic influences in the Inland Empire, see William Hudson Kensel, "The Economic History of Spokane,

Washington, 1881–1910" (Ph.D. dissertation, Washington State University, 1962).

2. The pre-World War I patterns of transportation were determined using various issues of *The Official Guide of the Railways* (issued monthly by the National Railway Publication Co. of New York).

3. Bernard McEvoy, *From the Great Lakes to the Wide West: Impressions of a Tour between Toronto and the Pacific* (London: Sampson Low, Marston & Company, 1902), p. 258; R. H. Roy, "The Early Defense and Militia of the Okanagan Valley, 1871–1914," *Pacific Northwest Quarterly* 57 (January 1966): 28–35. See also Peter G. Silverman, "A History of the Militia and Defenses of British Columbia, 1871–1914" (M.A. thesis, University of British Columbia, 1956).

4. *Mining*, January 1896, p. 14.

5. John S. Church, "Mining Companies in the West Kootenay and Boundary Regions of British Columbia, 1890–1900, Capital Formation and Financial Operations" (M.A. thesis, University of British Columbia, 1961); C. F. J. Galloway, *The Call of the West – Letters from British Columbia* (London: T. Fisher Unwin, 1917), p. 26.

6. William J. Wilgus, *The Railway Interrelations of the United States and Canada* (New Haven: Yale University Press, 1937), p. 18. See also the annual reports published by the Canadian Pacific and Great Northern railways between 1893 and 1910.

7. *Colonist*, 10 June 1887, p. 4; *Spokane Spokesman-Review*, 12 January 1902, p. 9; *Seattle Union Record*, 28 February 1903, p. 5.

8. *Spokane Review*, 2 November 1888, p. 3; James Leroy Hunt, "A History of the Central Labor Council in Spokane, Washington" (M.A. thesis, State College of Washington, 1940), pp. 3, 4.

9. *Spokane Review*, 6 February 1892, p. 3; 13 February 1892, p. 8; 15 February 1892, p. 3; *Spokane Falls Review*, 5 November 1889, p. 3; Marion Harrington, "The Populist Movement in Oregon, 1889–1896" (M.A. thesis, University of Oregon, 1935), pp. 17, 59.

10. *Freemen's Labor Journal* (Spokane), 26 June 1897, pp. 3, 7; 9 Decmber 1898, p. 8; 16 August 1901, p. 7.

11. *Spokane Review*, 3 September 1891, p. 3; 8 September 1891, p. 1.

12. Robert D. Saltvig, "The Progressive Movement in Washington" (Ph.D. dissertation, University of Washington, 1966), pp. 53, 56; *Spokane Review*, 17 April 1894, p. 1; *Spokesman-Review*, 26 April 1896, p. 3; 8 June 1896, p. 6.

13. *Spokesman-Review*, 8 June 1896, p. 6.

14. John H. M. Laslett, *Labor and the Left: A Study of Socialist and Radical Influences in the American Labor Movement, 1881–1924* (New York: Basic Books, 1970), p. 5.

15. *Rossland Industrial World*, 20 January 1900, p. 3; William D. Haywood, *Bill Haywood's Book: The Autobiography of William D. Haywood* (New York: International Publishers, 1929), p. 30; *Miners' Magazine*, April 1902, pp. 30, 31.

16. *Spokesman-Review*, 15 July 1897, p. 5; 22 July 1897, p. 6; 22 November 1899, p. 1; *Freemen's Labor Journal*, 2 August 1897, p. 1; 5 November 1897, p. 1.

17. *Nelson Miner*, 3 June 1893, p. 8; Theodore F. Allison, "History of Northwest Mining Unions Through 1920" (M.A. thesis, State College of Washington, 1943), pp. 55; *Colonist*, 9 August 1895, p. 3; Paul Phillips, *No Power Greater: A Century of Labour in British Columbia* (Vancouver: Boag Foundation, 1967), pp. 28, 29.

18. *Colonist*, 20 January 1900, p. 4; 7 February 1900, p. 3.

19. *Freemen's Labor Journal*, 9 June 1899, p. 1; *Sandon Paystreak*, 21 October 1899, p. 2; *Colonist*, 21 June 1899, p. 1; 1 September 1899, p. 4; 15 February 1900, p. 8; *Rossland Industrial World*, 20 January 1900, p. 3; "Convention of the Unions of the Western Federation of Miners District No. 6, Rossland, December 18, 1899," in Angus MacInnis collection, box 4, Special Collections Division, University of British Columbia Library.

20. Rodman W. Paul, *Mining Frontiers of the Far West, 1848–1880* (New York: Holt Rinehart and Winston, 1963); Robert W. Smith, *The Coeur d'Alene Mining War of 1892: A Case Study of an Industrial Dispute* (Corvallis, Ore.: Oregon State University Press, 1961).

21. R. E. Gosnell, *The Year Book of British Columbia and Manual of Provincial Information, 1897* (Victoria: Legislative Assembly, 1897), p. 27; George V. Ferguson, "Queen of the Kootenays," *Beaver*, Outfit 290 (Spring 1960), 18–23; Michael R. Booth, "Theatrical Boom in the Kootenays," *Beaver*, Outfit 292 (Autumn 1961), 42–46.

22. *Boundary Creek Times*, 6 May 1899, p. 2; *Colonist*, 29 July 1893, p. 4; Daniel J. Boorstin, *The Americans: The National Experience* (New York: Random House, 1965), pp. 65, 85; *Okanogan Record*, 28 April 1905, p. 4.

23. *Coeur d'Alene Barbarian* (Wallace) 30 April 1892, p. 4; *Miners' Magazine*, April 1900, p. 15; Clive Phillipps-Wooley, "Mining Development in British Columbia," *Canadian Magazine*, February 1897, 299–304.

24. Olga Osing, "Canada's Volcanic City: Rossland, B.C.," *Canadian Geographical Journal* 73 (November 1966): 166–71; *Labour Gazette*, February 1904, p. 768; *Rossland Industrial World*, 20 January 1900, p. 3; 14 July 1900, p. 1.

25. "Annual Report of the Minister of Mines, 1901," in *British Columbia Sessional Papers, 1901*, pp. 1216–21 *passim*; "State Inspector of Coal Mines Report," in the "Fourth Biennial Report of the Bureau of Labor of the State of Washington, 1903–1904," *Washington Public Documents, 1903–1904*, 2: 20–29 *passim*. Though conditions varied from camp to camp, hardrock miners lived in a basically male society. The manager of the Le Roi Mining Company reported as late as 1913 that at one of his mines all but 5 of the 130 male employees lived in the company boarding house. About 65 of the men were single; the remainder returned to their families when winter shut down mining operations. "Evidence before the Board of Arbitration, New Denver, January 14, 1913," in the Cominco papers, box 9, folder 2, Public Archives of British Columbia.

26. Marilyn Tharp, "Story of Coal at Newcastle," *Pacific Northwest Quarterly* 48 (October 1957): 120–26; Joseph F. Tripp, "Progressive Labor Laws in Washington State (1900–1925)" (Ph.D. dissertation, University of Washington, 1973), pp. 20, 21; "Eighth Biennial Report of the Bureau of Labor Statistics and Factory Inspection," in *Washington Public Documents, 1911–1912*, 3: 320; *Miners' Magazine*, March 1901, p. 19.

27. *Industrial Worker*, 12 August 1909, p. 1; *Union Record*, 9 October 1915, p. 2; *Nelson Miner*, 17 June 1893, p. 3; *Boundary Creek Times*, 31 May 1899, p. 7.

28. *Miners' Magazine*, October 1902, p. 13; *Freemen's Labor Journal*, 25 October 1901, p. 1; Haywood, *Bill Haywood's Book*, p. 23. Dubofsky notes that Haywood's autobiography was written "while the author was in exile in Moscow, a desperately ill and defeated man. Completed with the assistance of Communist party ghostwriters, the autobiography rings true in many places, yet it is replete with errors a healthy and observant Haywood would never have tolerated." Melvyn

Dobofsky, *We Shall Be All; A History of the Industrial Workers of the World* (Chicago: Quadrangle Books, 1969), p. 532.

29. Dubofsky, *We Shall Be All*, pp. 58–59. See also, Cominco papers, Labour Relations, 1905–1913.

30. *Miners' Magazine*, August 1901, pp. 29–32; October 1901, p. 7.

31. Paul Phillips, *No Power Greater*, pp. 33–34; *Rossland Industrial World*, 20 January 1900, p. 3; 14 July 1900, p. 1; *Miners' Magazine*, 10 August 1915, p. 4; Western Federation of Miners, *Convention Proceedings, 1903*, p. 8; idem, *Convention Proceedings, 1907*, pp. 136ff. See also International Union of Mine, Mill, and Smelter Workers (Canada) papers, box 155, folder 1. The striking Rossland miners lost the equivalent of 50,000 working days in 1901. *Report on Strikes and Lockouts in Canada, 1901–1912* (Ottawa: Department of Labour, 1913), p. 171.

32. *Miners' Magazine*, January 1902, p. 19; *Northport News*, 1 December 1 1902, p. 8; *Seattle Socialist*, 8 December 1901, p. 1.

33. Western Federation of Miners, *Convention Proceedings, 1902*, pp. 69, 166.

34. *Social Democratic Herald* (Chicago), 4 November 1899, p. 1; 11 November 1899, p. 1.

35. *Canadian Annual Review, 1902*, p. 87; *Independent* (Vancouver), 22 March 1902, p. 1; *Single Tax Review*, 15 July 1902, p. 58.

36. *Canadian Socialist* (Vancouver), 5 July 1902, p. 4; *Western Socialist* (Vancouver), 8 November 1902, p. 4; *Independent*, 28 June 1902, p. 1; 10 January 1903, p. 1.

37. *Independent*, 12 July 1902, p. 1; 20 December 1902, p. 2; *Canadian Socialist*, 16 July 1902, p. 4; *Citizen and Country* (Toronto), 30 May 1902, p. 2.

38. *Seattle Socialist*, 21 July 1901, p. 3; *Miners' Magazine*, November 1901, p. 45.

39. *Freemen's Labor Journal*, 25 February 1899, p. 1; 7 July 1899, p. 1; 13 October 1899, p. 4; 20 October 1899, p. 1; 20 July 1900, p. 4.

40. *Social Democratic Herald*, 31 March 1900, p. 3; *Pueblo Courier*, 12 October 1900, p. 1; *Weekly People* (New York), 8 July 1911, p. 5.

41. *Spokesman-Review*, 14 September 1902, p. 8; *Freemen's Labor Journal*, 1 May 1903, p. 4; *Idaho Daily Statesman* (Boise), 5 January 1895, p. 3; *New Time* (Spokane), 10 December 1904, p. 2; 7 January 1905, p. 4.

42. *Social Democratic Herald*, 31 March 1900, p. 3; *New Time*, 6 June 1903; p. 1; 28 March 1904, pp. 1, 4; 10 December 1904, p. 2; 7 January 1905, p. 4; Paul B. Bushue, "Dr. Hermon F. Titus and Socialism in Washington State; 1900–1909" (M.A. thesis, University of Washington, 1967), p. 33.

CHAPTER 9

1. *Freemen's Labor Journal* (Spokane), 7 February 1902, p. 1; Philip S. Foner, *History of the Labor Movement in the United States* (New York: International Publishers, 1964), 3: 413–27 *passim*.

2. *American Labor Union Journal*, 16 April 1903, p. 6; 3 September 1903, p. 3; *Freemen's Labor Journal*, 31 March 1899, p. 4; 2 March 1900, p. 1; 4 May 1900, p. 1; 17 August 1900, p. 1; *Spokane Spokesman-Review*, 26 April 1896, p. 3. Walker attended the 1899 convention of the WLU as one of the two delegates from the Spokane labor movement. Delegates were also present from Rossland and Kaslo, British Columbia. *Pueblo Courier*, 12 May 1899, p. 1.

3. *Northern Light* (Tacoma, Seattle, and Spokane), 11 October 1890, p. 2; *Spokane Industrial World*, 18 November 1892, p. 3; *Coast Seamen's Journal*, 14 June

Notes

1893, p. 9; *Directory of the Labor Unions of the State of Washington and Northern Idaho for 1898* (Spokane ?: n.p., ca. 1898), pp. 9–17 *passim*.

4. Minutes of the Western Central Labor Union, 15 November 1899, Archives and Manuscripts Division, University of Washington Library; *American Federationist*, February 1901, p. 62; Foner, *History of the Labor Movement in the United States*, 3: 415–16.

5. "Address of the State Labor Congress Delivered in the Committee of the Whole House in the Hall of Representatives, February 9, 1893" (Seattle ?: n.p., ca. 1893); *Directory of the Labor Unions of the States of Washington and Idaho for 1898*, pp. 17–21.

6. *Freemen's Labor Journal*, 28 January 1898, pp. 1, 2; James Leroy Hunt, "A History of the Central Labor Council in Spokane, Washington" (M.A. thesis, State College of Washington, 1940), pp. 8, 9.

7. *Seattle Union Record*, 29 June 1901, p. 4; 11 January 1902, p. 1; 18 January 1902, p. 4; 25 January 1902, p. 4; 25 October 1902, p. 3; 29 November 1902, p. 1; *Labor Clarion* (San Francisco), 28 February 1902, p. 1.

8. *Union Record*, 10 November 1900, p. 4; 7 December 1901, p. 4; 22 February 1902, p. 4; 1 March 1902, p. 4; 15 April 1902, p. 4; 1 November 1902, p. 4; 29 November 1902, p. 1.

9. Ibid, 1 Feburary 1902, p. 4; 15 February 1902, p. 4; 22 February 1902, p. 4; 15 April 1902, p. 4; *Freemen's Labor Journal*, 4 April 1902, p. 1; Minutes of the Western Central Labor Union, 12 February 1902.

10. *Freemen's Labor Journal*, 20 February 1903, p. 1; *Union Record*, 23 January 1904, p. 1; *Spokane Record*, 26 February 1904, p. 4.

11. *Freemen's Labor Journal*, 18 January 1901, p. 1; 10 January 1903, p. 1; 16 February 1903, p. 1; *Spokane Record*, 22 January 1904, p. 1; 29 January 1904, p. 4; 10 June 1904, p. 4; *Spokesman-Review*, 27 December 1903, p. 7; *American Labor Union Journal*, 19 May 1904, p. 2.

12. *Spokane Record*, 26 February 1904, p. 4; 15 July 1904, p. 1; *Portland Labor Press*, 30 August 1906, p. 1 (second section).

13. Details of the affiliation struggle in Spokane can be found in Hunt, "A History of the Central Labor Council in Spokane, Washington," pp. 14–25.

14. *Miner's Magazine*, January 1902, p. 19; *Union Record*, 13 October 1900, p. 4; 6 November 1901, p. 4; 20 November 1901, p. 4; 21 June 1902, pp. 2, 4; 1 November 1902, p. 4; 10 January 1903, p. 2; 6 February 1904, p. 4; *Labour Gazette*, January 1904, p. 675.

15. *Union Record*, 15 February 1902, p. 4; 25 October 1902, p. 3; 1 November 1902, p. 4; 17 October 1903, p. 1.

16. Robert L. Friedheim, *The Seattle General Strike* (Seattle: University of Washington Press, 1964), pp. 26, 27.

17. Allan Donald Orr, "The Western Federation of Miners and the Royal Commission on Industrial Disputes in 1903 with Special Reference to the Vancouver Island Coal Miners' Strike" (M.A. thesis, University of British Columbia, 1968), pp. 101–3.

18. Martin Robin, *Radical Politics and Canadian Labour* (Kingston, Ont.: Industrial Relations Centre, Queen's University, 1968), pp. 74–75; Thomas Robert Loosmore, "The British Columbia Labor Movement and Political Action, 1879–1906" (M.A. thesis, University of British Columbia, 1954), p. 159.

19. Trades and Labor Congress, *Convention Proceedings, 1902*, pp. 1, 56–57, 68. The best account of the 1902 Berlin convention is Robert H. Babcock, *Gompers in*

Canada, A Study in American Continentalism Before the First World War (Toronto: University of Toronto Press, 1974), pp. 85–97.

20. Trades and Labor Congress, *Convention Proceedings, 1900*, pp. 4, 23; Babcock, *Gompers in Canada*, pp. 51, 111–42 *passim*.

21. *Labour Gazette*, August 1901, p. 91; Babcock, *Gompers in Canada*, pp. 38–54 *passim*.

22. British Columbia suffered the loss of 512,433 workdays because of strikes and lockouts in 1903 as compared with 9,122 in 1902 and 5,150 in 1904. *Report on Strikes and Lockouts in Canada, 1901–1912* (Ottawa: Department of Labour, 1913), p. 73.

23. *Railroad Telegrapher*, April 1899, p. 320; June 1899, p. 518; June 1900, p. 518.

24. *American Labor Union Journal*, 3 September 1903, p. 14.

25. *Labour Gazette*, July 1903, p. 79; *Winnipeg Voice*, 9 May 1902, p. 6; 13 June 1902, p. 1.

26. *American Labor Union Journal*, 29 January 1903, p. 3; 3 September 1903, p. 14; *Western Socialist* (Vancouver), 17 January 1903, p. 1.

27. *Railroad Telegrapher*, July 1901, pp. 601–3; *Railway Trainmen's Journal* as quoted in the *Railroad Telegrapher*, January 1902, pp. 3, 4.

28. Foner, *History of the Labor Movement in the United States*, 3: 425; *Railroad Telegrapher*, January 1902, pp. 3, 4.

29. Trades and Labor Congress, *Convention Proceedings, 1903*, p. 10; *Winnipeg Voice*, 30 January 1903, p. 6; *Railway Employees' Journal*, 11 June 1903, p. 1; *American Federationist*, April 1905, p. 215.

30. *American Labor Union Journal*, 1 January 1903, p. 5; *Railway Employees' Journal*, 11 June 1903, p. 3.

31. *American Labor Union Journal*, 19 March 1903, p. 5; 3 September 1903, p. 12; *Labour Gazette*, May 1903, p. 796; *Winnipeg Voice*, 18 July 1902, p. 1; The Canadian Pacific strike was unwanted and unplanned. The UBRE had expected to organize in the West and then move east until it attained a membership of 100,000. Paul Phillips, *No Power Greater: A Century of Labour in British Columbia* (Vancouver: Boag Foundation, 1967), p. 40.

32. *Report on Strikes and Lockouts in Canada, 1901–1912*, p. 185. Phillips, *No Power Greater*, pp. 39–41; "Report of the Royal Commission on Industrial Disputes in the Province of British Columbia," in Dominion of Canada, *Sessional Papers*, 37, no. 36a (1903); "Evidence taken before the Royal Commission to Inquire into Industrial Disputes in the Province of British Columbia," in Dominion of Canada, *Sessional Papers*, 38, no. 13 (1904); Minutes of the Regular Meetings of the Vancouver Trades and Labor Council, 5 March 1903; 19 March 1903, Vancouver Trades and Labor Council papers, Special Collections Division, University of British Columbia Library.

33. *American Labor Union Journal*, 19 March 1903, p. 5; 3 September 1903, p. 12; Orr, "The Western Federation of Miners," pp. iv, 140, 151; *Fourth Annual Report on Labour Organization in Canada* (1915), p. 80.

34. *American Labor Union Journal*, 3 September 1903, p. 12; *Report on Strikes and Lockouts in Canada, 1901–1912*, p. 181; *Union Record*, 15 June 1901, p. 4; *Miners' Magazine*, May 1903, pp. 20, 21; "Evidence taken before the Royal Commission to Inquire into Industrial Disputes in the Province of British Columbia," pp. 239–46.

35. *American Labor Union Journal*, 3 September 1903, p. 12; *Union Record*, 5 April 1903, p. 4.

36. *American Labor Union Journal*, 9 April 1903, p. 1; 16 April 1903, p. 6; 9 July 1903, p. 2; *Western Socialist*, 8 November 1902, p. 4.

37. The Vancouver Trades and Labor Council rejoined the Dominion's Labor Congress in order to send delegates to the 1906 TLC convention in Victoria. John T. Saywell, "Labour and Socialism in British Columbia: A Survey of Historical Development Before 1903," *British Columbia Historical Quarterly* 15 (July-October, 1951): 144.

38. *Colonist*, 17 May 1903, p. 4; *Canadian Annual Review, 1903*, p. 527; American Federation of Labor, *Convention Proceedings, 1903*, p. 66; *Trades and Labor Congress, Convention Proceedings, 1903*, pp. 30–32.

39. A detailed analysis on the Royal Commission "Report" is contained in Orr, "The Western Federation of Miners."

40. *American Labor Union Journal*, 11 May 1903, p. 1; 3 September 1903, p. 12; *Labour Gazette*, June 1904, pp. 127ff; George Estes, *Railway Employees United: A Story of Railroad Brotherhoods* (Portland, Ore.: G. Estes, 1931).

41. Western Federation of Miners, *Convention Proceedings, 1904*, p. 274; *United Mine Workers' Journal*, 9 July 1903, pp. 2, 4; 3 March 1904, p. 4.

42. John H. M. Laslett, *Labor and the Left; A Study of Socialist and Radical Influences in the American Labor Movement, 1881–1924* (New York: Basic Books, 1970), pp. 192–94; Norman Ware, *The Labor Movement in the United States, 1860–1895* (New York: D. Appleton and Company, 1929), p. 218.

43. *Miners' Magazine*, 2 February 1905, p. 13; *Voice of Labor* (Chicago), February 1905, p. 1.

44. Industrial Workers of the World, *Convention Proceedings, 1905*, pp. 28, 543. Delegate Riordan objected to the word "American" in the title of the proposed industrial union organization; he argued that the name change from the Western Labor Union to the American Labor Union had hindered the union's organizational activities in Canada (*Ibid.*, p. 297).

45. Philip Taft, *The A. F. of L. in the Time of Gompers* (New York: Harper & Brothers, 1957), p. 159; Melvyn Dubofsky, *We Shall Be All: A History of the Industrial Workers of the World* (Chicago: Quadrangle Books, 1969), pp. 76–87 *passim*.

46. *Winnipeg Voice*, 14 July 1905, p. 1; *Union Record*, 3 November 1906, p. 3; Dubofsky, *We Shall Be All*, pp. 138–39; Harold H. Kolb, "Industrial Millstone," *Idaho Yesterdays* 16 (Summer 1972): 30–32.

47. Cloice R. Howd, "Industrial Relations in the West Coast Lumber Industry," in Bureau of Labor Statistics, *Bulletin 349* (1924), p. 63; *Industrial Worker* (Spokane), 22 July 1909, p. 2.

48. Howd, "Industrial Relations in the West Coast Lumber Industry," pp. 39, 40, 41. See also the material on the Pacific Northwest lumber industry in the C. D. Orchard papers, Special Collections Division, University of British Columbia Library.

49. Norman H. Clark, *Mill Town: A Social History of Everett, Washington, from Its Earliest Beginnings on the Shores of Puget Sound to the Tragic and Infamous Event Known as the Everett Massacre* (Seattle: University of Washington Press, 1970), pp. 92–93; James Rowan, *The I. W. W. in the Lumber Industry* (Seattle: Lumber Workers Industrial Union, [ca. 1920]), p. 7.

50. Clark, *Mill Town*, pp. 90, 91; Rowan, *The I. W. W. in the Lumber Industry*, pp. 22–25; Howd, "Industrial Relations in the West Coast Lumber Industry," pp. 55–61 *passim*; Vernon H. Jensen, *Lumber and Labor* (New York: Farrar and

Rinehart, 1945), p. 116; John H. Cox, "Trade Associations in the Lumber Industry of the Pacific Northwest, 1899–1914," *Pacific Northwest Quaterly* 41 (October 1950): 285–311.

51. Robert Tyler, *Rebels of the Woods: the I. W. W. in the Pacific Northwest* (Eugene, Ore.: University of Oregon Books, 1967); *Union Record*, 26 April 1913, p. 5.

52. *Historical Statistics of the United States: Colonial Times to 1970* (Washington, D.C.: Government Printing Office, 1975), 1: 12–37 *passim*. An excellent study of the political and judicial climate of opinion in Washington during the Progressive Era is found in Joseph F. Tripp, "Progressive Labor Laws in Washington State (1900–1925)" (Ph.D. dissertation, University of Washington, 1973).

CHAPTER 10

1. *Seattle Union Record*, 6 April 1901, p. 4; 17 August 1901, p. 4; *Seattle Socialist*, 25 August 1901, p. 1; Meryl E. Rogers, "The Labor Movement in Seattle, 1885–1905" (M.A. thesis, Pacific Lutheran University, 1970), p. 111.

2. *Union Record*, 27 September 1902, p. 1; 13 August 1904, p. 4; 19 November 1904, p. 4.

3. Ibid., 3 November 1900, pp. 1, 4; 5 January 1901, p. 4; 29 June 1901, p. 4; 20 January 1906, p. 1. Kearney, an outspoken leader of the anti-Chinese movement in California, had been widely admired by Sinophobes in the Pacific Northwest.

4. American Federation of Labor, *Convention Proceedings, 1901*, p. 22; idem, *Convention Proceedings, 1902*, p. 112.

5. Mable F. Timlin, "Canada's Immigration Policy, 1896–1910," *Canadian Journal of Economics and Political Science* 26 (November 1960): 519–32.

6. *B. C. Saturday Sunset* (Vancouver), 21 September 1907, p. 1; *Canadian Annual Review, 1909*, p. 581; *Western Clarion* (Vancouver), 27 October 1906, p. 2.

7. Joseph Gowen, "Canada and the Myth of the Japan Market, 1896–1911," *Pacific Historical Review* 39 (February 1970): 63–83.

8. *American Federationist*, November 1907, pp. 866–69; Howard H. Sugimoto, "The Vancouver Riot and its International Significance," *Pacific Northwest Quarterly* 44 (October 1973): 163–74. American influence was, to some degree, responsible for the riot. Branches of the newly formed Asiastic Exclusion League united American and Canadian workers in a common cause. According to the *Union Record*, hatred of Oriental labor was so intense in Vancouver that "a peaceable meeting held by organized labor proved the torch that started the anti-oriental bonfire, but the flames were fed by other than union men." *Union Record*, 17 September 1907, p. 2; 1 February 1908, p. 1; 19 May 1908, p. 2. Robert Wynne, "American Labor Leaders and the Vancouver Anti-Oriental Riot," *Pacific Northwest Quarterly* 57 (October 1966): 173, 174, 178. See also the Harry Cowan Scrapbooks, Special Collections Division, University of British Columbia Library. Cowan was secretary of the Asiatic Exclusion League in Vancouver.

9. *Labour Gazette*, September 1905, pp. 279–88; John H. Cox, "Trade Associations in the Lumber Industry of the Pacific Northwest, 1899–1914," *Pacific Northwest Quarterly* 41 (October 1950): 285–311; Clarence Bonnett, *Employers' Associations in the United States: A Study of Typical Associations* (New York: Macmillan, 1922).

10. William M. Dick, *Labor and Socialism in America: The Gompers Era* (Port

Notes

Washington, N.Y.: Kennikat Press, 1972), p. 35; *American Federationist*, August 1906, p. 542; January 1909, p. 37; *Union Record*, 4 August 1906, p. 1.

11. *Union Record*, 10 February 1906, p. 1; 17 February 1906, p. 1; 8 September 1906, p. 2; 22 February 1908, p. 1; 14 March 1908, p. 1.

12. Ibid., 16 July 1910, p. 4; 30 July 1910, p. 1; 20 August 1910, p. 5; Melvin G. De Shazo, "Radical Tendencies in the Seattle Labor Movement as Reflected in the Proceedings of its Central Body" (M.A. thesis, University of Washington, 1925), p. 25; *Workingman's Paper* (Seattle), 20 August 1910, p. 1; Donald D. Saltvig, "The Progressive Movement in Washington" (Ph.D. dissertation, University of Washington, 1966), pp. 403–6. Labor's endorsement of a candidate in the Seattle municipal elections of the pre-World War I era was of negligible importance except where combined with support from other groups. William J. Dickson, "Labor in Municipal Politics: A Study of Labor's Political Policies and Activities in Seattle" (M.A. thesis, University of Washington, 1928).

13. *Union Record*, 20 January 1906, p. 4; 19 May 1906, p. 1.

14. Patrons of Husbandry, *Convention Proceedings, 1902*, p. 198; Washington State Grange, *Convention Proceedings, 1905*, p. 10; idem, *Convention Proceedings, 1916*, p. 37; *Pacific Grange Bulletin*, November 1908, p. 1; George Shibley, "Progressive Farmers," *Arena*, January 1908, p. 97.

15. Charles S. Barrett, *The Mission, History and Times of the Farmers' Union* (Nashville, Tenn.: Marshall & Bruce, 1909); William P. Tucker, "Populism Up-to-date: The Story of the Farmers' Union," *Agricultural History* 21 (October 1947): 198–201.

16. *Union Record*, 12 January 1907, p. 1; 19 January 1907, p. 4; 20 June 1908, p. 1; *American Federationist*, October 1908, pp. 891, 893.

17. *Union Record*, 11 October 1913, p. 6; *B. C. Federationist* (Vancouver), 13 June 1913, p. 1; *Everett Commonwealth*, 27 December 1912, p. 1.

18. *Union Record*, 11 July 1908, p. 1; 20 February 1909, p. 4; *Colfax Commoner*, 28 January 1910, p. 1.

19. *American Labor Union Journal*, 11 May 1903, p. 1; 3 September 1903, p. 12; *Colonist*, 2 March 1902, p. 10.

20. *Boundary Creek Times*, 5 September 1903, p. 2; *International Socialist Review*, October 1903, p. 249. Hawthornthwaite won with 44 percent of the vote in a three-way race in the Nanaimo riding; Williams received 40 percent of the vote in a three-way race in the Newcastle riding. Ernest Mills, the Socialist candidate in the Greenwood riding, lost by only nine votes out of 648 cast. The Socialist candidate in the Fernie riding also ran well. *Canadian Parliamentary Guide, 1905*, pp. 440–43.

21. Peter R. Hunt, "The Political Career of Sir Richard McBride" (M.A. thesis, University of British Columbia, 1953), p. 52; Brian R. D. Smith, "Sir Richard McBride: A Study in the Conservative Party of British Columbia, 1903–1916" (M.A. thesis, Queen's University, 1959); H. F. Evans to Richard McBride, 28 October 1903, and H. F. Evans to Richard McBride, 31 October 1903, McBride papers, Private Letters, alphabetical no. 3, Public Archives of British Columbia.

22. *Canadian Annual Review, 1912*, p. 277; *Victoria Times*, 31 January 1907, p. 4; *Colonist*, 21 September 1907, p. 4; Dorothy Steeves, *The Compassionate Rebel: Ernest E. Winch and His Times* (Vancouver: Boag Foundation, 1960), pp. 16–17.

23. Capsule biographies of all the Socialists who served in the legislative assembly are available in Daisy Webster, *The Growth of the N. D. P. in B.C., 1900–1970* ([Vancouver: n.p., 1970?]).

24. *Western Clarion*, 11 August 1906, p. 2; Robert Harper Babcock, "The A. F. L. in Canada, 1896–1908: A Study in Labor Imperialism" (Ph.D. dissertation, Duke University, 1969), pp. 363–69 *passim*.

25. Trades and Labor Congress, *Convention Proceedings, 1906*, pp. 82–86 *passim*; *Labour Gazette*, October 1906, pp. 392–399; *Canadian Annual Review, 1906*, p. 269. Martin Robin details the conflict between the Laborites and Socialists in *Radical Politics and Canadian Labour, 1880–1930* (Kingston, Ont.: Industrial Relations Centre, Queen's University, 1968), pp. 81–86.

CHAPTER 11

1. *Seattle Socialist*, 1 August 1908, p. 4.

2. Ibid., 28 June 1903, p. 3; *Co-Operator* (Burley, Wa.), 11 September 1899, p. 4; *Miners' Magazine*, January 1901, p. 3; Paul B. Bushue, "Dr. Hermon F. Titus and Socialism in Washington State: 1900–1909" (M.A. thesis, University of Washington, 1967), p. 63.

3. *Seattle Socialist*, 12 July 1903, p. 1; *Co-Operator*, August 1903, p. 23.

4. Socialist Party of America, *Convention Proceedings, 1904*, pp. 16, 37; Bushue, "Dr. Hermon F. Titus and Socialism in Washington State," p. 76; *Seattle Times*, 19 February 1905, p. 20.

5. Melvyn Dubofsky, *We Shall Be All: A History of the Industrial Workers of the World* (Chicago: Quadrangle Books, 1969), pp. 96–105 *passim*; *Western Clarion* (Vancouver), 28 April 1906, p. 1.

6. *Victoria Times*, 24 March 1906, p. 4; *Socialist* (Caldwell, Id.), 7 July 1906, p. 1.

7. Bushue, "Dr. Hermon F. Titus and Socialism in Washington Sate," pp. 89, 92, 103; *Colfax Commoner*, 28 October 1904, p. 6; 2 November 1906, p. 4; *New Time* (Spokane), 7 November 1903, p. 2; *Socialist Party Official Bulletin*, February 1906, p. 3; E. B. Ault, "Autobiographical Sketch," in the E. B. Ault papers, box 6, folder 62, Archives and Manuscripts Division, University of Washington Library.

8. Bushue, "Dr. Hermon F. Titus and Socialism in Washington State," pp. 71, 72; *Portland Labor Press*, 26 November 1908, p. 1; *Citizen and Country* (Toronto), 9 May 1902, p. 3; *Canadian Socialist* (Vancouver), 16 July 1902, p. 4; *Direct Legislation Record*, July 1899, p. 49; Ira Kipnis, *The American Socialist Movement, 1897–1912* (New York: Monthly Review Press, 1952), p. 580.

9. *Saturday Evening Tribune* (Seattle), 15 June 1907, p. 5; *Labor and Socialist Press News*, 20 October 1906, p. 4; *Seattle Union Record*, 23 March 1907, p. 1.

10. Michael Harrington, *Socialism* (New York: Saturday Review Press, 1970), p. 122; *Seattle Socialist*, 1 August 1908, p. 3.

11. Ross Alfred Johnson, "'No Compromise — No Political Trading': The Marxian Socialist Tradition in British Columbia" (Ph.D. dissertation, University of British Columbia, 1975), pp. 279–81; *Saturday Evening Tribune*, 7 September 1907, p. 4; 12 October 1907, p. 1.

12. *Saturday Evening Tribune*, 11 May 1907, p. 7; 3 August 1907, p. 5; 7 September 1907, p. 4; 5 October 1907, p. 8; Bushue, "Dr. Hermon F. Titus and Socialism in Washington State," p. 108.

13. *Saturday Evening Tribune*, 27 July 1907, p. 5; 4 January 1908, p. 2; 25 April 1908, p. 1; Socialist Party of America, *Convention Proceedings, 1908*, pp. 43–61; *Seattle Socialist*, 13 June 1908, p. 4.

14. Kipnis, *The American Socialist Movement*, p. 372, *Seattle Socialist*, 25 July 1908, p. 4; 1 August 1908, p. 1; 9 January 1909, p. 2; 27 February 1909, p. 4.

Notes

There is no way to determine with certainty the exact Socialist vote in Washington in 1908. According to official sources there were approximately fourteen thousand Socialist votes cast, but because the party had balked at holding a primary as required by state law, the Supreme Court of Washington ruled that the party would not appear on the ballot. The Socialist party printed stickers that members affixed to the official ballot. "General Election Returns, 1908," in the "Tenth Biennial Report of the Secretary of State," *Washington Public Documents, 1907–1908*, 1: 20; Bushue, "Dr. Hermon F. Titus and Socialism in Washington State," p. 120.

15. *Seattle Socialist*, 27 February 1909, p. 4; 3 July 1909, p. 4; 10 July 1909, p. 1; 28 August 1909, p. 4.

16. Ibid., 24 July 1909, p. 4; 31 July 1909, p. 1; 28 August 1909, p. 4.

17. Ibid., 31 July 1909, p. 1; *Workingman's Paper* (Seattle), 6 November 1909, p. 1; 26 February 1910, p. 1; *Social Democratic Herald* (Milwaukee), 18 September 1909, p. 1; *Labor and Socialist Press News*, 14 August 1909, p. 5; 4 September 1909, p. 5; *Socialist Party Weekly Bulletin*, 21 August 1909, pp. 1, 2; 11 September 1909, pp. 1, 2; *Socialist Party Official Bulletin*, September 1909, pp. 1, 5.

18. *Seattle Socialist*, 11 September 1909, p. 1; 4 October 1909, p. 1; 23 October 1909, p. 4; *Workingman's Paper*, 30 October 1909, p. 1; 6 November 1909, p. 4; William Z. Foster, *From Bryan to Stalin* (New York: International Publishers, 1937), p. 37.

19. *Workingman's Paper*, 6 November 1909, p. 1; 26 February 1910, p. 1; 19 March 1910, p. 1; Foster, *From Bryan to Stalin*, pp. 26–39 *passim*.

20. Foster, *From Bryan to Stalin*, pp. 31, 38; Harvey O'Connor, *Revolution in Seattle: A Memoir* (New York: Monthly Review Press, 1964), p. 17. See also a copy of *The Four Hour Day* in Ault papers, part 1, box 5.

21. O'Connor, *Revolution in Seattle*, pp. 13, 17; Hulet M. Wells, "I Wanted to Work," manuscript in the Hulet M. Wells papers, box 2, Archives and Manuscripts Division, University of Washington Library, p. 127; Ault papers, box 5, folder 7.

22. *Spokane Spokesman-Review*, 2 May 1910, p. 13; Foster, *From Bryan to Stalin*, p. 31.

23. Members of the Vancouver executive committee of the former Socialist Party of British Columbia became the leaders of the SPC. They expected the new organization to unite the various socialist groups that had formed in other parts of Canada, but the SPC remained almost wholly a British Columbia organization. Because many of its leaders were convinced that socialists in other countries were deviating from correct policy, the SPC became very insular. Its rejection of immediate reforms lessened its appeal to most workers. Johnson, "'No Compromise — No Political Trading,'" pp. 190–91; *Winnipeg Voice*, 23 December 1904, p. 3.

24. *Colonist*, 17 December 1905, p. 4; 1 May 1906, p. 4; *Vancouver Daily Province*, 3 January 1905, p. 4; *Victoria Times*, 26 January 1907, p. 5; *Western Clarion*, 10 August 1906, p. 4; 3 November 1906, p. 1; 5 January 1907, p. 2; 2 February 1907, p. 3; 4 December 1907, p. 1; *Canadian Annual Review, 1907*, p. 607; John McInnis to Dorothy Steeves, 30 September 1958, Angus MacInnis collection, box 53, folder 8.

25. *American Labor Union Journal*, 3 September 1903, p. 12; R. P. Pettipiece to the Sandon Miners' Union, 11 August 1903, International Union of Mine, Mill, and Smelter Workers (Canada) papers, box 158, Special Collections Division, University of British Columbia Library; *Winnipeg Voice*, 8 February 1907, p. 6; *Western Clarion*, 22 April 1905, p. 2; Trades and Labor Congress, *Convention*

Proceedings, 1908, pp. 80–81; Tim Buck, *Our Fight for Canada* (Toronto: Progress Books, 1959), p. 24.

26. *Winnipeg Voice*, 10 May 1907, p. 1.

27. Johnson, "'No Compromise — No Political Trading,'" pp. 280–82; *Victoria Times*, 15 April 1907, p. 3; *Winnipeg Voice*, 3 May 1907, p. 1; 7 May 1909, p. 1; *Saturday Evening Tribune*, 18 May 1907, p. 3; *Social Democratic Herald*, 11 May 1907, p. 4; *Socialist Party Official Bulletin*, May 1907, p. 3.

28. *Weekly People* (New York), 4 May 1907, p. 1. For Ernest Burns's impression of DeLeon see Ernest Burns interview, April 1958, in the Angus MacInnis collection, box 53, folder 1.

29. Buck, *Our Fight for Canada*, p. 25; *Winnipeg Voice*, 30 April 1909, p. 1; 29 July 1910, p. 1; *Cotton's Weekly* (Cowansville, Quebec), 21 August 1913, p. 3; Johnson, "'No Compromise — No Political Trading,'" p. 289.

30. *B. C. Federationist* (Vancouver), 24 October 1913, p. 8; 9 December 1913, p. 2.

31. *Victoria Times*, 23 May 1911, p. 4; *Miners' Magazine*, 7 October 1909, p. 7; *Western Clarion*, 13 November 1909, p. 1; Dan Sproul, "The Situation in British Columbia," *International Socialist Review*, February 1910, pp. 741–44. John McInnis was not reelected in 1909, but he returned to the legislative assembly in 1945 as a Cooperative Commonwealth Federation representative from Ft. George. John McInnis to Dorothy Steeves, 30 September 1958, Angus MacInnis collection, box 53, folder 8.

32. *Social Democratic Herald*, 26 December 1908, p. 4; *Union Record*, 4 March 1911, p. 8; *Western Clarion*, 19 May 1906, p. 1; *Seattle Socialist*, 2 November 1907, p. 4.

33. The election statistics are taken from various issues of the *Canadian Parliamentary Guide*; occupational statistics are based on information in various issues of the *British Columbia Voters' List*. Before 1900 the *Voters' List* was included in the *Sessional Papers of British Columbia*.

34. Martin Robin, *The Rush for Spoils: The Company Province, 1871–1933* (Toronto: McClelland and Stewart, 1972), p. 114; Johnson, "'No Compromise — No Political Trading,'" pp. 49, 237.

CHAPTER 12

1. *Seattle Union Record*, 18 August 1909, p. 4; *Industrial Worker* (Spokane) 25 March 1909, p. 1; 22 June 1909, p. 4; 16 July 1910, p. 2; *Demonstrator* (Home, Wa.), 7 February 1906, p. 1; 20 June 1906, p. 2; 18 July 1906, p. 8.

2. William D. Haywood, *Bill Haywood's Book: The Autobiography of William D. Haywood* (New York: International Publishers, 1929), pp. 228–29; *Seattle Socialist*, 29 May 1909, p. 1; 12 June 1909, p. 1.

3. *Industrial Worker*, 18 March 1909, pp. 1–4; Robert C. Eckberg, "The Free Speech Fight of the Industrial Workers of the World, Spokane, Washington: 1909–1910" (M.A. thesis, Washington State University, 1967); Elizabeth Gurley Flynn, *The Rebel Girl: An Autobiography* (New York: International Publishers, 1955), pp. 95, 109.

4. *Pasco Express*, 18 November 1909, p. 4; Hermas John Bergman, "Progressive on the Right: Marion E. Hay, Governor of Washington, 1909–1913" (Ph.D. dissertation, Washington State University, 1967), p. 73; Philip S. Foner, *History of the*

Notes

Labor Movement in the United States (New York: International Publishers, 1965), 4: 183–85; Robert Tyler, *Rebels of the Woods: The I. W. W. in the Pacific Northwest* (Eugene, Ore.: University of Oregon Books, 1967), p. 39.

5. *Industrial Worker*, 20 May 1909, p. 1; 5 August 1909, p. 1; 16 July 1910, p. 1; *Miners' Magazine*, 26 May 1904, p. 11; *Colonist*, 4 June 1907, p. 4. Labor statistics were taken from the 1911 to 1914 issues of the Department of Labour's *Report on Labour Organization in Canada*.

6. Paul Phillips, *No Power Greater: A Century of Labour in British Columbia* (Vancouver: Boag Foundation, 1967), pp. 52–53; *Industrial Worker*, 15 June 1911, p. 1; Minutes of the Regular Meetings of the Vancouver Trades and Labor Council, 2 May 1912, Vancouver Trades and Labor Council papers, Special Collections Division, University of British Columbia Library; Foner, *History of the Labor Movement*, 4: 230–31. An excellent account of the IWW in Canada is A. Ross McCormack, *Reformers, Rebels, and Revolutionaries: The Western Canadian Radical Movement, 1899–1919* (Toronto: University of Toronto Press, 1977), pp. 98–117 *passim*.

7. *B. C. Federationist* (Vancouver), 20 April 1912, p. 1; 8 June 1912, p. 1; *Western Clarion* (Vancouver), 27 January 1912, p. 1; *Industrial Worker*, 8 February 1912, p. 1; Minutes of the Regular Meetings of the Vancouver Trades and Labor Council, 6 June 1912.

8. William Z. Foster, *Pages From a Worker's Life* (New York: International Publishers, 1939), p. 139. Foster's recollection is in error on one point, for Kamloops is situated on the Thompson River, which joins the Fraser River approximately seventy miles from the community. The Syndicalist League, which began as an offshoot of the IWW in Nelson, British Columbia, promoted syndicalism in the existing trade unions. *Agitator* (Home, Wa.), 15 May 1912, p. 4.

9. William Mackenzie and Donald Mann to William Bowser, 14 March 1913, McBride papers, Premier's Official Correspondence, 1913, box 296, folder 13, Public Archives of British Columbia; *Industrial Worker*, 13 March 1913, p. 1; *Vancouver Daily Province*, 2 February 1912, p. 1. Aside from a minute book for the IWW's Vancouver branch in 1912, the IWW collection at the University of British Columbia contains little material on the Wobblies in the province before 1917.

10. Tyler, *Rebels of the Woods*, pp. 44–48; *Union Record*, 1 September 1917, p. 4.

11. American Federation of Labor, *Convention Proceedings, 1910*, pp. 198–99; Trades and Labor Congress, *Convention Proceedings, 1911*, pp. 14, 41; Watters left British Columbia in 1913.

12. *Western Wage-Earner* (Vancouver), 15 June 1912, p. 1; *B. C. Federationist*, 15 June 1912, p. 1.

13. *B. C. Federationist*, 24 August 1912, p. 2; *Report on Labour Organization in Canada, 1911*, pp. 31, 80–83; Phillips, *No Power Greater*, pp. 169–70; Washington State Federation of Labor, *Convention Proceedings, 1911*, p. 23; *Union Record*, 8 July 1905, p. 7.

14. Harry W. Call, compiler, *History of Washington Federation of Labor, 1902–1954* (n.p.: [Washington State Federation of Labor], n.d.), pp. 43–44; Norman H. Clark, *Mill Town: A Social History of Everett, Washington, from Its Earliest Beginnings on the Shores of Puget Sound to the Tragic and Infamous Event Known as the Everett Massacre* (Seattle: University of Washington Press, 1970), pp. 93–95 *passim*, 148. Marsh remained president of the Washington State Federation of Labor until 1917.

15. *Colonist*, 7 July 1907, p. 25; 21 August 1910, p. 8 (Sunday section); *Week*

(Vancouver), 8 February 1913, p. 4; *Canadian Municipal Journal*, April 1914, p. 135; Trades and Labor Congress, *Convention Proceedings, 1913*, p. 88.

16. *B. C. Federationist*, 3 October 1913; *Colonist*, 31 December 1915, p. 4; 14 April 1916, p. 2; *Vancouver Daily World*, 19 October 1912, p. 40; *Champion* (Vancouver), August 1912, p. 12; *B. C. Saturday Sunset* (Vancouver), 7 November 1914, p. 1; B. C. Alcohol Research and Education Council, Minute Book 43, 1915–16, in Public Archives of British Columbia.

17. Joseph F. Tripp, "Progressive Labor Laws in Washington State (1900–1925)" (Ph.D. dissertation, University of Washington, 1973); *Industrial Canada*, July 1913, p. 1569; *Industrial Progress and Commercial Record*, April 1915, p. 264; *B. C. Federationist*, 14 August 1914, p. 1; Burton J. Hendrick, "Insurance for Workingmen: How Labor is Automatically Protected in the State of Washington," *McClure's*, December 1912, 169–77.

18. *Colonist*, 30 March 1900, p. 4; 7 March 1919, pp. 1, 4; *Victoria Times*, 13 March 1919, p. 11; *Winnipeg Voice*, 1 May 1908, p. 1; *Canadian Annual Review*, *1919*, p. 795; Keith A. Berriedale, "The Initiative and Referendum in Canada," *Journal of Comparative Legislation and International Law*, 3rd S., 2 (January 1920): 112–15.

19. *Victoria Times*, 15 July 1911, p. 1; 20 September 1911, pp. 1, 4; *Week*, 28 January 1911, p. 1; 16 September 1911, p. 1; *Colonist*, 21 September 1911, p. 2; Martin Robin, *The Rush for Spoils: The Company Province, 1871–1933* (Toronto: McClelland and Stewart, 1972), p. 119.

20. Margaret A. Ormsby, *British Columbia: a History* ([Toronto]: Macmillan of Canada, 1958), p. 363; *Vancouver Sun*, 12 February 1912, p. 6; 5 March 1912, p. 6; *Nelson Daily News*, 2 March 1912, p. 1; *Western Call* (Vancouver), 15 March 1912, p. 4; *Week*, 9 March 1912, p. 1; *Spokane Spokesman-Review*, 16 November 1910, p. 3.

21. Brian R. D. Smith, "Sir Richard McBride: A Study in the Conservative Party of British Columbia" (M.A. thesis, Queen's University, 1959), p. 313; Herbert Cuthbert to Richard McBride, 14 March 1913, McBride papers, Private Correspondence, 1913, box 311, folder 13; Richard McBride to Donald Mann, 17 August 1914, McBride papers, Premier's Correspondence Inward, Canadian Northern Railway, 1913–14; *Canadian Annual Review, 1915*, p. 730.

22. *Industrial Progress and Commercial Record*, January 1916, p. 146.

23. *Canadian Annual Review, 1916*, pp. 754, 755, 777; *Industrial Progress and Commercial Record*, January 1916, p. 143; Ormsby, *British Columbia*, pp. 391–93.

24. *Vancouver Sun*, 1 September 1916, p. 4; 11 September 1916, p. 17; Robin, *The Rush for Spoils*, pp. 162–73 *passim*; *Canadian Annual Review, 1916*, pp. 768–69; Ormsby, *British Columbia*, pp. 393–94. The Workmen's Compensation Act had actually been passed during the last days of the Bowser government but was reinacted because Brewster had doubts about the legitimacy of the original enactment. Robin, *The Rush for Spoils*, p. 171.

25. *Western Clarion*, 17 March 1906, p. 2; Miles Poindexter, "What Progressive Republicanism Stands For," *Man to Man*, July-August 1910, pp. 563–64; *Colonist*, 8 October 1910, p. 1; 26 September 1912, p. 4.

26. *Colfax Commoner*, 20 May 1904, p. 3; 27 May 1904, p. 4; C. Brewster Coulter, "John L. Wilson, Erastus Brainerd and the Republican Party of Washington," *Idaho Yesterdays* 4 (Summer 1960): 13; Robert D. Saltvig, "The Progressive Movement in Washington" (Ph.D. dissertation, University of Washington, 1967), p. 87; "First Message of Governor Albert E. Mead, Olympia, January 11, 1905," in *Washington Public Documents, 1903–1904*, 1: 15, 17.

27. Saltvig, "The Progressive Movement in Washington," pp. 116–38 *passim*; *Okanogan Record*, 2 November 1906, p. 2; *Pasco Express*, 16 August 1906, p. 1; *Union Record*, 9 February 1907, p. 2; Coulter, "John L. Wilson," pp. 18, 19.

28. H. J. Bergman, "The Reluctant Dissenter: Governor Hay of Washington and the Conservation Problem," *Pacific Northwest Quarterly* 42 (January 1971): 27–33. Details of Hay's life and an analysis of his relationship to Progressive reform are found in Bergman's "Progressive on the Right."

29. Bergman, "Progressive on the Right," pp. 240, 264; Saltvig "The Progressive Movement in Washington," p. 178; Keith Alexander Murray, "Republican Party Politics in Washington During the Progressive Era" (Ph.D. dissertation, University of Washington, 1946).

30. Howard Allen, "Miles Poindexter and the Progressive Movement," *Pacific Northwest Quarterly* 53 (July 1962): 115, 117; Helen O. Filson, "Miles Poindexter and the Progressive Movement in Eastern Washington, 1908–1913" (M.A. thesis, State College of Washington, 1941), pp. 51, 80. See also Howard W. Allen, "Miles Poindexter: A Political Biography" (Ph.D. dissertation, University of Washington, 1959).

31. Murray, "Republican Party Politics in Washington During the Progressive Era"; Saltvig, "The Progressive Movement in Washington," p. 149.

32. Murray, "Republican Party Politics in Washington During the Progressive Era," pp. 140, 141; *Colfax Commoner*, 3 May 1912, p. 1. See also Keith A. Murray, "The Aberdeen Convention of 1912," *Pacific Northwest Quarterly* 38 (April 1947), pp. 98–108.

33. Filson, "Miles Poindexter," pp. 105–7, 118; Allen, "Miles Poindexter: A Political Biography," pp. 175–180 *passim*; Norman F. Tjaden, "Populists and Progressives of Washington: A Comparative Study" (M.A. thesis, University of Washington, 1960), p. 58; "Twelfth Biennial Report of the Secretary of State" in *Washington Public Documents, 1911–1912*, 1: 180–83.

34. "Twelfth Biennial Report of the Secretary of State," pp. 180–83; Tjaden, "Populists and Progressives of Washington," pp. 65–66.

35. Tjaden, "Populists and Progressives of Washington," pp. 77–78, 100–14 *passim*; Murray, "Republican Party Politics in Washington During the Progressive Era," p. 197.

36. Saltvig, "The Progressive Movement in Washington," pp. 299, 300; Herman Sleizer, "Governor Ernest Lister, Chapters of a Political Career" (M.A. thesis, University of Washington, 1941).

37. Saltvig, "The Progressive Movement in Washington," p. 311; *Union Record*, 8 March 1913, p. 1; 15 March 1913, p. 1; 29 March 1913, p. 1; 25 October 1913, p. 3. The Legislature in 1914 outlawed collecting of fees from job seekers by private employment agencies, but the measure was struck down in 1917 by the United States Supreme Court as a violation of the Fourteenth Amendment.

38. Filson, "Miles Poindexter," p. 31; Saltvig, "The Progressive Movement in Washington," p. 370. The best account of the reconciliation between the Progressives and the Republicans is in Murray, "Republican Party Politics in Washington During the Progressive Era," chapter 5.

39. Saltvig, "The Progressive Movement in Washington," p. 349; *Union Record*, 4 February 1914, p. 3; 6 June 1914, p. 1; 10 October 1914, p. 1; 31 October 1914, p. 1.

40. Clark, *Mill Town*, pp. 149–50; "First Biennial Report, Election Division" in *Washington Public Documents, 1913–1914*, 2: 55–62; Thomas C. McClintock, "J.

Allen Smith, A Pacific Northwest Progressive," *Pacific Northwest Quarterly* 53 (April 1962): 49–59; *Union Record*, 20 March 1915, p. 1; 15 May 1915, p. 6; 4 December 1915, p. 4. In *The Spirit of American Government* (1907), Smith had been critical of the allegedly undemocratic character of the United States Constitution.

41. Saltvig, "The Progressive Movement in Washington," p. 435; *Union Record*, 16 September 1916, p. 1; 7 October 1916, p. 1; 4 November 1916, p. 4; *Spokane Labor World*, 29 September 1916, p. 1.

CHAPTER 13

1. *Greenwood Ledge*, 8 August 1907, p. 2; *Colonist*, 26 November 1910, p. 4; 13 May 1911, p. 16; 30 July 1915, p. 4; *Miners' Magazine*, 1 January 1914, p. 6; *B. C. Saturday Sunset* (Vancouver), 10 August 1915, p. 1; *Labour Gazette*, March 1915, p. 1062; Dorothy G. Steeves, *The Compassionate Rebel: Ernest E. Winch and His Times* (Vancouver: Boag Foundation, 1960), pp. 30–31; *Fifth Annual Report on Labour Organization in Canada (1915)*, pp. 223ff.

2. L. D. Taylor and the single tax in Vancouver were the subject of a special issue of the *Single Tax Review*, May-June 1911.

3. *Seattle Union Record*, 9 November 1912, p. 5; *Western Clarion* (Vancouver), 29 April 1911, p. 2.

4. Margaret J. Thompson, "Development and Comparison of Industrial Relationships in Seattle" (M.B.A. thesis, University of Washington, 1929), p. 33; "Ninth Biennial Report of the Bureau of Labor Statistics and Factory Inspection, 1913–1914," in *Washington Public Documents, 1913–1914*, 3: 119–21; Cloice R. Howd, "Industrial Relations in the West Coast Lumber Industry," U.S. Bureau of Labor Statistics, *Bulletin 349* (1924), pp. 58ff; Melvyn Dubofsky, *We Shall Be All: A History of the Industrial Workers of the World* (Chicago: Quadrangle, 1969), p. 341.

5. C. William Thorndale, "Washington's Green River Coal Company [Country]: 1880–1930" (M.A. thesis, University of Washington, 1965), pp. 108–9; Frederick E. Melder, "A Study of the Washington Coal Industry with Special Reference to the Industrial Relations Problem" (M.A. thesis, University of Washington, 1931); "Ninth Biennial Report of the Bureau of Labor Statistics and Factory Inspection," pp. 101–6.

6. *United Mine Workers' Journal*, 31 January 1907, p. 4; 4 January 1912, p. 6; *Union Record*, 6 September 1913, p. 1; Paul Phillips, *No Power Greater: A Century of Labour in British Columbia* (Vancouver: Boag Foundation, 1967), pp. 55–61.

7. J. Kavanagh, *The Vancouver Island Strike* (Vancouver: B. C. Miners' Liberation League, [1913]). The best account of the strike is Alan John Wargo, "The Great Coal Strike, The Vancouver Island Miners' Strike, 1912–1914" (B.A. thesis, University of British Columbia, 1962).

8. Kavanagh, *The Vancouver Island Strike*, pp. 6–13 *passim*; Phillips, *No Power Greater*, pp. 58–59.

9. Steeves, *The Compassionate Rebel*, pp. 22–23; *B. C. Federationist* (Vancouver), 17 July 1914, pp. 4, 6.

10. *Canadian Annual Review, 1914*, p. 689; *Union Record*, 21 November 1914, p. 2.

11. *Nanaimo Daily Herald*, 8 July 1914, p. 1, copy in McBride papers, Premier's Official Correspondence, 1914, box 16, folder 14; "Report of the Royal Commission on Labour," in *British Columbia Sessional Papers, 1914*, p. m-2.

12. Confidential memo to Richard McBride from the provincial secretary, 10 September 1914, McBride papers, Premier's Correspondence Inward, 1914–1915;

Notes

chief constable's office, Nanaimo, to superintendent of provincial police, 21 September 1914, McBride papers, Premier's Correspondence Outward, Unemployed 1914–1915; F. W. James to Richard McBride, 28 December 1914, McBride papers, Premier's Correspondence Inward, Unemployed 1914–1915; Saskatchewan Department of Labour to William Bowser, 6 July 1915, McBride papers, Premier's Correspondence Inward, Unemployed 1914–1915.

13. *Union Record*, 18 October 1913, p. 3. The cost-of-living information is derived from issues of the *Canada Year Book* and the *Statistical Abstract*.

14. *Union Record*, 2 May 1914, p. 8; 7 August 1915, p. 4.

15. James O. Morris, *Conflict Within the AFL: A Study of Craft Versus Industrial Unionism, 1901–1938* (Ithaca, N.Y.: Cornell University Press, 1958). Information on the voting pattern of delegates from the Pacific Northwest is derived from AFL *Convention Proceedings* between 1900 and 1917.

16. Trades and Labor Congress, *Convention Proceedings, 1911*, p. 73; *Convention Proceedings, 1912*, p. 82; *Canadian Annual Review, 1911*, pp. 337–39; *Report on Labour Organization in Canada, 1912*, pp. 12–13; *Industrial Worker* (Spokane), 29 August 1912, p. 4; *Union Record*, 14 December 1907, p. 1; 16 August 1913, p. 1; Washington State Federation of Labor, *Convention Proceedings, 1914*, p. 44. Little was ever done in the pre-World War I era to carry out the resolutions. Supporters of industrial unionism in Seattle and the state Federation of Labor in 1919 were thrown into confusion when they realized that implementation of industrial unionism would mean secession from the AFL and the inability of workers holding cards from industrial unions in Washington to work outside the state. Robert L. Friedheim, *The Seattle General Strike* (Seattle: University of Washington Press, 1964), pp. 31–33.

17. *Canadian Annual Review, 1912*, p. 595; *B. C. Federationist*, 6 May 1912, p. 1; *Colonist*, 14 March 1912, p. 1; Washington State Federation of Labor, *Convention Proceedings, 1914*, p. 42. The vote in the Vancouver Trades and Labor Council was 53 to 8 in favor of socialism. Minutes of the Regular Meetings of the Vancouver Trades and Labor Council, 21 March 1912.

18. *Union Record*, 2 September 1915, p. 4; Minutes of the Central Labor Council of Seattle, 2 September 1915, p. 4; Minutes of the Central Labor Council of Seattle, 12 July 1916, Archives and Manuscripts Division, University of Washington Library; *Young Socialist* (Spokane), July 1902, p. 30; E. B. Ault, "Autobiographical Sketch," Ault papers, box 6, folder 62, Archives and Manuscripts Division, University of Washington Library; Hulet M. Wells, "I Wanted to Work," manuscript in the Hulet M. Wells papers, box 2, Archives and Manuscripts Division, University of Washington Library, pp. 181, 192. In addition to Ault and Pettipiece, other prominent socialists or erstwhile socialists who edited labor organs in the Pacific Northwest at that time included H. L. Hughes of the *Spokane Labor World* and Maynard Shipley of the *Everett Labor Journal*.

19. The WFM had reentered the AFL in 1911, and it became a partner of the UMW in the newly formed mining department. Leaders of the WFM, soon to become the International Union of Mine, Mill, and Smelter Workers, argued that by joining the AFL the hardrock miners gave up none of their advanced ground but rather became a powerful voice for industrial unionism in the craft-dominated federation. *Miners' Magazine*, 30 June 1910, p. 4; 2 February 1911, p. 4; 18 July 1912, pp. 5, 6.

20. David J. Saposs, *Left Wing Unionism: A Study of Radical Policies and Tactics* (New York: International Publishers, 1926), p. 34; *American Federationist*, May 1911, pp. 388–89; *Union Record*, 25 September 1915, p. 4.

21. David A. Shannon, *The Socialist Party of America* (New York: Macmillan,

Notes

1955), pp. 69–80 *passim*; James Weinstein, *The Decline of Socialism in America, 1912–1925* (New York: Random House, 1969); Eugene V. Debs, "Dangers Ahead," reprinted in Jean Y. Tussey, ed., *Eugene V. Debs Speaks* (New York: Pathfinder Press, 1972), p. 180.

22. *Union Record*, 8 March 1913, p. 4; W. H. Kingery to Carl Dean Thompson, 24 July 1913, letter in Socialist party collection, Duke University, Durham, North Carolina. Peder Jensen, a Danish-born Tacoma Pharmacist, became the first declared Socialist in the Washington State senate when he switched from the Democratic party to the Socialist party midway during the course of his four-year term. *1913 Legislative Manual, State of Washington*, pp. 4–5.

23. *Union Record*, 10 December 1910, p. 4; *Socialist Voice* (Seattle), 25 November 1911, p. 1; *Everett Commonwealth*, 13 December 1912, p. 1; *Socialist Herald* (Seattle), 12 November 1913, 4 December 1914, clippings in the Socialist party collection.

24. *Coming Nation*, April 1911, p. 5; *Union Record*, 11 February 1911, p. 8; Wells, "I Wanted to Work," pp. 133–37; *Pasco Express*, 11 October 1912, p. 4; 5 December 1913, p. 1; 5 June 1914, p. 1.

25. *American Federationist*, November 1912, pp. 892–93; *Spokane Spokesman-Review*, 24 May 1911, p. 6; 8 August 1911, p. 6; 12 March 1913, p. 3; *History of the 1913 Secession in the Socialist Party of Washington* (n.p.), pp. 10–11, pamphlet in the Socialist party collection.

26. *Everett Commonwealth*, 31 January 1913, p. 4; Harvey O'Connor, *Revolution in Seattle: a Memoir* (New York: Monthly Review Press, 1964), p. 20; *History of the 1913 Secession in the Socialist Party of Washington*, pp. 1, 12; *Report of Committee on Investigation of Party Differences in the State of Washington to the National Executive Committee of the Socialist Party in Session, May 10, 1914* (n.p.), pamphlet in the Socialist party collection.

27. *Reasons for Division in Socialist Party of Washington* (n.p.: Trustees of the Party, ca. 1914), pamphlet in the Socialist party collection; *Washington Socialist* (Everett), 7 May 1914, pp. 1, 3. For further details on the Socialist party struggle see Barbara Winslow, "The Decline of Socialism in Washington: 1910–1925" (M.A. thesis, University of Washington, 1969).

28. *Union Record*, 18 December 1915, p. 4; O'Connor, *Revolution in Seattle*, p. 20; *Red Feather* (Seattle), January 1916, p. 4; *Socialist World* (Seattle), 14 July 1916, p. 4; Miriam Allen De Ford, *Up-Hill All the Way, The Life of Maynard Shipley* (Yellow Springs, Ohio: The Antioch Press, 1956), pp. 149–58 *passim*; *Everett Commonwealth*, 20 November 1913, p. 2.

29. *Colonist*, 21 May 1911, p. 6; 28 May 1911, p. 6; Martin Robin, *The Rush For Spoils: The Company Province, 1871–1933* (Toronto: McClelland and Stewart, 1972), pp. 118–19. Hawthornthwaite had apparently been speculating in land, for the *Vancouver Daily Province* reported in 1912 that he had made $65,000 on one transaction! Ross Alfred Johnson, "'No Compromise—No Political Trading': The Marxian Socialist Tradition in British Columbia" (Ph.D. dissertation, University of British Columbia, 1975), p. 286. Hawthornthwaite returned to British Columbia and won Parker Williams' old seat in the legislative assembly, but he was later expelled from the Victoria local of the party because he criticized the Bolsheviks. Paul Fox, "Early Socialism in Canada," in J. H. Aitcheson, ed., *The Political Process in Canada: Essays in Honour of R. MacGregor Dawson* (Toronto: University of Toronto Press, 1963), p. 97.

30. *Canadian Annual Review, 1912*, p. 612; *Grand Forks Gazettte*, 23 March 1912, p. 1; *Western Clarion*, 6 April 1912, p. 1.

31. *B. C. Saturday Sunset*, 25 January 1913, p. 5; 8 February 1913, p. 9; *Cotton's*

Weekly (Cowansville, Quebec), 5 March 1914, p. 3; *B. C. Federationist*, 25 February 1916, p. 1; 21 July 1916, p. 2; 8 September 1916, p. 4; Steeves, *The Compassionate Rebel*, pp. 33.

32. Trades and Labor Congress, *Convention Proceedings, 1917*, pp. 43–44; Steeves, *The Compassionate Rebel*, pp. 36–37; *B. C. Federationist*, 1 February 1918, p. 1; 8 February 1918, p. 1; 22 February 1918, p. 1; 8 March 1918, p. 1; 19 April 1918, p. 1. The SDP was absorbed into the Federated Labor party, but the SPC continued to lead a nominal existence. Johnson, "'No Compromise—No Political Trading,'" p. 323.

33. E. J. Brown Scrapbooks, Pacific Northwest Collection, University of Washington Library. On the evolution of political radicalism in Washington during the 1930s see Albert Anthony Acena, "The Washington Commonwealth Federation: Reform Politics and the Popular Front" (Ph.D. dissertation, University of Washington, 1975). On related political matters, see Fayette Florent Krause, "Democratic Party Politics in the State of Washington During the New Deal, 1932–1940" (Ph. D. dissertation, University of Washington, 1971).

34. Robert L. Tyler, "The United States Government as Union Organizer: The Loyal Legion of Loggers and Lumbermen," *Mississippi Valley Historical Review* 47 (December 1960); Harold M. Hyman, *Soldiers and Spruce: The Origins of the Loyal Legion of Loggers and Lumbermen* (Los Angeles: Institute of Industrial Relations, University of California, 1963).

35. Howard Allen, "Miles Poindexter and the Progressive Movement," *Pacific Northwest Quarterly* 53 (July 1962): 122; Washington State Federation of Labor, *Convention Proceedings, 1915*, p. 3; Joseph F. Tripp, "Progressive Labor Laws in Washington State (1900–1925)" (Ph.D. dissertation, University of Washington, 1973), pp. 111, 112; *B. C. Federationist*, 24 November 1916, p. 1; Robert L. Tyler, *Rebels of the Woods: The I. W. W. in the Pacific Northwest* (Eugene, Oregon: University of Oregon Books, 1967), pp. 132, 149.

36. *Union Record*, 23 January 1915, p. 1; 15 July 1916, p. 4; *Spokane Labor World*, 11 August 1916, p. 1; Washington State Federation of Labor, *Convention Proceedings, 1915*, p. 13; *Convention Proceedings, 1917*, p. 5; Norman Clark, "The 'Hell-Soaked Institution' and the Washington Prohibition Initiative of 1914," *Pacific Northwest Quarterly* 56 (January 1965): 1–16. Not all influential labor leaders in the state opposed prohibition. James Duncan, the secretary of the Central Labor Council in Seattle, led the anti-liquor forces in the state federation of Labor. Friedheim, *The Seattle General Strike*, p. 36.

37. The best study of the evolution of the farmer-labor coalition is Hamilton Cravens, "A History of the Washington Farmer-Labor Party" (M.A. thesis, University of Washington, 1962).

38. *Co-Operative News* (Everett), 9 May 1918, p. 1; Wells, "I Wanted to Work," p. 119. After release from McNeil Island Penitentiary, Wells became active in the Farmer-Labor party and was in 1925 its Washington state chairman; Herman, old and unable to work, killed himself in 1929. Wells, "I Wanted to Work," p. 119; De Ford, *Up-Hill All the Way*, p. 149.

39. Trades and Labor Congress, *Convention Proceedings, 1917*, p. 45; Johnson, "'No Compromise—No Political Trading,'" p. 336; Minutes of the *B. C. Federationist*, 4 March 1918, in Vancouver Trades and Labor Council papers. On the suppression of radicals in Canada see A. Ross McCormack, *Reformers, Rebels, and Revolutionaries: The Western Canadian Radical Movement, 1889–1919* (Toronto: University of Toronto Press, 1977), pp. 137–64 *passim*.

40. Robert L. Friedheim and Robin Friedheim, "The Seattle Labor Movement,

Notes

1919–20," *Pacific Northwest Quarterly* 55 (October 1964): 146–56; William Preston, Jr., *Aliens and Dissenters: Federal Suppression of Radicals, 1903–1933* (Cambridge: Harvard University Press, 1963), pp. 152–80; Phillips, *No Power Greater*, pp. 67–84. See also O'Connor, *Revolution in Seattle*; Friedheim, *The Seattle General Strike*; and Kenneth McNaught and David J. Bercuson, *The Winnipeg Strike: 1919* (Don Mills, Ontario: Longman Canada, 1974).

CHAPTER 14

1. *Week* (Vancouver), 18 July 1908, p. 1; *Social Democratic Herald (Milwaukee)*, 21 December 1912, p. 1.

2. David A. Shannon, ed., *Beatrice Webb's American Diary, 1898* (Madison, Wis.: University of Wisconsin Press, 1963), p. 144; Joseph F. Tripp, "Progressive Labor Laws in Washington State (1900–1925)" (Ph. D. dissertation, University of Washington, 1973).

3. Paul Phillips, *No Power Greater: A Century of Labour in British Columbia* (Vancouver: Boag Foundation, 1967), pp. 79–84, 87, 92–96; Earl Pomeroy, *The Pacific Slope, A History of California, Oregon, Washington, Idaho, Utah, and Nevada* (New York: Alfred A. Knopf, 1968), pp. 222–24, 240–41: Dorothy O. Johansen and Charles M. Gates, *Empire of the Columbia, A History of the Pacific Northwest*, 2nd ed. (New York: Harper & Row, 1967), pp. 486–87. From 1939 to 1953, the number of unionized workers increased from 41.3 to 53.3 percent of the nonagricultural labor force in Washington and from 12.7 to 35.4 percent of the nonagricultural labor force in British Columbia. Pomeroy, *The Pacific Slope*, pp. 245, 317n; Phillips, *No Power Greater*, pp. 120, 169–70.

4. Johansen and Gates, *Empire of the Columbia*, p. 504; Neal R. Pierce, *The Pacific States of America: People, Politics, and Power in the Five Pacific Basin States* (New York: W. W. Norton, 1972), pp. 240–41; John Gunther, *Inside U. S. A.* (New York: Harper & Brothers, 1947), pp. 98, 99.

5. Phillips, *No Power Greater*, pp. 85ff. See also Walter D. Young, *The Anatomy of a Party: The National CCF, 1932–61* (Toronto: University of Toronto Press, 1969).

6. For further discussion of the failure of American socialism, see Donald D. Egbert and Stow Persons, eds., *Socialism and American Life*, 2 vols. (Princeton: Princeton University Press, 1952); and John H. M. Laslett and Seymour Martin Lipset, eds., *Failure of a Dream? Essays in the History of American Socialism* (Garden City, N.Y.: Doubleday, Anchor Press, 1974).

7. Interview of Harold E. Winch by Glen Jenkinson, 1 March 1973, oral history transcript in the Special Collections Division, University of British Columbia Library, pp. 4–1, 4–2.

8. *Colonist*, 21 January 1906, p. 4; American Federation of Labor, *Convention Proceedings, 1910*, pp. 198–99; Trades and Labor Congress, *Convention Proceedings, 1911* pp. 14, 41. See also Gad Horowitz, *Canadian Labour in Politics* (Toronto: University of Toronto Press, 1968).

9. Farley's supposed sobriquet for Washington is mentioned in Richard L. Neuberger, *Our Promised Land* (New York: Macmillan, 1938), p. 277. "The Pacific Northwest," *Time*, 12 December 1977, pp. 26–36. The reference to British Columbia appears on "A Map of the Canadas" prepared by Terry Mosher to illustrate Mordecai Richler, "Oh! Canada! Lament for a Divided Country," *Atlantic Monthly*, December 1977, pp. 41–55.

Bibliographical Essay

The bibliographical essay that follows represents no attempt to list all the works consulted for this study. On the other hand, it includes a few titles not specifically cited in chapter notes. Primarily, this essay is intended to offer guidance to anyone pursuing the topics I have mentioned.

MANUSCRIPT SOURCES

For the history of the Seattle labor movement prior to the appearance of the *Union Record* in 1900, the minutes of the Western Central Labor Union are invaluable; they also supplement news appearing in the *Union Record* between 1900 and 1917. Unfortunately, no minutes were kept during the lean years of the mid-1890s. In addition to serving as a repository for the WCLU minutes (and those of its successor, the Central Labor Council of Seattle and Vicinity), the University of Washington Library in Seattle contains the papers of E. B. Ault and Hulet Wells, two collections relating to labor and socialism in western Washington, and the papers of the Oregon Improvement Company and Governor Eugene Semple. The latter two collections include a small amount of material on labor disputes in the Cascade-area coal fields in the late 1880s.

Complementing the minutes of the WCLU are those of the Tacoma Trades Council. Journals, ledgers, and many volumes of the *Labor Advocate* are available at the University of Washington Library.

The Angus MacInnis papers and the International Union of Mine, Mill, and Smelter Workers (Canada) papers are two large collections of labor and socialist materials deposited at the University of British Columbia Library in Vancouver. MacInnis, a prominent socialist politician in British Columbia, was primarily concerned with developments after 1917, but the collection, nonetheless, contains several items relating to the period from 1900 to 1917. The Mine, Mill, and Smelter Workers papers contain a mass of correspondence and the financial records of the Western Federation of Miners, as well as several local unions. The C. D. Orchard collection is a meticulously indexed compilation of material on all aspects of the forest industry in the Pacific Northwest. The Vancouver Trades and Labor Council papers, also at the University of British Columbia Library, contain the minutes of the council's regular meetings.

The Cominco papers, at the British Columbia Provincial Archives in Victoria, contain testimony relating to working conditions in some of the company's mines. The public papers of Sir Richard McBride, one of the Archives' larger collections, include a illuminating file on unemployment and the working classes in British Columbia in 1914.

A significant portion of the manuscript material relating to labor and socialism in the Pacific Northwest is located in archives outside the region. The Henry Demarest Lloyd papers and the Socialist Labor party collection are available at the State Historical Society of Wisconsin in Madison. Lloyd's papers contain a few letters relating to cooperative colonies on Puget Sound; more important are the items in the collection dealing with reform in America in the 1890s. The Socialist Labor party collection includes a scattering of broadsides, party platforms, letters, and minutes that pertain to party activities in Washington, and a small compilation of minutes from the Socialist Trades and Labor Alliance in Vancouver. The American Federation of Labor papers at the State Historical Society of Wisconsin are disappointing as a source of specific information on the development of trade unions in Washington and British Columbia. The State Historical Society of Wisconsin also is the repository for a number of published items used in this study, specifically the *Firebrand* and the *Saturday Evening Tribune*.

Materials on labor and socialism in the Pacific Northwest are also to be found in the Socialist Party of America collection at Duke University, and in the Burnette G. Haskell papers, the International Workingmen's Association papers, and the Silver City, Idaho, Miners' Union collection, all at the Bancroft Library in Berkeley, California. Like the State Historical Society of Wisconsin, the Bancroft Library also contains a large number of books and journals relating to Pacific Northwest history, including issues of the *Northern Light*, the *Spokane Industrial World*, and the *Coast Seamen's Journal*.

Periodicals and Newspapers

The single most important source of information for this study has been periodicals and newspapers. Only a few local labor newspapers were published in the Pacific Northwest prior to the turn of the century, and only infrequently were copies of these preserved for future study. Nonetheless, the scattered issues of the *Northern Light* (Tacoma, Seattle, and Spokane) and the *Spokane Industrial World* provide valuable information on the composition and membership of the early central labor bodies in Washington. The *Coast Seamen's Journal* contains a number of news items on early labor organizations in the Pacific Northwest, as do the trade union periodicals of national circulation such as the *Journal of United Labor*, the *Journal of the Knights of Labor*, and the Hamilton, Ontario, *Palladium of Labor*.

The *Seattle Union Record*, the *Independent* of Vancouver, and the *B. C. Federationist* trace labor developments in Washington and British Columbia from the turn of the century to World War I. Relating specifically to the labor movement in Spokane, the Inland Empire, and the Kootenays are *Freemen's Labor Journal* (and its successors, the *Spokane Record* and the *Spokane Labor World*) and the *Rossland Industrial World*. The *American Federationist* reflects the AFL's growing interest in organizing workers in the Pacific Northwest after the turn of the century, while the *Pueblo Courier*, the *Miners' Magazine*, *Railway Employees' Journal*, and *American Labor Union Journal* detail the challenge offered to the AFL by the Western Federation of Miners, the Western Labor Union, the American Labor Union, and the United Brotherhood of Railway Employees. The *Industrial Worker* presents the IWW's view of working conditions in the Pacific Northwest.

The region's growing interest in labor reform and socialism can be followed in the single tax, Nationalist, and direct legislation publications such as the *Standard*, the *Public*, the *Single Tax Review*, the *New Nation*, the *Nationalist*, and the *Direct Legislation Record*. News of early socialist activity in Washington and British Columbia can be found in Burnette Haskell's *Truth*; the *Model Commonwealth*, published by the Puget Sound Cooperative Colony; and Eugene Debs' *Railway Times* (and its successors, the *Social Democrat* and the *Social Democratic Herald*).

Although the *Seattle Socialist*, the *Everett Commonwealth*, and the *Western Clarion* (and its predecessors, *Citizen and Country*, the *Lardeau Eagle*, the *Canadian Socialist*, and the *Western Socialist*) are the best sources of information on the socialist movement in Washington and British Columbia in the early twentieth century, news items related to socialism in the Pacific Northwest also appeared occasionally in the *Appeal to Reason*, the *Coming Nation*, the *Winnipeg Voice*, *Cotton's Weekly*, and the *International Socialist Review*. The *New Time* of Spokane, available at the Washington State University Library, and Walter Thomas Mills' *Saturday Evening Tribune* presented the views of the reform socialists in Washington and British Columbia. Because the local socialist parties often slanted information related to their internal squabbling, one should also consult the *Labor and Socialist Press News*, published by the Socialist Party of America; the *People*, published by the Socialist Labor party; and the various journals published by the cooperative colonies on Puget Sound, particularly th *Co-Operator* (Burley) and *Industrial Freedom* (Equality).

The *Colfax Commoner* should be consulted for information on the unique relationship between farmers and workers in Washington from 1890 to 1917. The *Commoner* was ostensibly a general interest weekly newspaper, but like the *Victoria Daily Colonist*, the *Vancouver Daily World*, the *Spokane Spokesman-Review*, and a number of other newspapers cited in this study, it often contained information on labor, socialism, and reform not available elsewhere.

Convention Proceedings

The proceedings of the annual conventions of the American Federation of Labor and the Trades and Labor Congress of Canada, like the nationally circulating labor and socialist journals, help illuminate local developments. The reports from the annual meetings of the Knights of Labor, the Western Federation of Miners, and the United Mine Workers of America sometimes provide the only available information on the membership trends of these three influential unions in the Pacific Northwest. Without the proceedings of the 1908 national convention of the Socialist Party of America it would have been difficult fully to understand the outcome of the bitter conflict between Hermon Titus and Walter Thomas Mills. Important data on the formation and operation of the farmer-labor coalition in Washington can be found in the proceedings of the Washington State Federation of Labor, the Washington State Grange, and the Patrons of Husbandry.

GOVERNMENT DOCUMENTS

The best source of general statistical information on Washington and British Columbia is the decennial census reports issued by the federal governments of the United States and Canada. Unfortunately, however, since they used federal election districts as census districts in British Columbia, the compilers of the *Census of Canada* made it almost impossible for the researcher accurately to correlate election returns in provincial election ridings with the composition of the electorate in the pre-World War I era. The researcher can gather information on individual voters in each provincial election riding by using the periodically issued *British Columbia Voter's List.* Although not strictly a government publication, *The Canadian Parliamentary Guide* (issued annually in Ottawa) is a convenient source of information on provincial elections and on members of the legislative assembly. Errors, however, sometimes mar the election statistics in the *Guide.* Election returns in Washington were recorded by the secretary of state's office and published in the bound volumes of *Public Documents of Washington,* beginning in 1900. The *Legislative Manual* (sometimes entitled *Barton's Legislative Hand-Book and Manual*) contains election returns and capsule biographies of state legislators in Washington.

In addition to the *Labour Gazette,* a monthly compilation of labor news, the Dominion government published an *Annual Report on Labour Organization in Canada,* beginning in 1911, and issued a periodic *Report on Strikes and Lockouts in Canada* that provides summary information on labor disputes in British Columbia and other provinces after 1900. The "Biennial Report" issued by the Washington Bureau of Labor, beginning in 1897, is at best an uneven source of information on the state's labor movement. (Beginning in 1903 the "Biennial Report" was issued by the Bureau of Labor Statistics and Factory Inspection and generally bound in the *Public Documents of Washington*.) Labor statistics for Washington in the late 1880s and 1890s can also be found in the *Annual Report of the Commissioner of Labor*, a document issued by the federal government. Information on the perils of mine labor in Washington and British Columbia is contained in the reports issued by the territorial and state inspectors of coal mines and by the provincial minister of mines. Among the other relevant government documents used in this study are Cloice R. Howd, "Industrial Relations in the West Coast Lumber Industry," in U.S. Bureau of Labor Statistics, *Bulletin 349* (1924); Alexander Kent, "Cooperative Communities in the United States," U.S. Department of Labor, *Bulletin 35* (July 1901); and "Report of the Royal Commission on Industrial Disputes in the Province of British Columbia," in Dominion of Canada, *Sessional Papers*, vol. 37, no. 36a (1903).

MISCELLANEOUS UNPUBLISHED SOURCES

Dissertations and theses proved a rich source of information on labor and socialism in the Pacific Northwest. The interviews that Frederick E. Melder conducted for his "Study of the Washington Coal Industry with Special Reference to the Industrial Relations Problem" (M.A. thesis, University of Washington, 1931) contain primary source material available nowhere else. Of similar value are Margaret J. Thompson, "Development and Comparison of Industrial Relationships in Seattle (M.B.A. thesis, University of Washington, 1929), and William J. Dickson, "Labor in Municipal Politics: A Study of Labor's Political Policies and Activities in Seattle" (M.A. thesis, University of Washington, 1928). A number of dissertations are more far-reaching than their modest titles indicate. Robert A. Henderson, "The *Spokesman-Review*, 1883–1900: A Mirror to the History of Spokane" (Ph.D. dissertation, Washington State University, 1967), provides valuable information on the terminal rates controversy that agitated political life in Spokane for several decades. Alan A. Hynding, "The Public Life of Eugene Semple: A Study of the Promoter-Politican on the Pacific Northwest Frontier" (Ph.D. dissertation, University of Washington, 1966), details the labor disputes in the Cascade coal fields in the late 1880s. Most of this material is also contained in Hynding's *The Public Life of Eugene Semple: Promoter and Politician of the Pacific Northwest* (Seattle: University of Washington Press, 1973).

Melvin G. De Shazo, "Radical Tendencies in the Seattle Labor Movement as Reflected in the Proceedings of its Central Body" (M.A. thesis, University of Washington, 1925), discounts the radicalism of the labor movement in Seattle. Meryl E. Rogers, "The Labor Movement in Seattle, 1885–1905" (M.A. thesis, Pacific Lutheran University, 1970), concentrates on the formative years of the Seattle labor movement. The only extensive account of the Spokane labor movement is James Leroy Hunt, "A History of the Central Labor Council in Spokane, Washington" (M.A. thesis, State College of Washington, 1940). The best study of the Tacoma central labor body is James A. Halseth, "Social Disorganization and Discontent in Late Nineteenth Century Washington" (Ph.D. dissertation, Texas Tech University, 1974).

Three model studies of specific labor disputes are Harry K. Ralston, "The 1900 Strike of Fraser River Sockeye Salmon Fishermen" (M.A. thesis, University of British Columbia, 1965); Allan D. Orr, "The Western Federation of Miners and the Royal Commission on Industrial Disputes in 1903 with Special Reference to the Vancouver Island Coal Miners' Strike" (M.A. thesis, University of British Columbia, 1968); and Allan J. Wargo, "The Great Coal Strike, The Vancouver Island Coal Miners' Strike, 1912–1914" (B.A. thesis, University of British Columbia, 1962). Mark J. Stern, "'To Bring Forth the Hidden Wealth': The Knights of Labor in the Coalfields of King County, Washington, 1885–1891" (B.A. thesis, Reed College, 1973), is a social history of labor that offers a number of intriguing insights into western Washington's early radicalism. A related study is C. William Thorndale, "Washington's Green River Coal Company [Country]: 1880–1930" (M.A. thesis, University of Washington, 1965). An informative account of one particularly colorful dispute is provided in Robert C. Eckberg, "The Free Speech Fight of the Industrial Workers of the

World, Spokane, Washington: 1909–1910" (M.A. thesis, Washington State University, 1967).

Thomas Robert Loosmore, "The British Columbia Labor Movement and Political Action, 1879–1906" (M.A. thesis, University of British Columbia, 1954), and Ronald Grantham, "Some Aspects of the Socialist Movement in British Columbia, 1898–1933" (M.A. thesis, University of British Columbia, 1942), are two early studies of labor and politics in British Columbia. These two theses have been largely superseded by Ross Alfred Johnson, "'No Compromise—No Political Trading': The Marxian Socialist Tradition in British Columbia" (Ph.D. dissertation, University of British Columbia, 1975), and Andrew Ross McCormack, "The Origins and Extent of Western Labour Radicalism, 1896–1919" (Ph.D. dissertation, University of Western Ontario, 1973). McCormack's research is conveniently available as *Reformers, Rebels, and Revolutionaries: The Western Canadian Radical Movement, 1899–1919* (Toronto: University of Toronto Press, 1977).

There have been few studies of socialism in Washington. Charles P. LeWarne, "Communitarian Experiments in Western Washington, 1885–1915" (Ph.D. dissertation, University of Washington, 1969), covers an important aspect of the early socialist movement in the state. LeWarne's research, published as *Utopias on Puget Sound, 1885–1915* (Seattle: University of Washington Press, 1975), includes an excellent bibliography on early radicalism in Washington. Paul B. Bushue, "Dr. Hermon F. Titus and Socialism in Washington State, 1900–1909" (M.A. thesis, University of Washington, 1967), concentrates on socialist politics in the Seattle area. Continuing the story of socialism in the Puget Sound region is Barbara Winslow, "The Decline of Socialism in Washington, 1910–1925" (M.A. thesis, University of Washington, 1969).

The body of unpublished studies on Populism and Progressivism in Washington in growing. One of the best accounts of the three decades of reform in pre-World War I Washington is Robert D. Saltvig, "The Progressive Movement in Washington" (Ph.D. dissertation, University of Washington, 1966). Hamilton Cravens, "A History of the Washington Farmer-Labor Party" (M.A. thesis, University of Washington, 1962), supplements the Saltvig study.

David B. Griffiths, "Populism in the Far West: 1890–1900" (Ph.D. dissertation, University of Washington, 1967) is an excellent synthesis of published and unpublished studies of Populism in the western United States. Studes dealing primarily with Populism in Washington are Michael D. Boone, "The Washington State Legislature of 1897: A Study in Populism" (M.A. thesis, Washington State University, 1966); Margaret H. Thompson, "The Writings of John Rankin Rogers" (M.A. thesis, University of Washington, 1947); and Stephen Henry Peters, "The Populists and the Washington Legislature, 1893–1900" (M.A. thesis, University of Washington, 1967). Thomas Wayne Riddle, "Whitman County Populism and Washington State Politics: 1889–1902" (M.A. thesis, Washington State University, 1971), is a model study of the Populist movement on the county level. Riddle continues his study of Populism in "The Old Radicalism in America: John R. Rogers and the Populist Movement in Washington, 1891–1900" (Ph.D. dissertation, Washington State University, 1976). Norman F. Tjaden, "Populists and Progressives of Washington: A Comparative Study" (M.A. thesis, University of Washington, 1960), details the movement of former Populists into the Democratic party in Washington.

Progressivism in Washington is examined in Keith Alexander Murray, "Republican Party Politics in Washington During the Progressive Era" (Ph.D. dissertation, University of Washington, 1946). The unpublished biographies of political leaders in Washington during the Progressive Era include Hermas J. Berman, "Progressive on the Right: Marion E. Hay, Governor of Washington, 1909–1913" (Ph.D. dissertation, Washington State University, 1967); Helen O. Filson, "Miles Poindexter and the Progressive Movement in Eastern Washington, 1908–1913" (M.A. thesis, State College of Washington, 1941); Howard W. Allen, "Miles Poindexter: A Political Biography (Ph.D., University of Washington, 1959); and Herman Sleizer, "Governor Ernest Lister, Chapters of a Political Career" (M.A. thesis, University of Washington, 1941).

Eleanor Brown Mercer, "Political Groups in British Columbia, 1883–1898" (M.A. thesis, University of British Columbia, 1937), is an analysis of political developments in British Columbia before the introduction of party lines in the legislative assembly. The best unpublished studies of political activity in British Columbia in the early twentieth century are Peter Roberts Hunt, "The Political

Career of Sir Richard McBride" (M.A. thesis, University of British Columbia, 1953), and Brian R. D. Smith, "Sir Richard McBride: A Study in the Conservative Party of British Columbia, 1903–1916" (M.A. thesis, Queens University, 1959).

When studied in conjunction with Norman H. Clark, *The Dry Years: Prohibition and Social Change in Washington* (Seattle: University of Washington Press, 1965), Albert J. Hiebert's "Prohibition in British Columbia" (M.A. thesis, Simon Fraser University, 1969), adds a comparative dimension to reform in Washington and British Columbia. Joseph F. Tripp, "Progressive Labor Laws in Washington State (1900–1925)" (Ph.D. dissertation, University of Washington, 1973), and H. Fabian Underhill, "Labour Legislation in British Columbia" (Ph.D. dissertation, University of California, Berkeley, 1935), are valuable studies of the development of the welfare state in the Pacific Northwest. Robert E. Wynne's comparative study, "Reaction to the Chinese in the Pacific Northwest and British Columbia, 1850–1910" (Ph.D. dissertation, University of Washington, 1964), is an excellent study of working-class Sinophobia on the Pacific Coast. The best single study of an American labor organization in a non-American cultural and historical context is Robert Harper Babcock, "The A. F. L. in Canada, 1896–1908: A Study in Labor Imperialism" (Ph.D. dissertation, Duke University, 1969). Perceptively analyzing the influence of the AFL on the evolution of the Trades and Labor Congress of Canada, Babcock later published the essence of his research as *Gompers in Canada: A Study in American Continentalism Before the First World War* (Toronto: University of Toronto Press, 1974).

MISCELLANEOUS PUBLISHED SOURCES

The amount of travel and promotional literature relating to Washington and British Columbia is enormous. Dorothy O. Johansen, "A Working Hypothesis for the Study of Migrations "(*Pacific Historical Review* 36 [February 1967]: 1–12), enables one to understand this material in a comparative framework.

Many multivolume sets dealing with the Pacific Northwest were published at the turn of the century and sold by subscription to the region's prominent citizens. Although these works contained material of value to later researchers, the best general histories of the region appeared after 1940. Dorothy O. Johansen and Charles M. Gates, *Empire of the Columbia: A History of the Pacific Northwest*, 2nd ed. (New York: Harper & Row, 1967), is a narrative history of Oregon, Washington, Idaho, and Montana. Giving an urban interpretation to developments in the far western states is Earl Pomeroy, *The Pacific Slope: A History of California, Oregon, Washington, Idaho, Utah, and Nevada* (New York: Alfred A. Knopf, 1968). The two most recent histories of British Columbia present quite opposing views. Margaret Ormsby, *British Columbia: a History* ([Toronto]: Macmillan of Canada, 1958), concentrates on developments affecting primarily the middle and upper classes in the colony and province; Martin Robin, *The Rush for Spoils: The Company Province, 1871–1933* (Toronto: McClelland and Stewart, 1972), is a political history that is far more critical of the ruling "establishment" in British Columbia than is Ormsby's account. F. W. Howay, W. N. Sage, and H. F. Angus, *British Columbia and the United States: The North Pacific Slope from Fur Trade to Aviation* (Toronto: Ryerson Press, 1942), is an early and often superficial attempt to relate developments in British Columbia to those in the United States.

Paul Phillips, *No Power Greater: A Century of Labour in British Columbia* (Vancouver: Boag Foundation, 1967), is the best single source of information on the labor movement in British Columbia. No similar work exists for Washington, although Norman H. Clark, *Mill Town: A Social History of Everett, Washington, from Its Earliest Beginnings on the Shores of Puget Sound to the Tragic and Infamous Event Known as the Everett Massacre* (Seattle: University of Washington Press, 1970), is a fine introduction to labor history in western Washington.

In addition to *Mill Town*, there is information on the labor movement in Washington's forest industry in Vernon Jensen, *Lumber and Labor* (New York: Farrar & Rinehart, 1945). *Lumber and Labor* is not as substantial a study as Jensen's later tome, *Heritage of Conflict: Labor Relations in the Nonferrous Metals Industry up to 1930* (Ithaca, N. Y.: Cornell University Press, 1950). Melvyn Dubofsky, "The Origins of Western Working Class Radicalism, 1890–1905" (*Labor History* 7 [Spring 1966]: 131–54), and Richard E. Lingenfelter, *The Hardrock Miners: A History of the Mining Labor Movement in the American West, 1863–1893* (Berkeley: University of California

Press, 1974), discuss the influences that shaped the Western Federation of Miners. No study of radical unionism on the Pacific frontier would be complete without reference to Robert L. Tyler, *Rebels of the Woods: The I. W. W. in the Pacific Northwest* (Eugene, Oregon: University of Oregon Books, 1967), and Melvyn Dubofsky, *We Shall Be All: A History of the Industrial Workers of the World* (Chicago: Quadrangle Books, 1969). By minimizing the power of the AFL in the late nineteenth century, Melvyn Dubofsky, *Industrialism and the American Worker, 1865–1920* (New York: Crowell, 1975), offers a number of penetrating insights into the labor movement in North America.

Harvey O'Connor, *Revolution in Seattle, A Memoir* (New York: Monthly Review Press, 1964), is a fond recounting of the halcyon years of political socialism in Washington. O'Connor's emphasis on the revolutionary aspects of the Seattle General Strike contrasts with the tempered analysis offered in Robert L. Friedheim, *The Seattle General Strike* (Seattle: University of Washington Press, 1964). There is a chapter on the International Workingmen's Association in Chester McArthur Destler, *American Radicalism, 1865–1901: Essays and Documents* (New London, Conn.: Connecticut College, 1946), and local and regional socialist developments are also discussed in Howard H. Quint, *The Forging of American Socialism: Origins of the Modern Movement* (Columbia, S. C.: University of South Carolina Press, 1953), and Ira Kipnis, *The American Socialist Movement, 1897–1912* (New York: Columbia University Press, 1952).

John T. Saywell, "Labour and Socialism in British Columbia: A Survey of Historical Development Before 1903" (*British Columbia Historical Quarterly* 6 [July-October 1951]: 129–50), is a pioneer study of socialism in British Columbia. There is a more complete account of left-wing activities in British Columbia in Martin Robin, *Radical Politics and Canadian Labour, 1880–1930* (Kingston, Ont.: Industrial Relations Centre, Queen's University, 1968). The most readable account of socialism in British Columbia is Dorothy G. Steeves, *The Compassionate Rebel: Ernest E. Winch and His Times* (Vancouver: Boag Foundation, 1960).

John H. M. Laslett, *Labor and the Left: A Study of Socialist and Radical Influences in the American Labor Movement, 1881–1924* (New York: Basic Books, 1970), helps one to understand the influence of the AFL on the socialist movement in the Pacific Northwest. Also useful for keeping labor developments in the Pacific Northwest in perspective are Ira Cross, *A History of the Labor Movement in California* (Berkeley: University of California Press, 1935), and Gerald N. Grob, *Workers and Utopia, A Study of Ideological Conflict in the American Labor Movement, 1865–1900* (Evanston, Ill.: Northwestern University Press, 1961). Of the several general histories of the American labor movement, Philip S. Foner, *History of the Labor Movement in the United States*, 4 vols. (New York: International Publishers, 1947–1965), has the most pronounced ideological orientation, but it is also a very useful source of information on dual unionism in the American West.

Index

Index

Index

Index

Wagenknecht, Alfred, 174
Wages: statistics on, 19, 30, 51, 112, 123, 152
Waite, Davis (governor of Colorado), 63
Walker, Walter, 82
Walker, W. J., 122, 134, 136
Walla Walla, Wash., 6, 10, 55, 58
Wallace, Idaho, 112
Wardner, Idaho, 112, 113
Washington, Territory and State of: historical background of, 11–14, 75–76; constitution of, 32, 32n, 41, 55, 65; bureau of labor, 64, 66; supreme court, 64, 78; early political parties in, 75–76; weakness of political parties in, 162, 193. See also Labor movement, in Washington; Pacific Northwest; Socialist movement, in Washington
Washington, University of, 198–99, 209
Washington State Federation of Labor: organization of, 136; affiliation with American Federation of Labor, 136–37; cooperation with Washington State Grange, 160–62, 214; supports industrial unionism, 207, 207n; endorses socialism, 207; mentioned, 188, 189, 193, 198
Washington State Labor Congress, 137
Washington State Labor party, 160, 176
Watters, J. C., 188
Wayland, J. A., 84–85, 106
Waynick, W. H., 175
Weaver, James B., 54
Webb, Beatrice, 92, 219
Wegener, Otto F., 49
Wellington, B.C., 32, 33
Wells, Hulet M.: on Hermon Titus, 97, 177; as president of Seattle's Central Labor Council, 207; mentioned, 209, 213, 215, 215n
Western Central Labor Union: organization of, 49–50; and American Railway Union, 59; evolution of, 79, 137, 140; mentioned, 49, 50, 94, 156
Western Clarion (Vancouver), 44, 109, 111
Western Federation of Miners: formation of, 113–14, 123; and Knights of Labor, 113–14, 122; and American Federation of Labor, 114, 123, 127, 134, 136, 207, 207n; and Populist movement, 121, 129; and United Mine Workers of America, 150, 202; mentioned, 48, 151, 152, 170, 184
—and Pacific Northwest radicalism: role of, 4, 6, 113–14, 121, 127–30 *passim*, 141, 188, 218; supports regional unionism, 38, 114, 119, 134–36 *passim*, 139, 146; supports socialism in British Columbia, 98,

121–22, 127–31 *passim*, 139, 221. *See also* American Labor Union; Western Labor Union
—organizing activities in British Columbia: in Kootenay region, 4, 6, 7, 98, 122–24, 128–31 *passim*; among coal miners, 140, 146–47, 150
Western Labor Press Association, 37
Western Labor Union: organized by Western Federation of Miners, 134–35; seeks affiliation of Washington State Federation of Labor, 136–37; mentioned, 119, 184
Whitman County, Wash.: and Populism in Washington, 55–57 *passim*, 107; and socialist movement in Washington, 107–8, 170
Wilkeson, Wash., 29, 202
Wilks, James, 128, 131
Williams, Parker: activities in British Columbia legislature, 163, 165, 166, 178, 181, 211n, 212
Wilson, Woodrow (president of U.S.), 196, 199
Winch, Harold, 222
Wing, J. O., 161
Winnipeg, 124, 143, 145, 180, 220
Winnipeg Voice, 179
Winsor, Richard, 91, 96, 209
Women's Christian Temperance Union, 41. *See also* Temperance and prohibition
Women's rights: right to vote, 18, 42, 64, 65, 87, 189, 199; wage and hour laws, 78, 189, 192; mentioned, 81, 90
Working classes, in Pacific Northwest: immigration to the region, 3, 7–11; influenced by promotional and travel literature, 3, 7–11; political involvement of, 7, 49; Britons in, 13–14, 34; general working and living conditions of, 14–15, 17–21 *passim*, 118–19, 185; cultural influences on, 17–18, 124–28 *passim*; education of, 17–18, 26–27, 34–35, 43, 47, 48, 127–28, 219; anti-Oriental activities of, 23–27, 29, 80, 157–59 *passim*; and unemployment, 23, 51, 57–59 *passim*, 200–201, 205; and prohibition, 41–42, 127, 214, 214n. *See also* Lumberjacks; Miners, coal; Miners, metalliferous; Railway workers; Sawmill workers
Workingmen's party, 72
Workmen's compensation, 78, 189–90, 192, 192n, 194
World War I: impact on Pacific Northwest labor movement, 200–201; 212–16 *passim*; suppression of radicals during, 210, 214, 215; labor opposition to involvement in, 215.